*Urban Ministry in the 21ˢᵗ Century: Global Faiths*

*Volume 2*

# BAMBOO IN MIST

An Exploratory Understanding of Chinese Spirituality

Kaylene Powell, ed.

Andrew Wood, Series ed.

Urban Loft Publishers | Skyforest, CA

*Bamboo in Mist*

An Exploratory Understanding of Chinese Spirituality

Copyright © 2020 Kaylene Powell

All rights reserved. Except for brief quotations in critical publications or reviews, no part of this book may be reproduced in any manner without prior written permission from the publisher. Write: Permissions, Urban Loft Publishers, P.O. Box 6 Skyforest, CA 92385.

Urban Loft Publishers
P.O. Box 6
Skyforest, CA 92385
www.urbanloftpublishers.com

Senior Editors: Stephen Burris & Kendi Howells Douglas
Series Editor: Andrew Wood
Copy Editor: Marla Black
Graphics: Brittnay Parsons
Cover Design: Brittnay Parsons

Scripture quotations are taken from the *Holy Bible*, New Living Translation, copyright © 1996, 2004, 2015 by Tyndale House Foundation. Used by permission of Tyndale House Publishers, Inc., Carol Stream, Illinois 60188. All rights reserved.

ISBN-13: 978-1-949625-11-0

Made in the U.S.A.

## Acknowledgments

Special thanks to each dear volume contributor, and to all the wonderful people who cheered me on through the production of this volume, including Charles Weber, Rob and Jayna Gallagher, and Andrew Wood.

# Dedication

To the millions upon millions.

I cannot wait to see each face, and know each story, one day.

## Editors' Preface

*Urban Mission in the 21st Century* is a series of monographs that addresses key issues facing those involved in urban ministry whether it be in the slums, squatter communities, favelas, or in immigrant neighborhoods. It is our goal to bring fresh ideas, a theological basis, and best practices in urban mission as we reflect on our changing urban world. The contributors to this series bring a wide range of ideas, experiences, education, international perspectives, and insight into the study of the growing field of urban ministry. These contributions fall into four very general areas: 1--the biblical and theological basis for urban ministry; 2--best practices currently in use and anticipated in the future by urban scholar/activists who are living working and studying in the context of cities; 3--personal experiences and observations based on urban ministry as it is currently being practiced; and 4--a forward view toward where we are headed in the decades ahead in the expanding and developing field of urban mission. This series is intended for educators, graduate students, theologians, pastors, and serious students of urban ministry.

More than anything, these contributions are creative attempts to help Christians strategically and creatively think about how we can better reach our world that is now more urban than rural. We do not see theology and practice as separate and distinct. Rather, we see sound practice growing out of a healthy vibrant theology that seeks to understand God's world as it truly is as we move further into the twenty-first century. Contributors interact with the best scholarly literature available at the time of writing while making application to specific contexts in which they live and work.

Each book in the series is intended to be a thought-provoking work that represents the author's experience and perspective on urban ministry in a particular context. The editors have chosen those who bring this rich diversity of perspectives to this series. It is our hope and prayer that each book in this series will challenge, enrich, provoke, and cause the reader to dig deeper into subjects that bring the reader to a deeper understanding of our urban world and the ministry the church is called to perform in that new world.

Dr. Kendi Howells Douglas and Stephen Burris,
*Urban Mission in the 21st Century Series* Co-Editors

# Series Preface

## Global Faiths

In previous eras, knowledge of world religions and cultural proficiency in communicating with people of other faiths were within the purview of a select group of academics and missionaries with the motivation and means to travel internationally. In the 21st century, urbanization and globalization have brought large numbers of ordinary people of diverse cultures and religious beliefs into unavoidable daily contact in the workplace, educational institutions, local and national politics, and through social media.

For Christians, as for the rest of society, these social changes represent a challenge. Many church members are experiencing role conflict between their statuses as members of a particular nationality, class, and culture versus their status as citizens of the world-encompassing Kingdom of God. They waver between fear and faith as they try to reconcile the confusing and anxiety-provoking messages of the media with the imperatives of Scripture to love one's neighbor—even if one's neighbor seems like an enemy. Church leaders may find traditional means of evangelism and discipleship proving ineffective in demographically changing communities. Those who do succeed in bridging cultural divides in the community to communicate the Gospel compellingly may find it difficult to integrate ethnically diverse new Christians into the existing cultural majority of the church. Already overwhelmed with the demands of ministry, leaders typically do not have the time to do an in-depth cultural study to arrive at culturally appropriate, biblically sound, and effective means of communicating Jesus to people of non-Christian religious communities, especially given the great diversity of religious others one encounters every day in a major metropolitan area.

However, we must not allow the difficulties of rapid cultural change to overshadow the enormous opportunity this change represents to the church. For the first time, large numbers of ordinary Christians and members of other faiths can share and model their beliefs simply and directly with one another, unmediated by religious leaders. The "priesthood of all believers" (see 1 Pet. 2:9) can thus become a reality with respect to cross-cultural outreach in an unprecedented way. Moreover, learning and spiritual growth may very well go in both directions. As they lead religious others to become followers of Jesus, Christians themselves are challenged by the questions, devotional practices, and theologies of other faiths in ways that cause them to reexamine the reasons for their own beliefs and redouble their efforts to live consistently with their own profession of faith in Christ. The need to adjust ministry practices to communicate clearly to people of a wide variety of other faiths may cause Christian leaders to focus more carefully upon the true essentials of the Christian faith, stripping away the cultural syncretism that so easily entangles the church in materialism, nationalism, and other subtle idolatries. The result can be a church more focused on its mission with an increased capacity to love others in clearer emulation of the self-sacrificial model of Christ himself.

*Urban Ministry in the 21$^{st}$ Century: Global Faiths* is a monograph series intended to help the church overcome the challenges and rise to the opportunities represented by the growing religious diversity of the burgeoning cities of the world. Each volume focuses upon a different non-Christian religious faith, providing the reader with tools to understand that faith better as well as practical suggestions and examples for biblically faithful and culturally appropriate contextualization. The authors are ministry professionals and academics who write not only from a basis of careful research, but also from thoughtful reflection upon their own real-life experiences listening, dialoging, and sharing faith with people of religious backgrounds different from their own. We hope these volumes will be of practical assistance to ministers, educators, college students, Christian nonprofit workers, and inquisitive laypeople who will discern the Lord's hand at work in the cultural changes in their communities and respond eagerly to His call, "Here am I. Send me!" (Isa. 6:8 New International Version).

Dr. Andrew Wood

Series Editor

*Urban Ministry in the 21ˢᵗ Century: Global Faiths*

# Table of Contents

**Introduction: The Winding Path**
    By Kaylene Powell..................................................................................15

**Part 1: The Bamboo Forest: Distinctive Elements of Chinese**
    Spirituality.............................................................................................21

1. *Toward an Emic, Spiritually Based Perspective on Filial Piety*
    By Carl Roberts....................................................................................23

2. *Traditional Principles of Confucianism and Other Influences on My Life*
    By C.X..................................................................................................45

3. *Taoism's Influence on Daily Chinese Life*
    By Paul Thomas...................................................................................55

4. *One Woman's Experience and Beliefs*
    By Xie Baoli.........................................................................................87

5. *Observed Spirituality Among the Taiwanese*
    By David and Judy Newquist...............................................................91

6. *My Thoughts on Chinese Spirituality*
    By Josephine Qiu...............................................................................103

7. *Understanding and Ministering to Hui Chinese*
    By Kaylene Powell.............................................................................115

8. *What is "Chinese" Theology? Honor and Shame in Chinese Spirituality*
    By Jackson Wu...................................................................................133

**Part 2: Moving Mist: Historical and Modern Development of Chinese**
    Spirituality...........................................................................................157

9. *Neither Wheat nor Tares: The Problem of Sowing Seeds in Fields Deep with Traditional Chinese Spirituality and Chinese Nationalism*

By Nathan Faries...........................................................................................159
10. *A Brief Summary of My Life*
    By Ye Weijun..............................................................................................197
11. *Confucianism, Maoism, and Christianity: Chinese Intellectuals' Difficult Path to Christianity and Why it Emerged in the 1990s*
    By Franklin Wang........................................................................................199
12. *Key Steps on My Spiritual Path*
    By Wang Fei................................................................................................223
13. *Americans Through a Chinese Looking Glass: How Portrayals of Western Culture and Interactions with Americans Influence Chinese Students' Perceptions of Christianity*
    By Lucas Tian..............................................................................................227
14. *Chasing Knowledge: A Young Chinese Woman Reflects on the Empty Intellectual Spirituality of Her Generation*
    By Yang Xiaoxiao........................................................................................275
15. *Outside Influences and Personal Challenges: A Belief Journey*
    By Mia Pan..................................................................................................295

**Epilogue: A Clearing on the Way**
    By Kaylene Powell.......................................................................................311

# Introduction: The Winding Path

## By Kaylene Powell

"They asked you to do what? Are they crazy?" My teenage niece, Grace, eyed me with clear incredulity across the living room. "Auntie, how in the world are you supposed to write about the whole topic of Chinese spirituality in one small book?"

*How indeed?*

I smiled at the intelligence and wisdom displayed in her response—and equally at the measure of adolescent absolutism in her manner when she delivered it, rolling eyes and all. I smiled because her short reply so aptly summed up what I had thought and felt when first approached with the idea to spearhead this writing project.

Where Grace's simple questions and my earlier reaction intersected, this dilemma emerged: how is one to take a massive group of people and their non-linear culture developed over thousands of years of complex history and somehow separate one element of their psyche to explain it in understandable terms for mainly non-Chinese readers who will come from all different levels of background knowledge on the related topics—all in 300 pages or less?

The simple answer is: it cannot be done. Not if one wants to cover everything. And not if one wants to have the final product read with an engaging and perhaps at times entertaining cadence, comprehensible and still thought-provoking. Hence, the final work you hold in your hands is more like a collection of insightful snapshots than an exhaustive, comprehensive guide.

Am I a pessimist? No. Simply a realist. Let me explain.

I come from Western culture, a world where aspects of a person's life are fragmented and compartmentalized by medical professionals, by academics, and even by most average people (at least subconsciously). I have been conditioned to believe that everything can be explained logically and progressively if we will simply think about it long enough. I grew up repeatedly practicing higher order thinking skills in school: contrasting, analyzing, summarizing, and evaluating.

But Chinese culture, both past and present, is so completely opposite to this worldview, and includes such a conglomeration of interlaced ideas which often seem conflicting or contradictory in the minds of all non-Chinese, that even trying to begin to understand it, let alone explain or evaluate it, is an intimidating task. Contributor Paul Thomas highlights this conundrum well when he notes in Chapter 3, "It might be said that this confusion about definitions is a central theme of this book. As Westerners, we are driven to define and categorize, but the Chinese do not share this desire. Consider 'Taoism' as bamboo seen through a mist, perhaps in one of those delightfully suggestive Chinese ink paintings where a few strokes indicate the bigger picture. Seen through the mist, the bamboo stalks are indistinct, but they remain solid facts despite our hazy perspective. Chinese faith in Taoist ideas remains rock solid, despite the apparent vagueness of their organization or our inability to fix them to an organized faith system." The irony is that an individual Chinese, coming from a collectivist culture, is prone to speak in terms of "we" and "our" and "us" to answer inquiries with parroted lines memorized in school and sweeping generalizations that help keep the whole group bonded. And yet, as a Chinese student of mine pointed out in a class on Western culture, generalizations can be dangerous because of how myopic, limited, or inaccurate they often turn out to be.

Another reason it is difficult to cover every possible angle of this topic in one volume is because not only are there many aspects of traditional Chinese spirituality that are indigenous to Chinese culture, there are even more aspects of other religions and beliefs with "Chinese characteristics." For example, would a volume on the subject only discuss, say, Daoism, Confucianism, and the early hierarchy of Chinese gods including the Lord of Heaven? Even covering all those topics to a moderate degree of completeness in one large book would be a challenge. But to limit Chinese spirituality to such aspects without acknowledging all the foreign religious influences such as Buddhism, Christianity, and Islam that have also shaped and influenced Chinese culture both through the past and today is to ignore vitally important elements in the evolution of modern Chinese spiritual thought, and where that thought is headed in the future. The reader will see elements of both covered in the contributions of this book.

This leads to the fundamental question every writer or editor should ask: what is the scope of my writing project considering what I really want to communicate and what my readers most need or want to know about? Readers may open this volume out of curiosity or as part of an academic research project, but for many readers, there is something deeper fueling that curiosity. Some seek to know more about this topic because their family has some Chinese ancestry. Others may have a long-held or newly discovered interest in Eastern philosophy and mysticism; they are longing to explore the topic further with hopes of finding some peace or answers for how to improve their life. Still others may simply want to better understand the Chinese friends, neighbors, or co-workers who are now a part of their life. And then there is the group who strongly believe in a faith of their own and want to understand Chinese spirituality to find culturally sensitive ways to share their own beliefs with Chinese people they meet.

All those motives (and possibly others) are valid reasons for studying the topic. But to be clear from the start, my own perspective draws mainly from the last. For I believe that the Lord of Heaven created all things and all peoples through the first man and woman, and He has set eternity in the hearts of every person who has ever lived. As Pascal noted, there is a spot in our hearts that only He can fill. And while every culture has a different way of expressing that longing in words and dealing with that longing in customs, in the end, He supersedes culture and language. The world contains many religions and philosophies, yet only He can satisfy our spiritual hunger and resurrect our once-dead spirits, spirits of the Chinese and non-Chinese alike.

Turning back to the general challenge in my niece's question, my start and progress in taking on the project was not always clear and smooth. When the editors of a larger project first approached me and asked if I would take on this volume, it was poised more in terms of me being the sole author. My initial reaction was negative for two reasons—one based on limited time outside of my primary jobs and the other based on a sense that I did not possess enough knowledge and perspective to do the whole topic justice. Movement towards a "work of collected contributions and essays" seemed to alleviate the pressure from both objections and make the project a bit more manageable for tackling. However, as the lay of the land for contributors and their proposed contributions could finally be mapped out, it seemed that I needed to step in and do more editing, shaping, and contributing than I had first envisioned. As an English as a Second Language (ESL) instructor, I have come to see myself as a monolingual translator: I translate English of one sort into English my students can understand, and I translate my student's developing English into language the wider world can understand.

Looking back with a reflective heart, I see my own journey has equipped me uniquely for this task. Since I befriended my first Chinese roommate in 1997, I have spent most of my adult years living with, among, or near; teaching English to; worshiping with; praying for; and otherwise serving Chinese people in one capacity or another. I have faced the challenge of learning Mandarin, and though I am far from fluent, I have studied enough to begin grasping some of the deeper elements of the culture, worldview, and thought processes woven into the beauty of that language. I have wept for Chinese students, friends, and co-workers who struggle through life feeling empty, working so hard and yet somehow finding they are chasing the wind. And while I love all peoples of the world, the Chinese always hold a special place in my heart. The Chinese themselves might say fate put that special love there and I was destined to somehow connect with them. But I believe something greater than fate had a hand in it all.

At the beginning of this writing assignment, I saw myself as a journeyer trying to navigate a path and explain ideas which I knew would be so foreign and foggy for many of my readers. My initial mental picture of hiking through a bamboo forest and the resulting title phrase came as no surprise; from life experience, I was well-acquainted with the environment of southwest China so inspirational to classical

Chinese artists past and present. Their images of brush-and-ink paintings on scrolls, often including benign pandas lounging among slightly blurred stalks and leaves, have become one of the many enduring symbols of Chinese culture now appreciated worldwide. Among other things, for the Chinese, bamboo plants represent beauty or elegance, as well as strength, integrity, loyalty, and modesty. In addition to being the main food source of the mysterious giant panda, as long as Chinese culture has existed, bamboo has been an integral part of it, not only for decorative and culinary purposes, but also for much more practical purposes (e.g. a building material, a writing surface).

So, while I started this writing journey focusing much more on differences and ambiguous concepts, I rediscovered the beauty, goodness, and usefulness of certain aspects within the Chinese worldview. It reminded me of hiking along a path in Sichuan Province years ago, when the winter chill drew the fog of my breath into a dance with the mist around me right before my breath was taken away by the sight of a clearing before me, a clearing surrounded by great clumps of those green stocks. With the low ceiling of clouds above, the bamboo seemed on that damp morning to tower to the very edge of Heaven in silent, resilient grandeur.

It is from this heart and experience I have felt compelled to continue working on this project and to now present to our readers this collection of essays, from a variety of viewpoints: Christian and non-Christian, Chinese and Western, from various levels of academic research and lived personal experience. Given the span of the topic and the authors' perspectives, readers will likely find some material they agree with, while other material may create hesitation or even resistance. With an awareness of my own cultural and religious bias, I have endeavored to arrange and present viewpoints different than my own in a way that accurately represents the voice of each author for the reader's consideration. I ask the reader to approach the material with an open, inquiring mind and give a fair hearing to ideas that may challenge our preconceptions—a skill that is as necessary to practice with others of our own culture as it is with those of a vastly different background. In the end, I hope and pray that this volume will help readers better understand, converse with, and pray for Chinese people around them.

The essence of Chinese spirituality today is hard to pinpoint, but as we will see, it seems to revolve around a complex interweaving of plural philosophies and concepts, some deeply historical and some more recent. It is often felt more deeply than words can express, held more deeply than an individual will care to admit publicly, and engrained more deeply than most Chinese have ever fully explored. After all, which average members of any given society have taken time to deeply ponder what they do, why they do it, and whether their way of thinking is *really* superior to that of people from other cultures around the world?

I believe only one spirituality breeds ultimate truth and that anyone (Chinese or otherwise) who does not discover and receive it will never fully live in this life or the next. As dogmatic and judgmental as that may sound in our world today, I invite the reader to see that I and the contributors to this volume speak not out of cold narrow-mindedness but out of understanding, reason, and—most importantly—out of love. I want every person, including every Chinese man, woman, and child, to have the chance to know the Lord of Heaven and be named as His sons and daughters. But for any who would join me in sharing such an opportunity with them and helping them grow in such faith, we must first have a deeper understanding of and respect for where they are coming from: their worldview, their traditional ideas, and the complexities of how they think.

And I also urge the reader to understand my viewpoint and search their own heart. If we seek to understand another's ideas and views simply for the sake of changing them to be like "us" then we too are missing the point. We will run the risk of arrogance, manipulation, and misguided disappointment. We must not seek to understand simply for the sake of knowing facts or using that understanding to serve our own ends. Instead, we must learn a valuable lesson from the Chinese: to see each person in an integrated, holistic way. When we do so, we will cease to demand the job titles of "savior" or "truth-enforcer" and begin to find delight in offering our being-restored selves as companions to walk alongside the searching selves of our Chinese friends through the misty bamboo forest of life toward something better as we all carry on with this journey side by side, *yi bu yi bu* (one step at a time).

# Part 1

# The Bamboo Forest: Distinctive Elements of Chinese Spirituality

# 1. Toward an Emic, Spiritually Based Perspective on Filial Piety[1]

## By Carl Roberts[2]

There are lots of objections to various parts of the Bible and virtually all of them are based on high faith in your culture and the superiority of your culture. Years ago, I once talked about Christianity to a Chinese graduate student—a brilliant young man who was in Britain when I was at the time. And you know what, he had no problem with the idea that God would send people to hell. No problem at all because he says, 'You know I'm not a Westerner so the idea that God might have authority to send people to hell doesn't bother me. I have no problem with that exercise of authority. What I can't accept is this: the individualistic nature of Christian salvation means that if I believe in Jesus Christ then I would not be with my ancestors. And I don't want to believe in anything that would separate me from my ancestors.' Now my guess is that for the average Manhattan young professional, that is not the problem they have with the Bible . . . However, the average New Yorker's going to say, 'I just can't accept a God who can send people to

---

[1] *Editor's note: Filial piety (honor of and care for one's elders) is a particularly strong value in Chinese thinking, influencing the decisions of many Chinese from childhood into adulthood. Non-Chinese observers may struggle to understand how this value influences the spiritual development of young Chinese people today, so this author helps us to explore the issue from an emic (or insider) perspective. The author of the following piece was born and raised in the American Midwest before he moved to mainland China, where he works as an exemplary language educator. He has concentrated both his graduate and post-graduate work in the field of intercultural studies. - K.P.*

[2] *A pseudonym has been used to protect the identity of the contributor.*

hell." At that moment, what you're saying is this: 'My cultural location is superior to theirs. My culture is absolutely right.' (Keller, 2016)

Tim Keller shared the preceding anecdote while delivering a talk at Google. There are three primary reasons to begin this chapter with it. The first is that it highlights a flaw in just about everyone's thinking, which is that we tend to view the world exclusively through our own cultural paradigm. In context, Keller is saying that at the root of the doubt of Christianity for many people is a high faith in their own culture. In his example, he highlights how people from two cultures—American and Chinese—can generally interpret the doctrine of hell from different viewpoints. For many Westerners, the idea that a loving God could send people to hell is baffling. They simply cannot comprehend it; therefore, they deem it untrue and throw out Christianity along the way. Conversely, this Chinese graduate student had no problem whatsoever with God having the authority to send people to hell. His objection was from a different angle and there should be no doubt that each respective culture strongly shaped each of their perspectives.

The second reason to use this anecdote is that just as our cultural upbringing influences our worldview, so it also influences the way that we interpret others' worldviews. Upon hearing that the Chinese student's objection to Christianity had to do with potentially being separated from his ancestors, many Westerners might laugh at him for what they think is a foolish and ridiculous view. They, of course, think this way because of their own cultural upbringing and, most importantly, because of a lack of empathy. This idea will be drawn out and expanded upon later in this chapter.

A third reason this example is appropriate is that the student's objection to Christianity is also the primary focus of this chapter: filial piety. The goal of this chapter is to bring a better understanding of filial piety in general and how it can influence the lives of Chinese people with respect to their views toward Christianity. To accomplish this, we will begin with a historical introduction of the concept, its origins and how it has played out in Chinese society. Next, we will look at some modern thoughts on filial piety. The focus will then shift to how it can influence Chinese seekers and believers. To conclude, we will consider how Westerners should understand and respond to this important Chinese cultural value.

## Historical Introduction

孝 or *xiào,* known in English as filial piety, is a fundamental element of Chinese culture and society that can most simply be described as respect for one's parents and elders. Interestingly, the character that conveys the meaning of filial piety is actually comprised of two other characters: *lǎo* (老) and *zi* (子). *Lǎo* means "old" and is the top portion of the character and "zi," which means "son," is the bottom portion. Multiple interpretations of this meaning have been offered, but as Charlotte Ikels (2004) notes, the most commonly held belief is that it signifies a son carrying his elder. To put it another way, as one's parents get older, the child is responsible for taking care of and supporting his or her parents.

While the concept of filial piety exists throughout the world, it is more deeply rooted and prevalent in Eastern cultures - particularly in China. Two primary texts teach and display how it should be expressed, the first of which is the *Xiàojīng,* a classical treatise on filial piety that has been influencing Chinese culture for more than 2,000 years. Although the work was traditionally attributed to Confucius, it is now commonly accepted that it was put together by disciples of Confucius from his teachings. It is divided into eighteen different sections, each of which includes teachings on the importance of filial piety.

In the first section, Zhong Ni opens with a question to his disciple Zeng, asking if he is aware of the perfect virtue that the ancient kings had that, if practiced, would bring about peace and harmony. After Zeng says that he is not sure, Zhong Ni replies with this: "It was filial piety. Now filial piety is the root of all virtue, and the stem out of which grows all moral teaching . . . Our bodies—[down] to every hair and bit of skin—are received by us from our parents, and we must not presume to injure or wound them. This is the beginning of filial piety" (Legge, 1899).

As this first section illustrates, the concept of filial piety begins and ends with the recognition that all that we have is from our parents. Aris Teon (2016) clearly explains the impact of this value:

> The concept underlying the principle of filial piety is simple. Parents gave life to children, gave them food and clothes, an education, etc. For all the things that children received from parents, children have an eternal

obligation towards them. They have a debt towards their parents, a debt that can never be fully repaid. The only thing that children can do in order to repay at least a small part of this debt is to take care of their parents in their old age, to make them proud and happy, to obey and serve them.

Moving on in the *Xiàojīng,* in section seven, the servant Zeng acknowledges the greatness of filial piety, to which Zhong Ni replies, "Yes, filial piety is the constant method of Heaven, the righteousness of Earth, and the practical duty of Man" (Legge, 1899). In section ten, five common ways that a child can manifest filial piety are given:

> The service which a filial son does to his parents is as follows: In his general conduct to them, he manifests the utmost reverence. In his nourishing of them, his endeavor is to give them the utmost pleasure. When they are ill, he feels the greatest anxiety. In mourning for them dead, he exhibits every demonstration of grief. In sacrificing to them, he displays the utmost solemnity. When a son is complete in these five things, he may be pronounced able to serve his parents. (Legge, 1899)

The *Xiàojīng* has heavily influenced Chinese culture ever since it was first put together. Dr. Ulrich Theobald (2010), a senior lecturer in the Chinese Studies department at the University of Tübingen in Germany, summarizes it like this:

> The *Xiàojīng* gives concrete instructions for the display of filial piety. It had to penetrate all points that father and sons share and all social interactions in which both sides are involved. The body was given to a son by his parents, and filial piety meant not to harm the own body . . . The concept also implicates that sons had to revere and to [honor] the family name and the commemoration of their parents, as expressed in ancestor veneration. The highest form of venerating one's parents was to achieve a high position and a high social standing.

The second highly influential text was written more than 1,500 years after Confucius and is known as The Twenty-Four Filial Exemplars. It was written during the Yuan Dynasty sometime in the 13th or 14th century by a scholar named Guo Jujing. Tradition says that when Guo's father died, he grieved tremendously and "his depth of feeling prompted him to comb the histories in search of true stories of the finest examples of filial respect, as practiced by devoted children throughout the centuries" (Sure, n.d.). Each of these stories demonstrate intense devotion to one's parents, and while all Chinese people may not be intimately familiar with them, they have exerted a strong influence over Chinese society for centuries. We will highlight a couple of the stories to give a sense of the type of material found in The Twenty-Four Filial Exemplars.

Story Eleven tells of an eight-year-old boy named Wu Meng. His family was very poor and they could not afford mosquito netting. On hot summer nights when the mosquitoes were swarming, while his parents were sleeping Wu Meng would wake up, take off his shirt and allow them to bite him. Guo Jujing draws out the main point by first stating that Wu Meng was not foolish and then asking why he refused to shoo the mosquitoes away. The answer? "If he drove the mosquitoes away from his body, they would surely fly over and wake up his mother and father with their stinging. So the devoted son simply let the mosquitoes drink his blood instead" (Sure, n.d.). Wu Meng even did this all in secret, always putting on his shirt so that his parents would not know. However, one time he was so sleepy that he forgot to put his shirt back on afterwards. When his father woke up, he quickly perceived what his son had been doing and he and Wu's mother were moved to tears. All their neighbors heard the parents crying, word quickly spread, and Wu Meng was honored as a true filial son.

Story Nineteen tells of a nine-year-old boy named Huang Xiang who lived during the Han dynasty (206 BC-AD 220). After his mother died, he noticed that his father was in terrible grief. Seeing this, he was moved with great compassion and "resolved to make it his business to cheer up his father. After making that decision, there was no job in the house too troublesome for him, and he performed his chores with vigorous, positive energy" (Sure, n.d.). That was not enough in Huang's eyes, though. In the hot and humid summer, he would fan his father's bed so that when he went to sleep, the pillow and bed would be cool. In the cold winter, Huang would crawl into his father's bed to warm it for him before he went to sleep.

Story Twenty-Four tells of Huang Tingjing, who was said to have been the chief historian during Emperor Zhezhong's rule in the Song dynasty (AD 1085-1100). Guo Jujing begins the story by highlighting Huang Tingjing's fame as a calligrapher and poet, which had led to him having a house full of servants. However, "Despite his high status, he was not arrogant, or haughty. His nature, on the contrary, was respectful and compliant, especially in his filial regard for his mother" (Sure, n.d.). Although he had many servants for his own personal matters, he would never allow any of them to help with his mother's affairs. Instead, Huang Tingjing would personally scrub out his mother's chamber pot at the end of each day. Guo Jujing summarizes this story—and perhaps it is an inherent summary of the entire work seeing that it is the last example—by giving Huang Tingjing's reasoning for his actions in saying that parents "raise children to adulthood, sparing no efforts in accomplishing this difficult and often troublesome task, [so] the children in turn, by rights should personally see to the care of their parents. They should not pass the job on to others" (Sure, n.d.).

At least one thing to take from these stories is the language that is used by Guo Jujing. In Story Eleven, "the *devoted* son simply let the mosquitoes drink his blood instead." In Story Nineteen, "there was no job in the house *too troublesome* for him." In Story Twenty-Four, "his nature, on the contrary, was *respectful and compliant*, especially in his filial regard for his mother." In a society in which a high regard for family and filial piety has been ubiquitous century after century, it is not hard to imagine how these concepts and stories influence Chinese youth. A good son or daughter will be respectful, compliant, and devoted to their parents while recognizing that there is no task too troublesome to repay them for all they have sacrificed.

Now that we have had a brief historical introduction to the concept of filial piety and its foundations which have permeated Chinese society, let us shift from the historical influence and take a look at some contemporary vignettes of how filial piety impacts modern Chinese people.

## Modern Thoughts on Filial Piety

At the time of writing this chapter, I taught a course on writing to 49 students from mainland China. Each week, the students were required to write a journal entry in a notebook. One week, I gave them a prompt related to filial piety and asked them how they would explain the concept to a foreigner and describe what it means to them. Later, as I was conceptualizing this chapter, the idea of attempting to define or describe filial piety felt daunting. I felt tremendously inadequate to do so myself, so I thought it would be helpful to allow the students to speak for themselves. What follows are some of their answers (used with permission). Of the selections used here, to the best of my knowledge, none of the students were Christians.

*How would you describe filial piety and how has it impacted your life?*

> *Filial piety means a kind of responsibility to me. Sometimes I should obey my parents' wishes, like choosing [a] school and major, and even include choosing work. They didn't want me to go to a place far away from home. So they don't allow me to go to Beijing or Shanghai to study or work . . . Filial piety is a double-edged sword: It makes young people to take their responsibility but also makes them lose their independence.*

> *I should have gone to Yunnan province for college, but all of my family didn't agree with me and made the choice for me to come to our school.*

> *[Filial piety] has influenced my future deeply. Thus, I made a decision that I will go back to my hometown to be a normal English teacher. Although it is not my dream but my parent's, I accept it. Maybe that's a pity for my whole life to chase my own dream. But for my parents, I always wish they have a happy life, that's what I could do as a child.*

> *It is an important factor in big decisions that I have made in my life because I am the only child in my family and I am still dependent on them. If*

*someday I need to choose where to work or where to live, I would choose a place that is near to my parents. In this way, I can take good care of them.*

These are four authentic and raw depictions of what filial piety means and how it has impacted the lives of Chinese college students. Of course, it would be inappropriate to generalize the experiences of four students to all 1.378 billion Chinese people. They are not all the same, and there is certainly some nuance and variety in their views of filial piety. Having said that, in my experience these depictions are much closer to the norm than being outliers.

When I first began teaching in a Chinese college, it was common to have conversations with students either after class or during office hours. My students were all English majors, and a regular question that I would ask them is why they chose their major. In America, students typically choose a college major because it is an area of study that is of interest or perhaps because it will lead to a good job. If one finds that they are not overly satisfied with their selection, they will just switch majors. Neither of these are terribly common in China, where students are generally placed in an institution and study program based on their national college entrance exam scores. I was surprised to learn that many of my students actually did not like their major and did not choose it themselves but were simply obeying their parents' wishes. It was not uncommon to hear a response similar to this: "My parents think that being a teacher is a suitable job, and they wanted me to choose this major." The students do not say things like this begrudgingly or as if they feel greatly displeased. As filial sons or daughters, they are being respectful and compliant to their parent's wishes, not thinking about themselves, but about honoring their parents. As one of the students quoted above lucidly stated, "Filial piety is a double-edged sword: It makes young people to take their responsibility but also makes them lose their independence."

We will continue to allow our perception and understanding of filial piety to be informed from an emic perspective. What follows will be a series of questions and authentic responses. The questions will move from general in nature to an intersection of filial piety and faith. The respondents to these questions are all believers in Jesus Christ that were born and raised in China; therefore, their answers offer rich cultural insights through redeemed eyes.

## How would you explain filial piety to a Westerner?

> *It basically means children's identity is based in a community context rather than who he or she wants to be, as opposed to an individualistic culture. They are supposed to honor, respect and take care of parent's material needs, and excel in profitable business in order for the family to have face in other people's eyes. For 21$^{st}$ century Chinese people, money is the primary love language when it comes to the concept of filial piety. Parents are supposed to provide for their children's main material needs and discipline them to make more money and bring face to the whole family. Chinese parents love to compare how much their children make with their cousins.* - H.G.

H.G. gives incredible insight by juxtaposing Chinese and typical individualistic Western cultures. It is not uncommon at all in America to hear a parent say about their child, "Well, as long as she is happy." However, in Chinese culture, a child being happy is not the most important thing because it is not about the individual being happy, but about harmony in the family. And as H.G. states, the 21$^{st}$ century has brought shifts into how filial piety is expressed—
with the added dimension of money.

In my opinion, the former one-child policy has played a large part in making finances an important element of filial piety. As is the case in most of the world, as parents age, it is a child's responsibility to care for them. In China, most people— although certainly not everyone—born after 1979 are only children, meaning they are solely responsible for the care of their parents. Perhaps you can begin to see the economic responsibility that is looming over that child. In response, Chinese parents will typically spare no expense to try to give their child the best opportunities to be successful: after-school tutoring, music lessons, Saturday school lessons, etc.—all provided because that child will have the burden to care for his or her parents. H.G.

also gives us the great insight that mixed in with all of this is the desire for the child to give face and honor to their parents through their success.

### *In what ways has filial piety impacted your life and the decisions that you have made?*

> *I don't have a typical traditional mindset, luckily my parents [don't] either. So most of the time I make decisions myself; I decided my major in college, I chose Christian belief without their permission, and they respect my decisions. But I still feel afraid of my decision to go to graduate school and if I could stay in the US. Because that means I won't [stay] with my parents when they get older. And most of my relatives say, 'You're a girl, after graduating from your college, come back home and be a teacher and [stay with] your parents! Isn't that what you want and should do?'* - W.M.

Margaret Mead was an American cultural anthropologist. A simplified version of her research philosophy is "What people say, what people do, and what they say they do are entirely different things" (Miles, Blocher, & Corporon, 2000). W.M. claims to not have a traditional mindset regarding filial piety, and she very well may have assessed herself accurately. However, while she may think that filial piety does not play a significant role in her life, some of its influences and effects can still be seen clearly in her words and thought process. So, as Mead says, sometimes what people say they do and what they actually do is not the same thing. This does not inherently mean that it is hypocritical; it means that we are often unaware of just how deeply our own culture has permeated our thought processes and we may not even recognize its presence. From what I know of W.M., she is right in saying that she does not have a typical traditional mindset, yet the concept of filial piety still plays a significant, although perhaps undetected, role in her decision-making. It may not show itself in the actual final decision, but it is most definitely a part of the decision-making process. For example, she was just admitted to a graduate program in the United States and will soon begin a master's degree. While she undoubtedly wanted to go abroad for her postgraduate studies, the final decision was not easy as she had a few promising options to stay in China as well. For W.M., it was not simply that she was determined to go to America, but that road included the nuances of filial piety in the final decision.

> *I was considering to study in seminary, but my dad's strong opposition has been a hindrance and my major concern to take the next step. I am still trying to learn how to honor my dad, but at the same time answer God's call.* - H.G.

H.G.'s candor is wonderful, and it highlights a tension that many Chinese believers may feel and wrestle with in some important life decisions. There are some factors in their decision-making process that do not even enter the typical Westerner's mind. In H.G.'s example, it truly is not as simple as just saying, "You need to follow God and go to seminary now." That very well may be the Lord's call, but the timing is not ours to judge.

**In what ways may filial piety impact a typical Chinese person in respect to even being interested in Christianity? Do you think one may be reluctant to have any interest in Christianity due to a sense of filial piety?**

> *If the parents disagree with Christian beliefs or have their own belief, usually they won't support their children to get to know Christianity or even strongly oppose them to do so. The children will feel guilty if they make their parents annoyed.* - T.Z.

> *I would say filial piety is one of the hindrances which prevents some Chinese making that decision to live for Him. I think young people are less likely to be intimidated by the Confucius idea, but still they probably feel a sense of betraying their parents and humiliating the family when they make that decision to follow.* - H.G.

In order to truly understand how filial piety impacts the process of one being interested in the Lord, we must recall our historical introduction. As earlier summarized, a good son or daughter will be respectful, compliant, and devoted to their parents while recognizing that there is no task too troublesome in order to give back to them for all that they have sacrificed. Blended with this is the concept of bringing honor and face to one's parents. H.G. highlights this in his response and we cannot separate the two.

The impact of filial piety on a Chinese college student's interest in Christianity is best understood on a continuum, ranging from it being a true deciding factor to it being inconsequential. Having taught hundreds of students and discussed this topic with many of them, I can attest that its impact varies. However, it is nearly universally a part of the thought process of Chinese people. It absolutely does play a role, but how significantly will vary from person to person. The best a Westerner can do is to try to understand and empathize, not to pressure them to ignore or dismiss their feelings.

***Thinking back to when you were spiritually seeking, did filial piety play a role in your journey of coming to the knowledge of Jesus? If so, how? If not, why not?***

> *Yes, a little bit. My dad's consistent disapproval has been a pressure for me. I felt uncomfortable sharing deep things with him because he always has a very negative view on faith. He also kept pushing me to make more and more money because it means respect for him.* - H.G.

In typical Western individualistic cultures, if a parent disapproves of their child's interest in Christ, the son or daughter may feel hurt by the disapproval, but they are likely to keep moving forward regardless. At least, the disapproval is not something that would be described as "pressure." While it may appear as though this pressure has a negative impact on the decision-making process, this is not always the case. In fact, the opposite can be true. Take a look at the rest of HG's answer and how the Lord uses this situation for good.

> *But on the other hand, [my father's] consistent opposition has also helped me to count the cost before I committed to the Lord, and I have learned to rely on Him daily to be able to love my dad.* - H.G.

Clearly, the concept of filial piety can lead Chinese seekers to truly count the cost of following Jesus, which results in a stronger commitment. When a Chinese person commits to Jesus, it is not a casual decision to follow a social trend. On the contrary, it is often a deeply thoughtful decision in which they have truly counted the cost. Chinese believers understand Jesus' words in Matthew 10:37 far greater than those of us from the West: "Whoever loves father or mother more than me is not worthy of me, and whoever loves son or daughter more than me is not worthy of me" (ESV). Ultimately, the love of Christ compels them and although the process can be difficult, the decision is definite. To illustrate this, consider T.Z.'s words:

> *It made me sad sometimes, but it cannot stop me to do the right thing.* - T.Z.

**There are instances when new Chinese believers have felt reluctant to tell their parents about their decision. Do you think this is related in some way to filial piety?**

> *Yes. Before I told my parents my belief, I even calculated how many tutoring jobs I should do if they were too angry to give me my living expenses.* – W.M.

I have never heard anything quite like this before in America. This is from W.M., who considers herself to be a non-traditional Chinese person with regard to filial piety. Even though it did not hinder her decision for Christ, it is evident that the cultural expectations of filial piety were heavy on her mind after her decision. However, so as not to generalize, consider a more nuanced view as to why this can occur:

> *I think this issue also involves personalities. Not all Chinese students feel reluctant to share [about God] with their parents. Some students are very brave and straightforward by nature and they, despite the cost of angering their parents, have learned how to make [God] known through words and deeds.* – H.G.

As is the case with all these aspects of filial piety, there is a continuum. And as we can see, this can also lead to boldness and strong reliance on the Lord when navigating the issue. These potential challenges for new Chinese believers may be present; however, while the challenges may be foreign to Westerners, this does not mean that they are wrong. They are just different and provides a unique opportunity to trust more deeply in God.

## How are Westerners to Understand This?

At this point, we have gone through a historical introduction and heard a plethora of thoughts on filial piety covering a range of angles from Chinese people themselves. What we are to do with it all? In order to point us in the right direction, I want to offer three launching points: a posture of humility, a reluctance to be judgmental, and a learning attitude.

Our first response should be one of humility. If you are a Westerner, I hope that you are feeling that you do not truly understand how filial piety impacts Chinese people. True, we can understand the concept in general and how it may influence Chinese culture, and we can comprehend their stories, but not having grown up in the culture we will never fully understand. And that naturally means that no matter how close we may be with a Chinese friend, we will never truly grasp what they are feeling in regard to their relationship with their parents and how this influences them.

Second, we should have a reluctance to be judgmental. Because Westerners do not truly understand the impact of filial piety, a negative reaction to the immense concern that it brings to Chinese believers is not uncommon. In a typical scenario, a Chinese student living in America comes to faith through the efforts and witness of an American Christian. Everyone is ecstatic and rejoicing in the Lord's salvation. A couple of months go by, and, when the student's parents come up in conversation, the American asks if the Chinese believer has told their family. Upon learning that the student has not, the American immediately begins to question the salvation of the Chinese person, unable to fathom why they are keeping it a secret from their family. In some cases, the American keeps these thoughts private; but in other cases, they pressure the Chinese believer, telling them that they "must not deny the Lord by not telling your family."

Regarding this scenario, the first thing to note is that the Westerner's internal reaction is understandable. It is something they have not dealt with, so they are processing it through their own worldview—the only worldview they have. This is fine, when initial reservations are kept private until they have had more time to understand the situation. After that initial reaction, Westerners need to listen to their friend sincerely and do their best to empathize with them and understand their thought processes. For example, here is H.G. explaining how new Chinese believers process a decision to tell their parents about their faith:

> *In our thinking pattern, our parents are supposed to be our authority and ruler, so we try not to anger or irritate them. Sharing our Father usually irritates them. By doing so, we tend to avoid hard topics.* - H.G.

Harmony is an essential pillar of Chinese society, and filial piety is a means to that end. As H.G. states, Chinese children try not to irritate or trouble their parents, so they may avoid hard topics. The reason a new Chinese believer does not share their faith with their parents is not because they are ashamed of Jesus, but because they want to maintain a harmonious home life by not upsetting their parents.

Certainly, in some cases, individual need encouragement to be bold in proclaiming their faith, regardless of the consequences. However, as a rule of thumb, Westerners should approach the situation with humility and a recognition that it is almost certainly something that their Chinese friend already has been seriously processing. Just as Americans need time to work through different cultural influences that impact their faith—for example, how our individualistic tendencies inhibit communal life with other believers—so our Chinese brothers and sisters need time to work through the issues that come with living out Christian faith in their own context.

The third response is that we should adopt a learning attitude. We need to grow in our understanding of what the Bible has to say about filial piety and view Chinese filial piety through that Biblical lens to see what we can learn from it.

The concept of filial piety is present throughout the Bible, though with motivations and foundations vastly different from those of Chinese culture. We will analyze this from two vantage points: the first will be direct commands in the Scripture and the second will be observations of instances related to filial piety throughout the Bible.

The most plainly stated passage on filial piety comes in the Ten Commandments, "Honor your father and your mother, that your days may be long in the land that the LORD your God is giving you" (Exodus 20:12). This command was so pivotal that God reiterated it throughout the Law: "Whoever curses his mother and father shall be put to death" (Exodus 21:17); "You shall stand up before the gray head and honor the face of an old man, and you shall fear your God: I am the Lord" (Leviticus 19:32). In his letter to the Ephesians, Paul very succinctly sums up this command before quoting it by simply stating, "Children, obey your parents in the Lord, for this is right" (Ephesians 6:1). In short, obedience to parents is required in God's economy.

Now what is debatable and worthy of further analysis is how this plays out. In doing so, it is imperative to stay close to the text to continue to learn from it in order to formulate our application of it. A common topic in this realm that often comes up is providing for parents in their old age. The Bible is far from silent on this, as Paul tells Timothy that "if anyone does not provide for his relatives, and especially for members of his household, he has denied the faith and is worse than an unbeliever" (1 Timothy 5:8).

Both Matthew and Mark record the story of Jesus rebuking the Pharisees for dismissing the command in Exodus 20:12 and deflecting their responsibility. The Pharisees taught that instead taking on the responsibility of caring for their parents, one could just say "It is Corban." This would mean that whatever money they may have used to provide for their parents could instead be given to the Temple. This custom was cloaked in an air of holiness, but Jesus exposed the hypocrisy of their hearts and in the process condemned their actions. Jesus told them that with this practice, they were making the word of God void (Matthew 15:1-9; Mark 7:9-13).

We will now move on to observations of examples of the concepts of filial piety in practice throughout the Bible and will do so in chronological order. One of the first instances is the story of Abraham's call from God, which reveals that he did not exactly pick up and leave everything immediately. Yes, he did leave, but he brought his father with him (compare Acts 7:2-4 with Genesis 11:31 - 12:5). In Acts 7:4, Stephen recalls this event and comments that after Abraham's father died, the Lord called him again and it was then that he left for the Promised Land—a clear sign of caring for his father.

Fast forwarding to the New Testament, as Jesus was on the cross, one of his final requests was to his disciple John, telling him to take care of Mary (John 19:26-27). Even near the point of death, one of Jesus' primary concerns was his mother's well-being. He was most certainly a filial pious son. Lastly, Jesus was the ultimate example of filial piety with his devotion and obedience to God the Father. In essence, Jesus embodied a perfect combination of unrelenting obedience, joyous communion, and faithful steward.

One caveat to all this Biblical truth is that obedience to God precedes all notions of filial piety. It absolutely does not negate the responsibility as the Pharisees erroneously displayed, but instead it just means that obedience to God is preeminent. Jesus himself said, "If anyone comes to me and does not hate his own father and mother . . . he cannot be my disciple" (Luke 14:26). The teaching in mind here is not animosity toward one's parents, but ultimate allegiance to God even if that means rejecting the wishes of parents.

Next, we must next consider ways in which sin can enter the picture and how we should respond to the resulting distortion. A redeemed view of these Confucian concepts lived out in the life of a believer is also necessary in applying this knowledge. Some of these concepts could certainly be used in discussion or perhaps even discipleship with Chinese believers. Most importantly, they are things to pray about on behalf of our Chinese brothers and sisters.

The first thing to point out is that the traditional Chinese foundation for filial piety is not Biblical. The concept itself is, but the motivations and end goals are not. Because of this, it is important to reorient our way of thinking about filial piety.

Sherwood Lingenfelter (2016) offers a way of doing this, which he borrowed from Malcom McFee. The concept is to become a "150% person." The example he gives is of the Blackfoot Indians assimilating into American culture. In the process of becoming more "American," they did not lose their native culture. Instead, they became 75% Blackfoot and 75% American. Lingenfelter (2016) summarizes the idea like this: "They have added to their cultural repertoire and become bicultural, 150 percent persons, yet somehow less than 100 percent of any culture."

This concept needs to be amended slightly for Christians; we can do so by suggesting that we should become a 175% person. That is, a person who is 100% in Christ and 75% influenced by filial piety from a Chinese perspective. What follows are several vignettes of what redeemed filial piety can look like.

As noted above, the primary aspect of Chinese filial piety that needs to be redeemed is the foundation and incentive. Traditionally, the primary thrust of motivation to be a filial son or daughter is that of obligation. As my students so often say, "My parents brought me into this world, so how can I not give my all for them?" It is a sense of duty. There is nothing wrong with some semblance of obligation to obey parents, but where it comes from is vital. One should not seek to demonstrate filial piety solely for the sake of filial piety, but instead first and foremost to honor and glorify God. When Paul says, "Children, obey your parents, for this is right," he does not mean that it is right based on its mere virtue. Instead, he appeals to the Scripture. The motivation must come from honoring God and being a follower of Christ. This also does not mean stripping away the Chinese characteristics of filial piety, but as Carolyn Chen (2006) beautifully states, when encouraging filial behavior, we should "use the new moral language of Christian discipleship to achieve traditionally Confucian ends."

As discussed above, one of the functional aspects of filial piety is to keep peace and harmony in a family. However, because of sin this is not always possible. This may manifest itself externally, but more commonly the effects of sin can show themselves inside a person's heart. With sin in the picture and motives from parents that are not always pure, it is natural for a son or daughter to feel a sort of resentment toward their parents for decisions that have been made. This can lead to bottled-up disdain for one's parents that can never be expressed because it would be impious to voice such disdain. Dealing with these feelings can be a conundrum.

Susanne Breganbaek (2016) gives a great example of how such a situation can be redeemed. She tells the story of a woman in a house church in Beijing whose father had left her and her mother earlier in life for another woman. The daughter, naturally, had strong feelings of resentment toward her father for his past actions, but had bottled them up and had nowhere to release them. After coming to faith, she learned of the importance of forgiveness and the possibility to pray about the situation. After some time, she was able to work up the courage to meet with him to begin the process of reconciliation. Her faith allowed her to confront her father in a way that maintained some honor and respect for him, but that could also begin to heal her of resentment. Or as the author summarized, "forbidden feelings such as anger directed at parents found expression in this Chinese house-church." When sin enters and complicates aspects of filial piety, Christ can provide a way out of it (1 Corinthians 10:13).

Two final insights from Chen Dingliang will now be addressed: respect for and evangelizing one's parents. The first concept is respect for our parents. Chen (2014) adeptly notes that "Respect for parents is not merely in the form of etiquette, but also in grace. As they age, some of their habits and the way they do things might grow to be improper, and they might do a lot of things we would never expect them to do." He goes on to reference the story of Noah and his drunkenness after the Flood in Genesis 9. In the story, Shem and Japheth take great concern for their father's honor and cover his nakedness. In response to it all, when Noah awoke, he cursed Ham's lineage for neglecting his honor. Chen is absolutely right: showing respect for our parents as they age is most certainly in the form of grace and should be done in God-honoring way.

The second concept is in regard to evangelism. H.G. spoke to this in relation to his dad: "I am still learning how to walk in obedience with Him while at the same time, seeking to love my dad in whatever capacity I have been given. I cannot change his heart, but I can lift his soul to Him and lean on His strength to love him." D. Chen (2014) offers a great insight that encapsulates how this all works together: "It's not only about helping them receive salvation, but also letting them grow spiritually; you have to care about their spiritual growth and maturity." This perspective is transformational—a Christian is not only concerned with simply honoring their parents, but with their spiritual condition as well.

By becoming a 175% person and adopting the spirit that is present in these few vignettes, a Chinese Christian can have a redeemed sense of filial piety. As Christians—regardless of our geographical location or cultural upbringing—we should be concerned about these elements that are related to filial piety. I contend that Chinese Christians understand what it means to "honor your father and mother" much better than those of us in the West. Christians from a more Western culture would do well to first approach the issue of filial piety with humility, then be reluctant to judge Chinese believers on immerging issues related to that virtue, and lastly to learn from our Chinese brothers and sisters on the topic itself.

## Conclusion

When a person comes to Christ, they become a part of God's family (John 1:12-13). A key concept of being a child of God is loving others, and this is both spiritually and functionally done by putting the needs and interests of others above our own, as Christ did for us (Philippians 2:1-11). Of special concern to God are those that are poor and weak (James 1:27; 1 John 3:17) and followers of Christ should care for, honor, and help those in such states. This naturally spills over into the realm of the parent-child relationship. When children are young, they are in many respects "poor and weak" and are cared for by their parents and other adults. Later, as the parents age and become weak, the adult children care for them. Going further, in a Christian community elderly people not only have their own children to rely upon for their support, but the whole Christian family.

A lot has been covered in this chapter, but much else is left to be learned. It is my hope that you feel as though you have a greater understanding of what the concept of filial piety is in Chinese culture and how to interact with it in relation to both your Chinese friends and also for yourself. If possible, I would highly recommend trying to talk to a Chinese friend about some of these concepts. For more information, please see the reference list below. Above all else, as believers, may it be our sincere desire to be filial sons and daughters of our true Father.

## References

Bregnbaek, S. (2016). From filial piety to forgiveness: Managing ambivalent feelings in a Beijing house-church. *ETHOS, 44*(4), 411-426. American Anthropological Association.

Chen, C. (2006). From filial piety to religious piety: Evangelical Christianity reconstructing Taiwanese immigrant families in the United States. *International Migration Review 40*(3), 573-602. DOI: 10.1111/j.1747-7379.2006.00032.x

Chen, D. (2014, March 18). *Filial piety: A Christian perspective.* Retrieved from: http://www.chinasource.org/blog/posts/filial-piety-a-christian-perspective Article originally posted in Chinese on January 18, 2014 on www.gospeltimes.cn

Ikels, C. (2004). *Filial piety: Practice and discourse in contemporary East Asia.* Stanford: Stanford University Press.

Keller, T. (2016, October 9). *Tim Keller: "Making sense of God: An invitation to the skeptical" | Talks At Google* [Video File] Retrieved from: https://www.youtube.com/watch?v=4uIvOniW8xA

Legge, J. (1899) *The sacred books of the East: The texts of Confucianism, vol. III, part I:* 2nd edition, Oxford: Clarendon Press. Retrieved from: http://www.anselm.edu/homepage/athornto/xiaojing.htm

Lingenfelter, S. (2016). *Ministering cross-culturally.* 3d ed. Grand Rapids, MI: Baker Academic.

Miles, R. B., Blocher, L., & Corporon, E. (2000). *Teaching music through performance in band, Vol. 3.* Chicago, IL. GIA Publications.

Sure, H. (n.d). *The twenty-four paragons of filial respect: Their stories & verses in praise* Translated by Dharma Master Hung. Retrieved from: http://www2.kenyon.edu/Depts/Religion/Fac/Adler/Reln270/24-filial2.htm

Teon, A.(2016, March 14). Filial piety (孝) in Chinese culture. *The Greater China Journal.* Retrieved from: https://china-journal.org/2016/03/14/filial-piety-in-chinese-culture/

Theobald, U. (2010, July 24). "*Xiaojing 孝經*". ChinaKnowledge.de: An encyclopaedia on Chinese history, literature and art Retrieved from: http://www.chinaknowledge.de/Literature/Classics/xiaojing.html

Yep, Jeanette, et al. (1998). Following Jesus without dishonoring your parents Retrieved from:

http://www.chinasource.org/blog/posts/filial-piety-a-christian-perspective

# 2. Traditional Principles of Confucianism and Other Influences on My Life[3]

## By C.X.[4]

Most of my relatives do not have any spiritual [religious] belief. As far as I know, only my maternal grandmother, who passed away several years ago, has believed in God. The God she believed in is not the same one from any other ideologies I have heard of. I have looked at the book, distributed by the group she joined, which describes her God. What is explained there sounds like a combination of Christianity, Islam, Confucianism, and superstition. Most of its main theory has positive ideas; for example, the concepts guide people to love others and to not do anything evil. However, it also includes some impossible ideas; for example, it says God will protect and heal believers, so they do not even need to take medicine when they are ill. They also believe that the only people God will take to join Him when they are dead are those believers who only did good things while they were alive. There are not too many followers of this particular group in China.

Our other family members do not have any belief. I think this is a very common situation in China now. More and more youths in China realize this, but nobody can tell if it is good or not. In the modern days, people get huge pressure from many sources, challenging work, increasing commodity prices, a high

---

[3] *Editor's note: This Chinese contributor is a highly educated middle-class professional approaching middle age. Here, he reflects upon what has shaped the spiritual aspect of his thinking, especially in his earlier years. This is a good illustration of how deeply ingrained the previously-discussed basic concepts of Confucianism remain in the mind of an average Chinese people, even over time. - K.P.*

[4] *The contributor's full name has been withheld to protect his identity.*

unemployment rate, etc. How to release bad emotions, how to stay at peace in one's heart, and how to self-motivate have become critical problems. Therefore, spiritual health is becoming more and more important at the present time.

Now, I am an adult and have had to choose my own personal beliefs. I do not believe in any specific religious ideology. When I was a child, modern China was in the very beginning phase of more open economic development. At that time, Chinese people were still deeply influenced by Marxism, which was brought to China by some of the well-educated foreign ideologists and proved to be effective for guiding the Chinese economy at that time. As the "political" result, children of my generation were educated with Marxism in school, though few children could understand it clearly. Through all of my years in school, Marxism was a compulsory course. Even though there have been several new theories set up by some of our Chinese leaders corresponding to the real conditions of China, they are still based on Marxism. Gradually, people have realized that every theory has its limitations and there is no one theory which can cover all situations. So, the current younger people in China, including me, do not have concrete beliefs.

With our country's further development, Chinese people have begun to know more and more information and new ideas from all over the world and are have also been influenced by various ideologies. People are starting to think and distinguish between viewpoints for themselves. They have the right and possibility to choose what they need. When making their selection, personal background and living environment really help to influence the choices people make.

Though most Chinese people do not believe in anything formally, we cannot deny that the theory of Confucianism influenced generations of Chinese people. As far as I know, there is not a concrete group of people in China now who get together to learn Confucianism or to teach other people Confucianism. When we talk about Confucianism in China, most of the time, it is just a theory or ideology that guides people to be kind and perform other positive actions. Confucianism is deeply rooted in the Chinese blood and mentality; it is a part of what makes someone Chinese.

Though I learned about Marxism at school, I was educated by my parents in the essentials of Confucianism at home. But I believe it does not really matter if I believe in one or the other. The theory one accepts is not so important. Doing right things, loving family, and being kind to others: these things are more important.

I am willing to talk with my good friends and discuss some things related to different ideologies. However, it has not happened often in the past years. Most of the friends around me show less interest to deeply learn about any particular ideology, especially different religions. Regarding most major religions and types of belief, we only know a little about the core concepts. Subconsciously, we do not believe these theories are true.

Many traditional Chinese ideas are tied to spiritual beliefs and superstitions, including following some of the medical practices we use, consulting a fortune teller before making decisions about the future, and believing in concepts like fate and good luck. In the old days, fortune tellers really had lots of followers. But nowadays, with the development of science and the expansion of education, more and more Chinese people regard the practice of fortune telling as superstition and believe more in scientific methods instead of going to visit a fortune teller. In this way, the spiritual world of Chinese people has changed a lot.

China is a big country with a very long history. Therefore, it is understandable that we do have many belief systems represented within our culture. In the history of China, there were various kinds of spiritual theories, especially in the Spring and Autumn and Warring States Periods, in which various theories were set up by advanced thinkers who cared about our nation, people, and nature. There is Taoism, which focuses on harmony between human being and nature, as well as a strong objection to war. Another major one is Legalism, which requires the nation's government to maintain strict laws. Finally, there is Confucianism, which is concerned with self-management and showing mercy to others. Of those three, Confucianism has had the greatest effect on the formation of Chinese beliefs.

With the development of society and civilization, Confucianism has changed to adapt to its environment. However, it is still the most important guidance for a Chinese person to use to deal with themselves and others. Generation by generation, children have been educated in Confucian ideas by either their parents or teachers.

Let me summarize some of the most important points of Confucianism:

1. Filial piety (孝 xiào)

Filial piety is regarded as the most important virtue in Chinese culture. We have a very famous saying: The first place of goodness is filial piety (百善孝为先). Thus, you can see filialpiety takes a very important role in the Chinese mind. Filial piety reflects the respect shown by children to their parents in a family. Since the parents give birth to the children and raise them up with great kindness, filial piety has two general layers of meaning. The first one is that children should feel grateful to their parents. And the other meaning is that children should follow the will of their parents.

In the old days, parents had a higher hierarchy than children in the family. Sometimes the parents' will was just like the imperial edict, and the children had to obey their parents' orders completely. For example, marriage was arranged by parents in the old days, instead of including consideration of the children's wishes as we do today. "Butterfly Lovers" is one of the most popular tragic stories in Chinese culture, and it clearly demonstrates the power of the parents' will. Nevertheless, presently, in most families, parents and children have a closer level of equality. They respect each other's thinking and decisions. Parents would like to encourage and support children to do what they are willing to and ask them to be responsible for their own lives. So, the second layer meaning of filial piety mentioned above is getting weaker and weaker now. But the first layer of meaning still plays a very important role, and in fact filial piety is still one of the most important and influential factors guiding young adults who are choosing a spouse in China.

2. Kindheartedness (仁 rén)

Kindheartedness, sometimes translated as "benevolence," is one of the virtues to guide people in how to get along with others (friends, colleagues, children or even strangers). The main idea is that everyone lives in a complex social environment in which it is impossible to avoid at least some form of communication with others. So being kind, sympathetic, and helpful to others will make those interactions and relationships harmonious. From the national point of view, if everyone shows kindheartedness, our society will be peaceful and happy.

3. Loyalty (忠 zhōng)

Loyalty, a character with two elements that point to what is at the center of one's heart, is a virtue of showing consistency or uniformity in devotion to country, other people, or beliefs. Most of the time, it means loyalty to one's country. Everybody has his or her own nationality; that is a part of our personal identity. So, for a lifetime, one should be loyal to their country and should not do anything that would harm the nation. Because of this important virtue, wars have been fought in past years, to help protect the country. Through their loyal defense, the Chinese people showed firmness of will to defend our country from aggression and drive invaders away.

    4.   Integrity (信 xìn)

Integrity, a character synonymous with faith and being worthy of belief, is also one of the virtues that helps us get along with others. Generally, it emerges when people promise something to others. It is the basis of gaining trust from others. Without integrity, it is hard to maintain friendships, do business, and govern a country. Therefore, it is very important for children to start learning about integrity while they are still young.

    5.   Politeness (礼 lǐ)

Foreigners commonly praise Chinese people for being polite. Indeed, to be polite is one of the very first lessons learned by a child in China. Politeness not only concerns the words or actions one extends to others, but it also means the behavior one demonstrates in front of people. In China, we have many aspects of being polite. For example,

- At the family dinner, children are not allowed to start eating before their parents.
- An umbrella should not be given to a couple as a wedding gift, and a clock should not be given to an old man. Unless it is an absolute emergency, it is rude to call people in the middle of the night.

Customs such as these reflecting the Chinese virtue of politeness are passed on by parents in the Chinese family so that their children will show good manners and leave a good impression on others.

The virtues we have discussed so far are only a part of Confucianism, and there are also many other aspects. Confucianism today is the fruit of cultural participation and evolution over thousands of years. Every Chinese person learns Confucianism by word of mouth. That is why it is deeply rooted in the Chinese psyche. But when you talk with any Chinese person about Confucianism, the virtues mentioned above will likely be a part of their speech. These basic concepts are used daily by the Chinese as a part of our reasoning method, as guidance for our actions, as fundamental values of our lives, and as a marker of our distinct identity in the wider world as "Chinese."

Growing up with the seeds of Confucianism in mind, most Chinese people will tell you they do not have a personal belief when you directly ask them about spirituality. However, this does not mean there are no spiritual or religious beliefs existing in China.

Let us return to my family as an example. As mentioned earlier, though the rest of us do not have strong personal beliefs, my grandmother still believed devotedly in her God. From some of my friends, I have heard of some other beliefs which are similar to my grandmother's even though I do not know the names of them. Most followers of these groups are old women who have less education, have no job, and always stay at home without participating in any other activities. And most of them live in small cities just as my grandmother did. When she was old, she probably often thought about where she would go after she died, and there was a need to fill her spirit with something. When this "God" came into her life, she became a follower immediately. She worked as housewife her entire life. Without good education in her younger years, she could hardly be expected to correctly distinguish between right or wrong spiritual theories. So, she just believed her "God."

When talking about my parents' generation, it seems in the past they have mainly believed in the Communist Party, especially in Chairman Mao when they were young. After Mao died, they did not have a personal belief anymore. I have talked with my mother about the Mao period. She said Mao was just like a "god" in China during her childhood. Every family had Mao's statue, picture, and red quotation book. All Chinese people believed that Mao would lead them into a communist society and to live a happy life. When news of Mao's death spread to the small city where my mother lived, everyone was shocked and felt the future was unclear or empty. My mother said the city was full of crying that day. When she recalled these things so many years later, she said she did not understand why everyone was crying so much. And after Mao's death, my parents really did not have anything left to believe in.

But what about other organized religions? Modern China contains 56 different ethnic people groups. The largest one, the Han, makes up 91% of the whole Chinese population. Most of the other minority peoples have their own beliefs. For example, Hui people believe in Islam. Muslims have many limitations with food. As the most widely known example, they are not allowed to eat pork.

When I was in senior middle school, I was classmates with a Hui girl named Miao. She had lunch together one day with several girls in our classroom, eating the food each of them had brought from home. Another girl kindly put a piece of pork made by her mother into Miao's lunchbox and asked Miao to have a taste. Of course, she did not know Miao was Hui; she just wanted to be friendly. Miao told her that she was Hui so she could not eat pork and gave the pork back to the other girl with her chopsticks. When Miao got home after school and gave her lunchbox to her mother to wash, her mother smelled the box and knew there had been pork inside. She got very angry with Miao and refused to talk to Miao for several days even though she knew it was not Miao's mistake. All the classmates who heard this story later exclaimed that her mother was very devout!

Another example concerns one of my colleagues who lives in the same housing block as I do and is very close to me in age. We usually have meals together. He is also Hui. When we eat together, we do not separate the pork from other foods intentionally. If there is pork nearby, that does not bother him. He says when he has meals at home, there is no pork at all since all his family members are Muslims. And his father has told him that when he has meals apart from his family, his relatives' one request is simply that he not actually eat pork since his father knows it is very difficult to guarantee there is no pork smell or pork oil existing in the cooking pans or on the dishes. In my opinion, his father is more kind to him, changing the rules according to the real situation. Maybe his father was influenced by Confucianism before. Who knows?

Minority peoples have their own beliefs formed from their specific living background and culture. Since young people from these groups leave their hometowns and move to bigger cities for educational or professional reasons, they interact further with Han people. So, some traditional habits or beliefs are influenced or changed, or even disappear.

In modern times, Chinese people face huge pressure from many sources, including challenging work, increasing commodity prices, high unemployment rates, and expensive medical costs. Therefore, we have heard of many emerging physiological disorders in recent years, such as depression, paranoia, mania, and insomnia. Interestingly, though many of us do not have a strong spiritual belief, we can see that a focus on spiritual and emotional health has really grown in importance. How should we release bad emotions, keep peace in our heart, and find sustaining self-motivation? These are critical problems for us.

Is spiritual belief a kind of medicine to help people conquer all of these pressures or make them feel at ease about life? I am not sure. But I think the person who faces a spiritual or mental illness could either have a personal belief or not. We cannot judge a man as being mentally sound or ill based on his beliefs, just like we cannot judge which belief is the best one in the world. The therapy used to treat such a person should not include throwing any kind of belief at the patient and getting the pathologic diagnosis by checking whether he could answer all the questions about that belief.

Chinese medicine attempts to prescribe a medicine especially for the disease in question, which means the doctor needs to know the symptoms clearly and specifically so as to cure the disease effectively. No single medicine can ever cure all kinds of disease! Human beings are complicated. For example, medical science still knows little about how the brain works and how to stimulate its potential, so it is still difficult to cure spiritual or mental diseases through medical means.

According to the news, more and more hospitals in China are setting up psychotherapy rooms to help those who have spiritual or mental illnesses. These patients may not have any physical injury, but they are suffering from disorders that make them feel bad in the spirit. But I seldom hear that anybody around me goes to the hospital to receive psychotherapy. One of the reasons is that the cost of seeing a professional for diagnosis is too high. Another reason is that psychotherapy is not recognized or understood as widely as other therapies in China. Possibly, with society's continued progress, an increasing number of people with these needs will be willing to get therapy from psychologists in the future.

I had an interesting experience discussing with one of my colleagues about which was better, Chinese medicine or Western medicine. I used to believe that even though Chinese medicine would take longer than Western medicine to cure the same disease, Chinese medicine is still better because it relies upon ingredients from nature that have fewer negative effects on the body. Western medicines, on the other hand, are chemically synthetic, so side effects are much more common and often worse than with any from Chinese medicine. Western medicine may even cause another disease after the original one is cured because of how that medicine affected the body.

My colleague had another point of view. He said Chinese medicine relies on the experience of millions of doctors and patients for thousands of years, which means it must have large enough experimental samples to find the most effective application for each medicine. The doctors draw from their experience to practice various therapies on patients without always knowing which will work. But Western Medicine is chemically based. When the patient is diagnosed as having a particular infection or illness, certain medicine will be applied against that infection or illness. The treatment is direct and precise, allowing for no exceptions. Therefore, Western medicine is much more effective and efficient than Chinese medicine.

In that discussion, there was no winner or loser. We considered the issue from different perspectives and both made some very good points. That may be the reason most Chinese medicine prescriptions now have chemical ingredient indications in the instruction papers and also why most of our hospitals combine Western medicine and Chinese medicine together to do therapy on patients across the Mainland. That is also a good example to further conclude that there is no "best" thing in the world as long as we could use the proper way or effectively combined way to think about and deal with things.

    The above contribution was my attempt to share personal feelings and opinions about belief in present-day China from a Chinese person's perspective. These paragraphs are not highly academic, but they are honest. I hope the things I have shared will help you to more deeply understand Chinese people as a whole and communicate more easily with specific Chinese people you meet.

# 3. Taoism's Influence on Daily Chinese Life[5]

## By Paul Thomas

Imagine someone from the West who has just moved to China—we will call her Jill. Although she enjoys her new life, she is quickly struck by the constant presence of curious customs, the sort of thing that Westerners would label "superstitions." Jill leaves her apartment to jog before work around dawn and passes middle-aged women on her school's basketball court making slow, synchronized movements with swords or fans. Next, Jill jogs through the public square, passing grandmothers who gingerly circle a potted tree, their hands outstretched as if casting a spell.

Later, at work, a friend pops by to generously give Jill a box of fresh lychees. "But be careful!" her friend says, holding back the box of fruit as if Jill is not yet ready to handle it. "Don't eat more than nine at a time, or you will *overheat*." Confusing as the warning sounds, the lychees are welcome, and Jill gobbles down a few.

Around eleven, Jill still feels peckish, so she invites the coworkers in her little office to grab an early lunch. Everyone stops and stares at her in horror. One of them explains (as if talking to a child) that lunch takes place *at noon* . . . followed by a

---

[5] *Editor's note: The author spent several years teaching literature to college students in southeast China, where he also served as a deacon in one of the few churches nationwide allowing Chinese nationals and foreign citizens to freely participate in all roles together. In addition, his long-time acute interest in Chinese culture, history, and religion has driven him to learn more about those topics in his leisure time. Though he is speaking primarily to readers who may live or work in China in the future, there are many useful points from his observations that will also be applicable to readers interacting with Chinese outside the Mainland. As the reader will note, here is another case where a blend of life experience as well as research from a non-Chinese perspective has combined to form a meaningful non-Chinese explanation of an otherwise dauntingly complex topic in the minds of most non-Chinese. – K.P.*

nap. Disturbing this routine might *endanger their health*. Unwilling to contradict them, Jill goes out in search of early lunch, and ends up eating stale fish balls at her local 7-Eleven.

At first, Jill finds all this charming and exotic, but it becomes more difficult to accept once she realizes that such seemingly irrational behavior extends to far more serious subjects. For example, her friends' wedding dates are chosen based on numerology. Their parents insist that their children be married on "auspicious" dates (usually including lucky number 8, and never including 4, which sounds like "death"). Wedding venues crank up their prices to capitalize on such lucky dates, but the parents pay nonetheless. Jill's friends consult fortune tellers for serious life decisions, such as who their daughter should be allowed to marry, when to lay the foundation of a new business, or even what day is best for a haircut. Even real estate is affected by obscure rules. An apartment with a front door which faces northeast or southwest will be cheap, compared to one with "good feng shui"—one that faces in a more spiritual direction. Even tombs must be constructed according to the laws of feng shui, placed on a hill (and hopefully facing a body of water) for the better repose of the deceased.

Amid all these seemingly antiquated practices, Jill finds herself talking with a Chinese friend one day, and spiritual subjects arise: God, the resurrection, angels, and miracles. Jill knows that her friend observes many traditional Chinese customs. She had told Jill that she burns paper money, houses, and cell phones to comfort her grandparents' souls on Tomb Sweeping Day. Yet today, to Jill's surprise, her friend shrugs off the idea of God and the rest as fairy tales. "How can you be so sure?" Jill asks. "Because we Chinese are atheists," her friend responds, without a hint of irony.

Jill pursues the subject—asking about lucky "8"s, unlucky "4"s, feng shui, the 9-lychee rule, and the rest—but her friend is unfazed. She smiles inscrutably and replies, "You do not understand our Chinese culture."

Clearly, Jill's friend is right. Something is amiss.

This chapter aims to help bridge the cognitive dissonance between these ideas and show how Taoism—the least visible but perhaps the most deeply entrenched of China's three traditional religions—influences daily life in China. By explaining some of the basic influences Taoism has had on Chinese life, I hope also to explain why understanding these deep Taoist roots is crucial if one hopes to communicate with mainland Chinese people about faith.

## Common Taoist Iconography

In mainland China, Taoism is both ever-present and unperceived. Unlike Buddhism, with its ubiquitous temples and priests, Taoism's presence seems relatively subtle. Many young people will confess that their grandmother is a die-hard Buddhist, but rarely will you meet anyone who calls himself a die-hard Taoist. Taoist monasteries exist, but (aside from some sacred mountains) people tend to go on pilgrimages to Buddhist, not Taoist, sites. And while Confucius remains China's most revered sage, the great Taoist writers Lao Tzu (in Chinese *Lao Zi*) and Zhuangzi remain a bit too esoteric for the people (or the government) to rally behind *en masse*. Both writers are famous and important, of course, but they are difficult to understand. Any Chinese citizen will tell you that Taoism is central to Chinese culture, but few will offer concrete examples of how.

Taoist symbolism, on the other hand, is everywhere. The *yīn-yáng* symbol, which most readers will recognize, appears painted on sidewalks and carved on charms. At Wudangshan, one of Taoism's holiest sites, a theater to showcase Wu-Tang Sword demonstrations was recently constructed in the shape of a gigantic yin-yang, with the theater itself forming the yang and the empty courtyard outside forming the yin (with a circle of dancing fountains forming the yang dot in its middle).

Taoist heroes also appear frequently. The religion's quasi-mythical founder Lao Tzu (Komjathy, 2012) is often seen, either relaxing in loose-fitting robes or riding on the back of an ox. Lao Tzu is said to have been a teacher during the tempestuous Warring States period, around the 6$^{th}$ century B.C. Taoist scriptures tell of how Lao Tzu tried to teach Confucius the importance of rising above worldly affairs. Confucius, of course, resisted; Confucianism focuses on laws to guide human relations in a very material, hierarchical way, whereas Taoism attempts to show a Way (the Tao, *Dao* in Chinese) above earthly ways, a way of emptiness and balance (Kohn, Livia, & LaFargue, 1998; Alexander, 1895). Lao Tzu is the archetypal "holy fool" whose wisdom defies logical boundaries.

Images of Lao Tzu riding an ox allude to a legend about the sage's lack of interest in worldly matters. As he rode through China's westernmost gates to leave the civilized world forever, the story goes, a guardsman asked Lao Tzu to write down his wisdom. Lao Tzu tossed off his ideas on some scrolls, thus casually authoring the *Tao Te Ching* (*Dàodéjīng* in modern pinyin spelling), the greatest Taoist scripture and one of the most important classics of Chinese literature (Kohn & LaFargue, 1998). The sage relaxing on the back of a lowly ox shows both Lao's humility and his desire to leave the world behind.[6]

Also commonly seen are paintings and carvings of the "Eight Immortals." These colorful folk heroes each attained immortality through Taoist practices and are usually represented crossing the ocean together to a faraway paradise (Williams, 1974). (Notice again the emphasis on leaving earth's petty cares behind.) Often the Eight Immortals are shown grouped in a boat, but more memorably they are depicted each using their signature magic objects to cross the waters—a sword, a flute, a gourd, a lotus, a crutch, a basket of flowers, a fan, and even a pair of castanets (Maspero, 1981).

The other common Taoist hero one comes across is Zhuge Liang, the ingenious imperial councilor from the great novel *Romance of the Three Kingdoms*. Based on a real military advisor who lived around A.D. 200 (Tillman, 2007), Zhuge Liang has grown into a figure who is at once Merlin, Benjamin Franklin, and Sun Tzu. A master strategist, Zhuge Liang could predict or control the weather, build mechanical cattle to transport supplies, save his country countless times, and even lay out plans to win battles long after his own death (Lo, 2002). At one point in the classic novel, he uses the *bāguà* (discussed below) to design a nigh-invincible battle formation, (Tillman, 2007) and later uses the same concept to build a stone maze that confounds his enemies (Lo, 2002). This maze, according to a taxi driver I met once in Hong Kong, made Zhuge Liang the patron saint of those who need directions: the driver had glued a small plastic Zhuge Liang to his dashboard in respect for the wily saint.

---

[6] See, for example, the description by Taiwan's National Palace Museum of a Sung Dynasty-era scroll picturing Lao Tzu riding his ox: https://www.npm.gov.tw/exh94/form9407/english/page02_05.html

Easily recognized by his Taoist robes, headdress, and crane-feather fan, Zhuge Liang is among several Taoist mystics in *Three Kingdoms* whose brilliance verges on being supernatural. This connection between Taoists and esoteric wisdom is common in Chinese folk culture.

## Taoism Resists Definition

Although Taoist imagery abounds in Chinese culture, Chinese people tend to offer certain stock responses if one asks them about the religion. They will say that Taoism plays an important role as one of China's three traditional religions, and that they admire the wisdom of Lao Tzu and the "freedom" of the other major Taoist author, Zhuangzi (Zhuangzi, 2003). They label it as such because Zhuangzi's wild writing celebrates the wisdom of those whom society considers fools with near-psychedelic imagery that can baffle both Chinese and Western readers (Zhuangzi, 2003). Beyond that, they are sometimes unable to identify Taoism's role in their daily life, or will disagree among themselves about what Taoism is, exactly.

Part of the confusion comes from Taoism's history. Central concepts of the religion, including yin and yang, predate Lao Tzu, who is generally cited as the founder of the religion (Kohn & LaFargue, 1998). The *Yijīng* (also called the *I Ching* in older romanization), a crucial work for Taoism, has been adopted outside of the religion as a holy book by Buddhists and as a repository of wisdom by secular scholars (Kohn & LaFargue, 1998). More importantly perhaps, folk stories and practices have melded over thousands of years with belief in the *Yijīng*, Lao Tzu's *Tao Te Ching*, and the general concept of balance between yin and yang to become the general framework of Taoism today (Kohn & LaFargue, 1998). One might compare this melding to the meshing of pagan and Christian symbols in Christmas and Easter. In China, however, culture has simmered for so long that it is difficult to sift these elements apart.

There have been attempts, especially in the 20th century, to separate "philosophical" Taoism from "religious" Taoism. If such a division is accepted, philosophical Taoism would include the writings of Lao Tzu, Zhuangzi, and others, and a secular pursuit of the Tao. Religious Taoism would include the pursuit of immortality, veneration of Taoist saints (such as the Eight Immortals), Taoist monasteries (such as the Quanzhen and Zhengyi schools) (Komjathy, 2012), and other supernatural beliefs (Kohn & LaFargue, 1998).

This splitting of Taoism into two parts is quite popular in the United States, where images of the Eight Immortals zipping over the waves on magical castanets and flower baskets would sit uneasily with Americans' emphasis on empirical science and Enlightenment thinking. The *Complete Idiot's Guide to Taoism*, for example, relates Taoism to Einstein (Toropov, 2002) but is conspicuously silent on the concept of immortality or the Eight Immortals. In fact, the guidebook's section on Zhuangzi (eschewing the Taoist master's characteristic spirituality) emphasizes commonsense platitudes such as that "death is inevitable" and touts a "must-visit" website that claims that mysticism is merely an attempt to find "a clear vision of reality," thus cutting off the religious aspects of Taoism entirely (Toropov, 2002). Similarly, the 1980s bestseller *The Tao of Pooh*, which used A. A. Milne's beloved children's books to explain Taoism, avoided Taoism's supernatural elements to make the religion more palatable to a western audience (Kohn & LaFargue, 1998).

The division between philosophy and religion was also encouraged in Communist China during the 1950-60s. When villagers and county officials rushed to destroy the "Four Olds" (Old Customs, Old Culture, Old Habits, and Old Ideas), Taoism naturally was attacked along with other religions. Enthusiastic Maoists raided Wudangshan in 1955 and 1956, and its treasures were "sold as scrap metal to help provide funds for the county budget" (Bush, 1970, p. 395). Taoism was accused of trying to mislead youths into pursuing non-useful lives as hermits, and later Taoist sects were linked (fairly or not) to rightist sedition groups that favored the defeated Nationalist Party (Bush, 1970).

Around this time, Beijing University debated whether Lao Tzu could be considered a materialist (thus making his writing Marxism-friendly). Some Communist scholars found the *Tao Te Ching* comfortingly unreligious and declared that Lao Tzu and Zhuangzi's dualistic way of understanding the world (rich and poor, dark and light) could perhaps be acceptable for a socialist China (Bush, 1970). Nevertheless, Taoism did not clearly advocate struggle for the people's material good, and some Party intellectuals condemned Zhuangzi for "subjective idealism" because "he views *Tao* as emptiness and his total focus is introspective" (Bush, 1970, p. 403). Thus, even philosophical Taoism remained on rocky ground.

In the 1970s, after the death of Mao and the fall of the Gang of Four, the Chinese government began to relax its persecution of religions and embrace its cultural past. Repressed Taoist beliefs resurfaced (Palmer, 2006), creating the current confusing mishmash of spiritual practices—practices which seem to have no organized faith-system to unify them. In China today, the division between Taoist philosophy and religion is much less clear than it is for Western Taoists. More confusingly, some aspects of Taoism that have so saturated the Chinese worldview that the Chinese themselves feel more comfortable describing the beliefs as "Chinese" rather than "Taoist."

It might be said that this confusion about definitions is a central theme of this book. As Westerners, we are driven to define and categorize, but the Chinese do not share this desire. Consider "Taoism" as bamboo seen through a mist, perhaps in one of those delightfully suggestive Chinese ink paintings where a few strokes indicate the bigger picture. Seen through the mist, the bamboo stalks are indistinct, but they remain solid facts despite our hazy perspective. Chinese faith in Taoist ideas remains rock solid, despite the apparent vagueness of their organization or our inability to fix them to an organized faith system.

Despite this vagary, it is worth examining the most central Taoist ideas that have become a part of daily Chinese life, and their ramifications for the Christian trying to reach out to his or her Chinese brothers and sisters.

### Yin, Yang and the *Yijīng*

Most readers are familiar with the yin-yang symbol: two intertwined paisley shapes, each dotted in the center with a circle of the opposite paisley's color. I recall in junior high school being taught that the yin-yang demonstrated the central idea of Taosim: there is good and bad, positive and negative, in all things. Taoists, my teacher explained, seek equilibrium and balance. As a starting place, this description was not terrible. Still, it reframed Taoism in terms that would be rather unclear for Chinese people.

Saying there is "good and bad in everything" misses the point that Taoism is generally unconcerned with the concept of evil. "Positive and negative" would be far more accurate Taoist terms: yang is "positive" in the sense of a hill, and yin is "negative" in the sense of a valley. Yin is all that is receptive, dark, soft, and female; yang is all that is intrusive, bright, hard, and male. The two halves need each other. They may wrestle, but a healthy life requires both.

A Christian, who views earth as a battlefield where good tries to eradicate evil, may be confused by the Taoist concept of dualism. Opposites in Taoism need only balance: hot balancing cold, light balancing dark, sky balancing earth. Just as we need daylight for health and happiness, we need nighttime for sleep and repose. The thing to be avoided, for a Taoist, is imbalance. Evil does not really play a role in this paradigm, but unhealthiness (too much or too little of anything—sleep, meat, alcohol, or sunlight, for example) certainly does.

Dualism is merely the beginning, however. Usually when the yin-yang is shown in China, it is surrounded by a set of eight symbols. Each symbol consists of three lines, some broken and some whole. These eight symbols are called the *bāguà*, or "Eight Diagrams"—or sometimes "Eight Trigrams," since each diagram contains three lines. Readers may have seen four of these eight symbols on the Korean national flag around a red and blue yin-yang. Anyone staying in China for any length of time will quickly come to recognize the *bāguà* encircling the yin-yang almost every time it appears. It illustrates the basic Chinese conception of the universe, breaking everything that exists into eight basic symbols[7]

---

[7] Image source: https://commons.wikimedia.org/wiki/File:Eight_Trigrams.jpg

Each set of lines represents a concept: "Heaven," "Earth," "Water," etc. Each also represents the physical manifestations of that concept. Thus "Heaven" also includes the ideas of "father," "strength," and "head," while "Earth" includes the ideas of "mother," "pliancy," and "belly" (Lynn, 1994). Within the *bāguà*, each set of lines faces a contrasting set on the far side of the circle—three whole lines vs. three broken lines, or one broken and two whole lines vs. one whole and two broken lines. Thus, for example, "Heaven/Father" (three whole bars ☰) stands opposite of "Earth/Mother" (three broken bars ☷), or "Fire/Stealthy Thief" (unbroken-broken-unbroken ☲) contrasts with "Water/One with a Big Belly" (broken-unbroken-broken ☵) (Lynn, 123). Some of these opposite concepts might not occur to a westerner (wind vs. thunder) while others may seem obvious (lake vs. mountain) (Lynn, 1994).

This system dates back to Chinese prehistory. The *bāguà* is said to have been discovered by a legendary sage named Fuxi, who is also claimed to be the author of the *Classic of Changes* (*Yìjīng*). Fuxi used his own observation and common sense to understand the concept of balance in the universe, and then embroidered it in the *Yìjīng* to describe sixty-four permutations of the *bāguà* (Cleary, 1986) by combining two trigrams together: "wood + gold" or "water + heaven," thus creating eight times eight symbols. These combinations are called hexagrams, since they are formed by a series of six lines (Cleary, 1986).

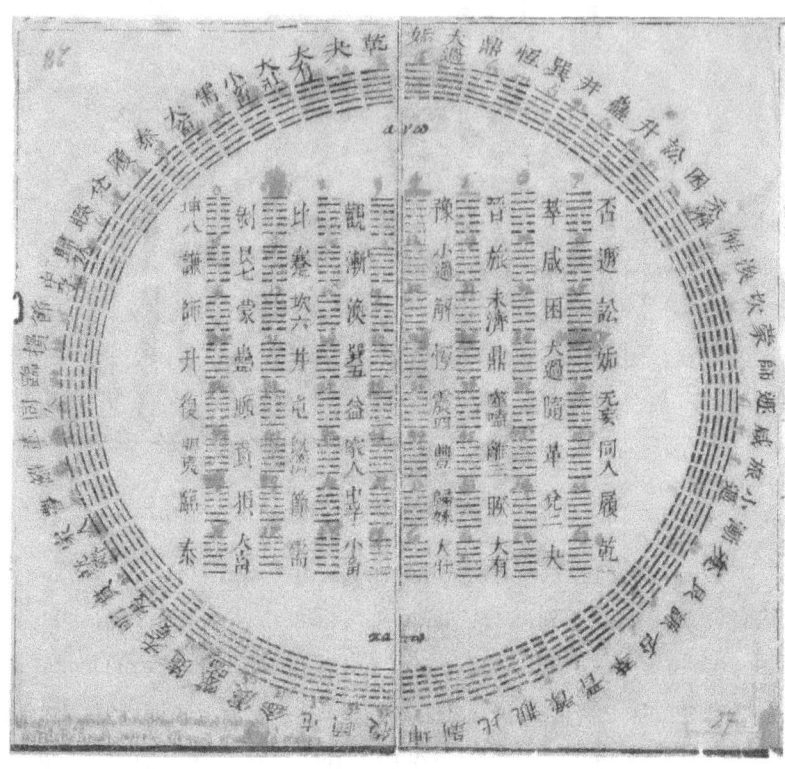

(Perkins, 2004)

The first section of the *Yijing* consists of a series of answers for divination questions. With the aid of a trained fortune teller and some divination sticks, a particular hexagram and its description is given as the answer to a question (Lynn, 1994; Santschi, 2011). This practice is common both in China and with "New Age" practitioners in the western world. The second portion of the *Yijing*, often referred to as "the Ten Wings," is a philosophical meditation on the sixty-four hexagrams and what they tell us about how the world functions. Like the *Tao Te Ching* and Zhuangzi, the "Ten Wings" are often read as philosophy instead of as soothsaying (Lynn, 1994). These two sections of the *Yijing* were probably written at vastly different times (Lynn, 1994) and demonstrate again how Taoism might be divided between folk magic and philosophy.

Many Chinese regularly consult the *Yijing* through fortune tellers. Sophisticated, educated Chinese friends have warned me not to underestimate its power. However, the focus of this chapter is not on the merits of fortune tellers, but on the effect which the *Yìjīng* and Taoist concepts have had on daily life in mainland China.

## Balance

The concept of balanced opposites is pervasive in China, appearing as a central value of Chinese life: to seek "the Middle Way." China has always sought peace through compromise. Sometimes this means the compromise of the weaker party accepting a ruler's views, but sometimes this is the compromise of *no one* getting quite what they want, so as to find middle ground for all. This is the opposite of, for example, the American tendency to assume that one true answer is supreme. The American ideal grew from the Puritan attempt to escape European corruption in their "pure" new Garden of Eden in Massachusetts—a starkly binary idea of good and evil. Both country's ways of seeking truth and conducting discussion reflect ancient traditions. Obviously, I am generalizing cultural ideals here. There have been plenty of one-sided purges committed in China, just as there have been plenty of American compromises based on moral gray areas. At heart, however, the Chinese believe that too much of any one thing is problematic, and a blending of two opposites is good. This is the basic meaning of yin and yang.

To illustrate it another way, at Shanghai's Disneyland, I once witnessed two Chinese mothers—obviously uncomfortable with the American/Disney system of waiting several hours in a single-file line—come close to blows on a hot, cranky afternoon. Each claimed that the other had cut ahead in line. The employees' response was classically Chinese: rather than deciding which mother was telling the truth (or ejecting them from the park), they pulled the squabbling families aside and forced them, after a lengthy wait, to ride at the same time as each other. Judging "right and wrong" was ignored in favor of compromise.

Traditional Chinese medicine (TCM) offers an ideal example. The *bāguà* forms the backbone of TCM, which stresses balance in one's diet and habits. Our bodies, according to TCM, require a balance between natural elements. Thus, whereas a Western person who needs to care for their heart may jog (eventually destroying their knees) and take anti-cholesterol drugs (eventually destroying their liver), a Chinese person will take up tai chi and other soft forms of *gōngfu* (kung fu).

A visit to a Chinese doctor may feel frustratingly ineffectual to a Westerner, but a lifetime of living with TCM ideas can avoid the excesses found in America: diabetes, heart disease, and other signs of one-sided living.

A similar concept of four balanced "humors" in the human body once thrived in the West. While considerably less complex than TCM, the four humors functioned largely in the same way. Europeans, following the Hippocratic tradition, believed that every person was dominated by one of four fluids. Each fluid corresponded to a particular organ, a type of personality, and even seasons of the year. The humors' names (phlegmatic, choleric, sanguine and melancholic) still appear in modern English to describe personality types. This theory dominated much of western medicine until the Enlightenment (Levine, 1971). Echoes of "humorism" continued through 19th century medicine, and Westerners only abandoned the theory around the time the Chinese gave up on imperial government (Arikha, 2007).

The positive results of this balanced (if not entirely scientific) thinking are easy to see. While Americans have statistically longer lifespans than the Chinese, it is common to see 70-year-old Chinese men doing gymnastics in the public park that would be beyond the abilities of Americans in their twenties.

Still, even balance can be taken to excess, and some disadvantages spring up as well. For example, painkillers are sometimes difficult to find in mainland China. The Chinese distrust anesthetics, because telling one's body to ignore pain (which exists to warn the body of danger) is a surefire way to invite imbalance. When we lived in Guangzhou, my family stocked up on aspirin any time we went outside the mainland. I even had a dentist who refused to give me anesthetics before drilling my teeth.

At times, the insistence of "balance" for health can seem a bit excessive. Earlier I mentioned the "nine lychee rule." Because lychees are said to be a "warm" fruit, they are believed to give heat to the body. People with "yin deficiency" (a "warm constitution" in Hippocratic terms) are strongly cautioned against eating them, especially in summer. Anyone who eats nine lychees at once is believed to be taking a serious health risk. I will admit that I have, in a fit of culture shock, peevishly defied this law and eaten ten or more lychees without suffering any noticeable effects.

For Western Christians interacting with Chinese, it is important to not confuse cultural differences with resistance to the Gospel. For thousands of years, Europeans believed in Hippocrates' "four humors." I doubt that belief interfered with their acceptance of Christ. God created our bodies in mysterious and wonderful ways, many of which are still not understood by Western science. If, in the church according to Colossians 3:11, there are neither "Greeks nor Jews, barbarians nor Scythians," it is important to remember the God is calling people to believe in His Son, not to embrace western culture or western science.

It is also important to recognize that, at times, the lines between religion and culture become blurred. We still say "bless you" when someone sneezes without meaning to honor the superstitions from which this custom arose. Before telling a Chinese person that their habits are "superstitious," we must consider how much of their behavior is simply custom and how much reflects deeply held beliefs. (A humorous aside: I used to ask my students to say "bless you" whenever I sneezed, because the practice is strangely comforting to a westerner abroad and might help them please future clients. Inevitably, a few students in each class would abstain, afraid that I was trying to trick them into praying!)

It also helps to remember that, despite all our scientific rigor, we in the West are sometimes wrong. The dentist who drilled my teeth without anesthetic was right: the process was painless, and a shot would have been an expensive (and slightly unhealthy) waste. Those old Chinese men in the park doing gymnastics well into their seventies know something which Americans do not.

### Pursuing Long Life: Magic Potions and "Qì" (Energy)

Since its murky beginnings, Taoism has always married the philosophy of balance with folk stories about sages pursuing immortality by channeling their energy or "*qì*." Taoist masters of old were said to transcend death through alchemy, potions, and intense breathing techniques that freed the flow of *qì* through one's body. Lao Tzu himself was said to have achieved eternal life this way (Kohn & LaFargue, 1998). In the classic novel *Journey to the West*, Lao Tzu is portrayed as a sort of divine alchemist who brews potions in a mighty stove engraved with the *bāguà* (Wu, 1997). Even China's first emperor (who lived around 200 B.C.) was obsessed with Taoist immortality potions (Roberts, 1996), which many believe eventually led to his death (Wright, 2001).

In modern China, alchemy and elixirs still surface occasionally, though the government works hard to curtail the killing of sharks, tigers, and elephants in the name of magic potions. Many pharmacies, however, still showcase a taxidermy deer in their front window as an advertisement for the curative powers of deer horn, and some of the ingredients found in Chinese prescriptions bear little resemblance to what a Westerner would expect from a doctor. Modern Chinese people may not believe in magic, but their ideas about medicine have roots in non-Vesalian formulas.

Taoist breathing techniques have endured in a much more public way. Anyone watching Chinese action films will have seen Kungfu heroes leap over walls and perch on treetops, performing exaggerated feats that exhilarate or baffle audiences. These feats (as described in the works of novelists such as Jin Yong and Gu Long) are allegedly accomplished through breath control. According to Taoist folk wisdom, intentional control of one's *qì*, especially via breathing techniques, can make the body lighter or stronger (Palmer, 2006). In the late 1800s, Boxer Rebellion fighters believed that these breathing techniques would make them impervious to bullets—a misconception that did not work out well for the Boxers (Palmer, 2006).

In everyday culture, the art of breathing and the manipulation of *qì* is practiced as *qìgōng*. *Qìgōng* is somewhat equivalent to yoga, though practiced standing up. In its most common form, *qìgōng* appears as tai chi (*tàijí quán,* in Chinese). Legends claim that tai chi was created by a Taoist monk (immortal, of course) inspired by the graceful movement of a snake fighting a crane. By observing the movements of the natural world, the monk created an exercise regime that also served as a form of self-defense (Galante, 1981). Many elderly people in mainland China spend mornings practicing their breathing together and exercising their limbs in graceful, balletic movements, often in village squares or public parks. Occasionally, these exercises are done with fans or swords, or (in a trendy modern incarnation) with a badminton racket and a ping-pong ball.

As with yoga, Christians are divided about the healthiness or danger of tai chi. Some see it as useful exercise that happens to be a harmless byproduct of ancient superstitions, no more sinister than Santa Claus or the Easter Bunny. Observing and copying the movements of God's creatures is not in itself a dangerous practice. Others see tai chi as a secular mask covering heathen worship.

What is certain, however, is that the Chinese government is wary of the spiritual overtones of *qigōng*. After being suppressed as "old culture" during the Cultural Revolution, the practice was rehabilitated in the 1970s and became quite popular, even with high-level Party officials, in the 1980s (Palmer, 2006). This changed dramatically when one *qigōng* organization, the now-infamous Falun Gong, grew to intolerable levels of popularity. In 1999, in an eerie and silent show of power, thousands of Falun Gong members surrounded the seat of the Chinese government in Beijing and publicly practiced tai chi (Tong, 2009). The government, never enthusiastic about rival power groups or freedom of assembly, declared the Falun Gong a dangerous cult (Xinhua, 1999). The group's leaders were driven out of the country, its leader seeking asylum in the United States (Ownby, 2008; Palmer, 2006).

An ugly propaganda war soon sprang up between the Falun Gong and the Communist Party. One can witness this continuing conflict outside Chinese embassies across the world, or in tourist hubs in Hong Kong, where both sides showcase horrific photos of atrocities allegedly committed either against or by Falun Gong members. In the 2000s, the Falun Gong went on a propaganda offensive (Palmer, 2006), sending the spectacular and propaganda-tinged stage show "Shen Yun" around the Western world to raise awareness of their persecution—and to advance their belief that the Falun Gong can bring peace and health to all of China.

While teaching in southern China, I had an obnoxious neighbor who was disliked by others in our apartment block for having loud, late-night arguments with her boyfriend. Another resident, in attempt to get the woman evicted, spread the rumor that her morning tai chi exercises were evidence of Falun Gong membership. Such an accusation was serious enough to have the police come and investigate. To their credit, the police sniffed out the truth and left the irritating neighbor alone after a stern warning. Still, the swiftness of their arrival was a clear sign of how seriously the officials take this *qigōng* sect.

*Qi* is not only for those who practice *qigōng*. Most Chinese people firmly believe in *qi*, the internal energy that allows us to live. Homes are arranged for the maximum flow of *qi*, including the placement of furniture, windows, and doors—what Westerners know as feng shui, literally "the balance of wind and water." People's daily lives (meals, naps, break times, and exercise) are arranged so that one's *qi* is collected and disbursed without any shock to the body's systems.

The nine-lychee problem cited above is entirely about hot vs. cold *qi*. Some western friends of mine, to get out of debating about why they did not want to follow TCM principles, have simply said that "our *qi* is different from yours", a response that satisfied their Chinese friends immediately and left the Westerner free to eat as many lychees as they liked.

One aspect of *qi* is the need to "*tuo qi*" (expel energy) by opening windows, to maintain balance in one's workplace or home. It is common to find shops, doors wide open, blasting air conditioning into the street on a hot day. My university's office regularly cranked their air conditioner to maximum capacity, opened their windows to the muggy outside air, and placed fans by the window to expel AC-cooled air as quickly as possible. At my church, I (as an energy-conscious Californian) engaged in many accidental summertime battles with my Chinese brothers and sisters over air conditioner management. They would open the church doors, which I would then close, and they would reopen. Each of us thought the other point of view was a little crazy.

My natural inclination as an American is to grab my Chinese friends and debate the scientific merits and weaknesses of *qi*. Manipulating one's own *qi* strikes me, in my Enlightenment core, as painfully unscientific. However, I eventually decided that debating the existence of *qi* was not a good use of my time. After all, plenty of things in the Bible suggest that Western science does not tell us everything there is to know about the universe. My job is to ask for the Holy Spirit to help both me and my Chinese friends with discernment whenever spiritual energy is discussed, not to prove that their assumptions on the subject are wrong because those assumptions do not match my own.

## Taoism as a Chinese Religion: The Concept of Originalism

The origin of things matters in China. This cannot be overstated. I used to joke with my students that Chinese people talked about "5,000 years of history" because one's own strengths are always beautiful to them. "What does a giraffe think is beautiful?" I would ask. "A long neck. But monkeys do not think long necks are beautiful. Monkeys think agile tails are beautiful." This silly example was given to underline a core assumption they held as a particularly Chinese value: because China is an old country, old things are beautiful to the Chinese. Old Chinese things are even more beautiful. I will illustrate this point with two frivolous examples.

When Yao Ming, the basketball phenomenon from Shanghai, became famous, China fell in love with the NBA. Students across the country spent hours glued to the television, fascinated to see their native son perform incredible feats on the world stage. Chinese kids eventually developed a passion for Kobe Bryant, LeBron James, and other foreign stars, but without Yao to lead the way, the NBA would have remained a foreign oddity (Wan, 2016).

When Yao finally retired, the NBA shrewdly attempted to keep the Chinese profits coming by shining a light on Jeremy Lin. Lin—born and raised in California, educated at Harvard, but still "originally" Chinese—appeared on the scene at just the right time, filling the gap left by Yao's retirement and blazing a brilliant trail in the 2012 season. For a brief time, it worked, and Lin was the new darling of Chinese youth (Jessop, 2012). My students positively glowed when they talked about him.

Then he fell sharply from grace. Lin (in typical American fashion) and his grandmother (in typical Taiwanese fashion) declared themselves to be, respectively, "Asian-American" and "Taiwanese" as opposed to "Chinese" (Bradsher, 2012). Instantly, my students lost all desire to discuss "Linsanity."

While it is true that Lin's explosive scoring slowed around that same time, similar slumps did little to cool the Chinese fervor for athletes such as tennis champion Li Na or track star Liu Xiang, who remained heavily in the public eye even when their best years were past. Yao Ming continues to appear in countless advertisements, a symbol of Chinese success, though he has not played basketball since 2011. Although there are many factors in the contrasting reputations of Yao and

Lin, Yao's commitment to the "motherland" and Lin's distancing himself from it were crucial to my students' perception of who was a hero and who was not.

Similarly, there is a curious anger among many Chinese youths regarding Koreans and the Dragon Boat Festival. The Dragon Boat Festival has existed for millennia in various forms. At some point in the distant past, the festival became tied to the story of Qu Yuan, a poet who, according to legend, drowned himself in sorrow when his beloved emperor passed away. Mourning citizens dumped rice dumplings into the river to distract fish, so they would not eat the body of the heroic Qu Yuan. Thus, for Chinese people, the Dragon Boat Festival carries heavily nationalistic overtones as the celebration of an idealized patriot.

In 2005, a village in Korea asked to register its *Gangneung Danoje* Festival with UNESCO, to signify its importance as a piece of Korean heritage. This relatively obscure village festival shares its date with the Dragon Boat Festival—unsurprisingly, since holidays in both countries follow the lunar calendar. To the surprise of Korean netizens, the Chinese Internet burst into righteous fury against Korea for trying to "steal the Dragon Boat Festival" and "pervert its true origins" (Liu, 2017). Tempers flared on both sides, since Koreans are also sensitive about origins. An Internet flame war began (Lixinski, 2014). To this day, if you ask young Chinese people about Korea, many will respond that they dislike Koreans because they "don't respect the Chinese origins of our Dragon Boat Festival."

As an American, it is well-nigh impossible for me to comprehend the passion behind such feuds. My country is less than 300 years old and prides itself on being a melting pot of immigrants. We are monkeys who find agile tails, not long necks, beautiful. However, if I hope to be taken seriously by Chinese friends, it is crucial for me to take their views seriously. I cannot empathize, perhaps, but I must understand that their passion is genuine and that people's feelings were honestly hurt in the two instances above.

The origin of things, especially intangible things, matters in China to an extent that no Westerner can fully understand. A New Zealander might defend pavlova as their national dessert, against the Australians' claim to have invented it, or a Frenchman might scoff at Italian or German wines. The British may sometimes claim that Americans have no ownership of the English language. However, there is a hint of self-mockery and implied kinship in these half-serious cultural skirmishes. In the case of the Dragon Boat festival, there is no irony or camaraderie. Westerners might understand to some extent Asian pride, but we cannot feel the hurt.

All of this is to emphasize the importance of Taoism as a "native" Chinese religion. Before considering what this means for Taoism, let us look briefly at the other two traditional belief systems of China.

Buddhism originally came to China, according to the quasi-historical story, when the monk Tripitaka undertook a perilous journey to India to bring sacred scriptures back to the Tang Dynasty court. This journey is the subject of the popular "Journey to the West," which all Chinese children have seen on television. If one visits the ancient cave monasteries in Dunhuang, guides point out that all Buddha statues dating from the religion's earliest years in China wear a "foreign" mustache. This marked Buddha as a "foreign god," acceptable for converts but not truly a part of Chinese culture. Only after centuries had passed and the religion was considered properly Sinicized could Buddha could finally be portrayed as "truly Chinese." Later statues had east Asian features and, of course, no foreign mustache. (Tang, 1994) The god was no longer a foreigner, but much time and tolerance were needed for him to be accepted.

Confucianism, for its part, gets its value partially because of its Chinese origin. China is proud of Confucius' heavy influence on the Korean and Japanese cultures, which demonstrates the overwhelming potency of Chinese ideas. When the Communist government named its worldwide university outreach program "The Confucius Institute," it was Confucius' role as an original Chinese thinker that they had in mind. Confucianism itself is somewhat at odds with Marxism, since it stresses rigid hierarchies and class structures, but Confucius as a Chinese-born genius trumps Confucius' actual teachings, in this case.

Taoism, like Confucianism, benefits from its status as a "native" Chinese religion. Its origins go deep into the "5,000 years of history" which Chinese people are so proud to tell others (and each other) about. One reason it is so difficult to clarify what Taoism is and is not is that, to the Chinese, many aspects of Taoism have shifted from being religious into being a part of culture. For many mainlanders, "religion" is an embarrassing relic of their feudal past, but "being Chinese" is the center of life. Displaying a statue of the Eight Immortals is often not a faith statement so much as a national one. Obeying the laws of feng shui, caring for one's *qi*, and keeping balance in one's life are not religious practices to a Chinese person; they are assumptions of living a natural Chinese life.

I say all of this as a warning. It is nearly impossible for a westerner, especially one from the immigrant nations of the last 300 years (the USA, Canada, New Zealand, and Australia) to comprehend the importance origins have for a Chinese person. If one criticizes practices which have grown out of Taoism, its folklore, TCM, or tai chi, one's audience may not hear an educated friend fighting against superstition. They will probably hear a foreigner attacking China. Once you have set yourself in opposition to China, you have lost your audience forever.

## Balance Between Mutually Exclusive Beliefs

If you do have a conversation regarding "superstitions" with a Chinese friend, you may be surprised. Your Chinese friend may agree with you enthusiastically. They might exclaim that China has too long been subject to "feudal" superstitions, and that they are glad that the Party has finally and completely rid their country of such nonsense.

"But I meet people every day who believe these things," you may respond.

If this conversation takes place in a setting with many Chinese people listening, it is likely that no one else will contribute, or that those who do respond will agree, perhaps meekly, with the person condemning old superstitions. Several things are happening in this situation.

First, members of the group may in fact disagree with each other but may be unwilling to say so. The majority, in fact, probably disagrees with the person condemning superstition. However, it would be in extremely bad taste to insult him by vocally disagreeing, thus implicitly claiming that the dissenting person has more value than the speaker. The speaker would lose face, which is serious business. Worse yet, it would not be "harmonious" for the group to have disagreements, especially in front of a foreigner. Harmony, a close cousin of balance, is crucially important in China. Thus, unity is preserved by any dissenters remaining silent.

Secondly, there may be a sense of shame among those who do believe in the old ways but fear that this makes them seem like ignorant peasants. It is even possible that the person who has agreed with you is speaking out of tacit shamefacedness. China progressed at an astounding rate over the $20^{th}$ century, changing from what many Chinese people feel was a downtrodden, underdeveloped nation into one of the world's most powerful economic forces. There is a lot to be proud of, but there is also a deep sense of shame about having held onto feudal rule until 1911. This shame is heightened by China's intense rejection of its own past during the Cultural Revolution and complicated even further by the frustration most Chinese people feel about how much culture was lost during that era. By attacking "superstitions," you are tapping into a complex and sensitive place in Chinese hearts.

For your Chinese listeners, your criticism lays out a very dangerous set of options for them when responding. They could deny their own culture publicly, and in front of a foreigner, which would be treasonous. They could publicly reject Maoism by defending antiquated parts of their culture, which is politically dangerous. They could, by directly telling you that you are wrong, embarrass themselves by making you lose face. Alternatively, they could say nothing.
Most people, understandably, will say nothing.

This may even be a problem between close friends. While preparing to write this chapter, I recalled a conversation with one of my closest Chinese friends. As I was moving into my first apartment in Guangzhou in 2011, my friend warned me that the place to which my family had been assigned had unsuitable feng shui. I wanted to cite his advice in this chapter, but since several years had passed, I wrote him to check if I had my facts straight.

His reply was pragmatic, scientific-sounding, and quietly defensive. All the feng shui had been removed from his advice:

> I don't know if northeast or southwest is good. But what I know for sure is it is better to have windows and doors facing south because we are living in northern hemisphere and the sun is always south to us. And especially in

mainland China, the wind from southeast is warm because the ocean is southeast to the continent. So, a southeast facing house is cool and chill in summer and warm in winter . . . But this may vary in other continents. When I was in Bay Area [of California], people like to have their house facing west so that they can see the ocean. (J. R. He, March 6, 2017, personal communication)

This may seem rational on the first read-through, but given the size and geographical complexity of China, the weather argument only holds true for some regions. Sub-tropical Guangzhou is barely affected by the direction a house faces; the sun rises and sets without any particularly southern bent, and the weather is still, flat, and muggy everywhere. When storms do move in from the South China Sea, people feel the humidity, but not the wind's direction. Finally, to be honest, our concrete-block apartment felt freezing in summer and winter alike. Our tiny windows, facing any direction, made little difference.

A westerner could call my friend's response evasive. He replaced the potentially embarrassing references to feng shui, which he had originally warned me about but was now avoiding, with more acceptable "scientific" explanations. These days, my friend knows me well enough to know I am dubious about feng shui, so his answer simultaneously downplays our differences and attempts to build common ground. This is polite and also saves my friend the embarrassment of appearing "superstitious." I know that (despite being a serious Marxist) he believes in feng shui, the *Yìjīng*, and similar things. However, my friend (who studied IT at Berkeley and USC) is an avid fan of American science. As he considered the possible responses to my question about feng shui, he decided to skip the meat of my question and instead look for common ground between us. This is a sign of respect in China. For me to contradict him, to push him to repeat what he had said years ago, would have been an insult. I would be seeking uncommon ground, thus rupturing the important bonds he was trying to reinforce.

Between good friends, similarly defensive (but affectionate) answers will arise quickly if you challenge the rationale of Taoist-inspired beliefs. Worse, it is possible that you may, by challenging deep-seated beliefs, accidentally sever the ties of trust built thus far in your relationship. If you are seeking to win over hearts, minds, and souls, consider choosing your battles, even when culture shock sets in and you want to eat those ten lychees in protest.

In the examples given above, the thing that may sit uneasily with a westerner (especially an American) is that the Chinese person has offered *the right answer at the right time*. Given a different approach, a different situation (with fewer listeners, for example), or a different stage in the relationship, another answer—totally different but equally sincere—might be given. To a westerner, this is dishonesty. To a person steeped in Chinese culture, it is discretion.

A common racist stereotype of the Chinese proclaims that they are "wily" and deceptive. This offensive simplification overlooks the subtlety of Chinese culture, and implicitly supports the Western (especially American) penchant for binary thinking. Especially in the United States, things are black or white, right or wrong. For most Westerners (especially Americans), the Pauli Principle that "two objects cannot occupy the same place at the same time" extends to intangible concepts. One can be Protestant OR Catholic, believer OR nonbeliever, right OR wrong.

The Chinese tradition promotes a different model, however. Confucianism and Taoism, for example, seem to be incompatible opposites. Confucianism, with its practical, hierarchy-focused rules, could not occupy the same space as Taoism, which stresses the importance an organic freedom in which no citizen is above another. The hero of Confucianism is the scholar who studies all things and respects the ruler, conforming to rigid social rules. The hero of Taoism is the idiot-savant who respects nothing but the Tao and breaks all social rules to demonstrate this. Two such diametrically opposed beliefs could not, for a Westerner, coexist.

In China, however, they can coexist in one person—but not in the same place and time. A Chinese adage says that a gentleman (the highest compliment Confucius could give a man) is "Confucian at court and Taoist in the countryside." In other words, a wise man will accept the necessary, hierarchal Confucian order of society when it is natural for city living, but if he ever manages to escape from such restraints—as any successful man would—he will follow the Tao and seek the wisdom of anti-hierarchal madmen like Lao Tzu and Zhuangzi. Following this ideal, the "ideal" Chinese person today is simultaneously Confucian, Taoist, probably Buddhist, and probably also Marxist. It simply depends on where and when you ask for their opinion.

If asked about ghosts, feng shui, or other non-scientific traditions, many Chinese people will give a colloquial response that perfectly sums up their beliefs: "*bàn xìn bàn yí,*" "Half believe, half doubt." Notice that this response does not mean the speaker is unsure; it literally means that they both believe *and* doubt. For a westerner, this is hypocrisy. One cannot obey two masters or two belief systems. For a Chinese person, following the system that works at this moment is common sense. A parent may teach strict honesty to their child, then shamelessly cheat someone who does not belong to their ingroup. The example of my friend's response concerning feng shui demonstrates this "flexibility." My friend would never lie to me, but given the awkward situation I had accidentally forced him into, he twisted his original words to a point which Americans might label as dishonesty.

One could argue that these situational ethics go back as far as the *bāguà* and the Taoist concept of the universe as a series of balanced opposites. A person lost in the desert has enough air but wants water to survive. A person drowning has too much water and needs air. It would be idiocy to offer water to a drowning man, even if we all need water to survive. Pursuing anything—even ethics—too far in one direction leads away from balance and health, according to Taoist ideals.

The casual disregard for rules in China also follows this pattern. Occasionally, the Chinese government will crack down on jaywalking, movie piracy, or other common infractions. During the ensuing public awareness campaign, everyone takes the law very seriously and will cluck their disapproval at those who continue to break it. Once the campaign is over, though, people return to "business as usual," resilient as ever and perfectly happy to jaywalk or illegally download films when it suits them.

As the person in charge of our afternoon lunch fellowship at a bicultural church in Guangzhou, one of my most painful duties was to create and enforce policies to keep lunch ticket sales fair. We tried many arrangements but were constantly faced with people who wanted to skip church and come only for the afternoon luncheon. These people often saw the lunch fellowship as a means to bring their friends into the Christian community—despite the fact that bringing their twenty friends to lunch (and not church) meant twenty regular church members would be unable to get tickets, and their twenty friends would almost definitely not mingle with the believers to learn a deeper understanding. Generally, a policy such as "one ticket per buyer," or "tickets only for those who had attended church" would work for a short time before someone from the local community found a way to subvert it. If I insisted on enforcing the letter of the law, I was inevitably met with confusion, embarrassment, and sometimes even deep hurt. My Chinese brethren recognized that rules were important but felt that my Western rigidity had pushed into territory that should be decided by relationships. Why would a rule be more important than my relations with the person who wanted to buy 20% of all available tickets for her friends? As one brother frequently told me in Chinese, "You foreigners are crazy."

However, these same "flexible" people sometimes suddenly insist on one fixed, immutable answer. In school, there is always one correct answer (a Marxist one). On television, there is always a good side (the Chinese) and a bad side (usually the Japanese). In history, if one of the "good guys" (Mao or Stalin, for example) committed atrocities, a student will simply say that "he *made some mistakes*" or "He was 70% good, 30% bad" (and never any other percentage). The absolute nature of some facts (such as the nine-lychee rule) seems like an unlikely intrusion of black and white thinking into what is otherwise a relativistic Chinese world.

However, this emphatic "black and white" mentality represents only one voice among the many a Chinese person may have. It comes out at school or at work when needed, especially when faced with an exam, since on Chinese exams, there is never more than one correct answer possible. Nevertheless, a proud Party member may go to her Buddhist grandmother's on weekends to pray. One student of mine (who mistakenly named himself "Max" after the philosopher "Karl Max") was a stalwart socialist at school, but in his free time he pursued the most enthusiastically capitalist career I have ever seen. In different contexts, people will give different answers, and they believe each of those answers fully.

If we are totally honest with ourselves, we will find that shades of this behavior exist in the West as well. Social psychologists Sonia Roccas and Marilynn Brewer studied this phenomenon in 2002 and branded it "social identity complexity" (Roccas & Brewer, 2012). People normally identify with multiple groups—national, religious, generational, political, ethnic, family—which usually coexist without much internal conflict. For example, one can easily identify simultaneously as American, white, and Christian, and not be concerned that many Americans are not white, or that most Christians are not American. However, when our ingroups come into conflict with each other, an individual must rationalize their allegiance to one of these groups above the others. For example, in a time of national emergency or tragedy, we tend to view all our compatriots as "one of us" because of an outside threat, be it a natural disaster or foreign conflict. However, when a conflict comes from within the national in-group, we tend to perceive different configurations of those who are "like me"—others with similar beliefs, regional background, or ethnicity, for example.

In pragmatic terms, this allows us a psychological space in which we can rationalize internal conflict. Sometimes this means that we may merely frown when politicians we agree with behave badly but become outraged when "the other side" behaves in a similar way. Although I feel a strong allegiance to "our" country, I may emotionally redefine who "we" are when, for example, another state passes laws I am opposed to. Our most useful or threatened identity tends to rise to the forefront.

In this sense, the "Confucian at court, Taoist in the countryside" doctrine is describing what modern social psychology has diagnosed. When surrounded by other urbane, law-abiding citizens, a gentleman feels the importance of membership in a Confucian community: allegiance to the emperor, rigid family rules, clarity, and order. When isolated in his comfortable retreat, the Taoist in him emerges because it helps process the needs of his isolation: oneness with nature, completeness in himself, harmony, and balance. Yet when confronted with new ideas—foreign ideas— the gentleman will defend his Chinese roots, whether they be Taoist, Confucian, Buddhist, or indeed Communist.

Accepting *your* role as the "Other" is an important step in understanding your interactions with the Chinese.

## Ministry Application

Already in this chapter I have offered some advice about how to deal with the many places where Taoism's influence bubbles to the surface of daily Chinese life. Here are, briefly, five things which I wish I had been told before moving to China:

1. Be cautious about immediately contradicting people regarding practices that sound like superstition to you. You may unwittingly be setting yourself up in their eyes as a stubborn foreign imperialist.

2. Be equally cautious when someone tells you that they look down on traditional folk religion. They may be only saying this to please you. By immediately accepting what they say at face value, you may inadvertently force your friend into feeling that they must hide their true beliefs. Chinese politeness may set up a barrier of embarrassed prevarication between you. Listen carefully and be slow to respond—relationships take a long time to build, and you may see several sides of your friend before you fully understand their beliefs.

3. Try to imagine what you look like from their perspective. Just like your Chinese friends, you are a scientifically minded, modern person. *They* believe that the universe relies on balanced sets of opposites and that humans and objects possess an invisible energy which can be channeled. *You,* as a Christian, believe that a Jewish peasant could walk on water, heal the sick with a word, and come back from the dead. This is more of a stretch than believing in *qi*. You are intelligent, modern and rational, so trust that they are, too.

4. Do not expect that you will understand China quickly. Even the Chinese do not understand China. The Chinese people you meet will not be experts, and most have probably never thought about the rationale behind habits and beliefs which seem strange to you, so making them defend these beliefs may be counterproductive. Chinese culture is very old and complex. Many contrasting traditions have blurred together into what you are now witnessing, and it would require decades of study to get a firm grasp on it.

For six years, my wife and I studied and discussed Chinese culture all day, every day: with each other, with our Chinese friends, and with expatriates who had far more experience than us. I read countless books about culture, religion, history, and art, including most of the great classics. At the end of it all, I feel only barely qualified to write this brief chapter. Accept that you may be wrong about the conclusions you piece together, and that no one you meet will ever be able to clearly explain certain cultural ideas.

5. Above all, *listen.* The one repeated comment I heard from my students was that they appreciated that my wife and I respected them. We were always open about our faith, but we also took the time to hear about what they believed. Touring missionary teams would come and go, sometimes turning our students off, although the Chinese undergrads were far too polite to say as much. The missionaries' logic, enthusiasm, and charm set some students on edge. Earning trust can take a long time. In a culture where words are adapted to fit the situation, a steadily Christ-like life can speak much louder than a singalong or a persuasive discussion.

However, there is a time and place to take a stand. I simply wish to remind readers Who they should take a stand for—not Isaac Newton or Marie Curie, not Thomas Jefferson or the concept of political liberty, and certainly not for yourself or the alleged superiority of your own culture.

Unfortunately, there will be days for any Western expatriate in China when the culture they left behind will seem rational and warm, and the Chinese culture they are surrounded by will seem chaotic and superstitious. Just try to remember that Christ did not die in the name of Western rationalism. He died for the Chinese, with all their quirks and seemingly bizarre assumptions, just like He died for you, with all the cultural baggage you carry.

## References

Alexander, G. G. (1895). *Lao-Tsze the Great Thinker.* London: Kegan Paul, Trench, Trubner & Co.

Arikha, N. (2007). *Passions and tempers: A history of the humours.* New York, NY: HarperCollins Publishers.

Bradsher, K. (February 15, 2012). An odd game a grandmother can appreciate. *NYTimes.com*. Retrieved from http://www.nytimes.com/2012/02/16/sports/basketball/jeremy-lins-grandmother-watches-along-with-taiwan.html

Bush Jr., R. C. (1970). *Religion in communist China*. New York, NY: Abingdon Press.

Cleary, T. (1986). *I Ching*. Boston, MA: Shambhala Publications, Inc.

Galante, L. (1981). *Tai Chi: The supreme ultimate*. York Beach, MN: Samuel Weiser, Inc.

Jessop, A. (July 27, 2012). The NBA's unprecedented growth in China fueled by Jeremy Lin and media platforms. *Forbes*. Retrieved from https://www.forbes.com/sites/aliciajessop/2012/07/27/the-nbas-unprecedented-growth-in-china-fueled-by-jeremy-lin-and-media-platforms/#4478bde777aa

Kohn, L., & LaFargue, M. (editors) (1998). *Lao-tzu and the Tao-te-ching*. Albany, NY: State University Press of New York, Albany.

Komjathy, L. (2012). The Daoist tradition in China in R. Nadeau (Ed.), *The Wiley-Blackwell Companion to Chinese Religions* (171-196). Chichester, UK: Wiley-Blackwell.

Levine, E. B. (1971). *Hippocrates*. New York, NY: Twayne Publishers, Inc.

Liu, C. (May 30, 2017). The forgotten history of dragon boat festival: How China nearly lost its own tradition. *The Beijinger*. Retrieved from https://www.thebeijinger.com/blog/2017/05/30/forgotten-history-dragon-boat-festival-how-china-nearly-lost-its-own-culture

Lixinski, L. (2014). A tale of two heritages: Claims of ownership over intangible cultural heritage and the myth of "authenticity". *Transnational Dispute Management 11(2)*. Retrieved from http://www.academia.edu/21706690/A_Tale_of_Two_Heritages_Claims_of_Ownership_over_Intangible_Cultural_Heritage_and_the_Myth_of_Authenticity

Lo Kuan-Chung (2002). *Romance of the three kingdoms, Volume 1.* (C. H. Brewitt-Taylor, Trans.). North Clarendon, VT: Tuttle Publishing.

Lo Kuan-Chung (2002). *Romance of the three kingdoms, Volume 2.* (C. H. Brewitt-Taylor, Trans.). North Clarendon, VT: Tuttle Publishing.

Lynn, R. J. (1994). *The classic of changes: A new translation of the I Ching as interpreted by Wang Bi.* New York, NY: Columbia University Press.

Maspero, H. (1981). *Taoism and Chinese religion.* (F. A. Kierman, Trans.). Amherst, MA: University of Massachusetts Press.

Ownby, D. (2008). *The life and times of Li Hongzhi in China, 1952 - 1995. Falun Gong and the future of China.* New York, NY: Oxford University Press.

Palmer, D. (2006). Body cultivation in contemporary China. In J. Miller (Ed.), *chinese religions in contemporary societies* (pp. 147-173). Santa Barbara, CA: ABC-CLIO, Inc.

Perkins, F. (2004). *Leibniz and China: A Commerce of Light.* Cambridge, UK: Cambridge University Press. Image retrieved from public domain version https://commons.wikimedia.org/w/index.php?curid=36231359

Roberts, J. A. G. (1996). *A history of China: Volume 1, Prehistory to c. 1800.* New York, NY: Saint Martin's Press.

Roccas, S. & Brewer, M. (2002). Social identity complexity. *Personality and Social Psychology Review, 6*(2), 88-106.

Santschi, R. (Producer) & Wilhelm, B. (Director). (2011). *Wisdom of changes: Richard Wilhelm and the I Ching* [Motion picture]. Germany: Triluna Films AG.

Tang, W. (1994). *Dunhuang art through the eyes of Tang Wenjie,* (T. Chung, Ed.). New Delhi, India: Indira Gandhi National Center for the Arts Press.

Tillman, H. C. (2007). Selected Historical Sources for *Three Kingdoms*: Reflections from Sima Guang's and Chen Liang's reconstructions of Kongming's story. In K. Besio and C. Tung (Eds.), *Three Kingdoms and Chinese Culture* (pp.53-69). Albany, NY: The State University of New York Press.

Tong, J. (2009). *Revenge of the forbidden city: The suppression of the Falungong in China, 1999-2005*. New York, NY: Oxford University Press.

Toropov, B., & Hanson, C. (2002). *The complete idiot's guide to Taoism*. Indianapolis, IN: Alpha Books.

Wan, M. (September 9, 2016). Chinese basketball fans will always thank Yao Ming. *ESPN*. Retrieved from http://www.espn.com/nba/story/_/id/17503441/what-yao-ming-means-basketball-fans-china-2016-nba-hall-fame

Williams, C. (1974). *Chinese symbolism and art motifs*. North Clarendon, VT: Tuttle Publishing.

Wright, D. (2001). *The history of China*. Westport, CN: Greenwood Press.

Wu, C. (1997). *Journey to the west, volume I*. (Y. His Trans.). Chicago, IL: The University of Chicago Press.

Xinhua (2009). China bans Falun Gong, *The People's Daily 22 July 1999*. Beijing, China. Retrieved from: http://heinonline.org/HOL/LandingPage?handle=hein.journals/chinelgo32&div=46&id=&page=

Zhuangzi. (2003). *Zhuangzi: Basic writings*. (B. Watson, Trans.). New York, NY: Stanford University Press.

# 4. One Woman's Experience and Beliefs[8]

## By Xie Baoli[9]

I am thirty years old and grew up in a family that was—and continues to be—loving and supportive. About five years ago, in 2011, I became very sick. At that time, I was thinking a lot about life, death, and the treasure of good health. I talked with some friends and read some books while I was recuperating.

The books were about a kind of religion or spirituality. It is not one of the major world religions today, so I am not sure what English-speakers would call it. I guess you could call it "spiritual energy" or "the universe" in English. I think this kind of belief has always existed, but recently we are seeing it become more popular in a new form, and in China it is far more popular among women than among men.

The author of the first book I read, a man named Bijan Anjomi, is originally from Iran but now lives in the United States. He has held seminars in 14 countries, including China. One of my close friends attended one of his lectures and met him in person. She told me I should read his book, *Absolutely Effortless Prosperity*, and I did, especially the contents of volume 2. I also read a book that was written by a Chinese person and has no English title, but the title touches on the concept of deeply knowing oneself.

Some of my family members believe in a mixture of Buddhism and spiritual energy, while others, especially in my aunt's family, believe a purer form of

---

[8] *Editor's note: This short personal essay is based on a 2016 interview between an American teacher and a Chinese woman from Sichuan Province. Sichuan is the modern name for the geographic area where Taoist thought became more formally gathered and understood so long ago. - K.P.*

[9] *A pseudonym has been used to protect the identity of the contributor.*

Buddhism. My younger sister has not really chosen one specific religion yet, but has studied several faiths and is now leaning more towards Buddhism. Actually, I think it is possible and even fine for a person to believe in more than one religion at the same time. My sister really believes in both Buddhism and the universe, and it is possible and fine for her to believe in both while she thinks about whether she will ultimately choose to follow only one of those beliefs because she finds one of them is best. After studying more about spiritual energy, however, I think that is the personal belief I want to follow. Now, I consider myself to be a devout follower of this religion.

The most important concept to understand in this religion is the congruence of body and soul; this congruence is most basically achieved with the balance of being healthy in the body, mind, and soul. This belief does not have any buildings such as churches or temples. Neither is there any god nor any one special book such as the Bible or Qur'an. We do not pray to a god, but we can recite incantations or say prayers; in this case, we are speaking to our own hearts.

These prayers can be about illnesses—focusing on a specific part of the body that is unwell—or about other people. For example, if my knee is hurt, I can touch it and say: "I'm sorry I have not treated you well recently. Please forgive me. Thank you. I love you." When I was so sick back in 2011, a friend introduced me to this central concept, and it really made a big difference and helped with my healing. That is a part of why I decided to adopt this faith.

In this belief system, we say that we can know whether a person is good or bad based on that person's mind and thoughts. We also say that evil originates in the hearts of people. So, I believe that the Law of Attraction is a paramount law to observe. It says that if I think positively, good things will happen, but if I think negatively, bad things will happen. In this way, my belief really impacts my daily choices and behaviors. After someone dies, we believe that their soul will continue to exist somewhere within the universe, but we do not believe in reincarnation or a return to material existence.

Currently, I am not married, and I think I could accept a potential marriage partner who believes differently than I do. However, I strongly feel that if we have the same beliefs, he and I will have an easier and better relationship. Likewise, if I were to have children one day, I would do my best to teach them about goodness, kindness, thankfulness, and the Law of Attraction (positive thinking). I think this would help us maintain a strong and peaceful family unit and help my children face their future successfully.

# 5. Observed Spirituality Among the Taiwanese[10]

## By David and Judy Newquist

We served as educators on the island of Taiwan between 1976 and 2010. That certainly does not make us experts on the amazing and complex ancient Chinese culture. But we would like to share some of our thoughts and experiences, to provide a unique perspective: that of non-Chinese long-term observers and friends who care deeply about people from that culture. We ask the reader to bear in mind that there are numerous and strong consistencies between the spiritual beliefs of people of Chinese descent from Taiwan and the people of Mainland China. However, in the following chapter, we will be referring to the Taiwanese people specifically, and while people from Taiwan do have a connection to the Mainland through language and cultural history, they still see their identity and current culture as being distinct or separate.

We believe that everyone, no matter what culture they come from, is lost without a mended connection to our Creator and His love and grace. And so, while every culture promotes beauty and some virtuous traits, we believe that people can only do so much on their own to be good, and each culture also has its own

---

[10] *Editor's note: Non-Chinese who have lived among or near Chinese for extended periods of time can help explain spiritual and cultural elements to other non-Chinese in terms that we would find more understandable. The authors of the following chapter are two such cultural interpreters. Their observations provide food for thought for those who befriend the Chinese, especially those with Taiwanese roots. – K.P.*

weaknesses and makes its own mistakes. Cultures in Western countries are no different. We do not want to criticize Taiwanese people or culture. We simply want to share our observations of what we saw happening to those who came from a society where most of the people practiced a spirtualty apart from Jesus Christ.

If you asked us to give an overview of Taiwanese spirituality, here is what we would say. They call it all Buddhism, but it is in fact a mixture of Confucianism, modified Buddhism, Taoism, and animism. Confucianism claims to be a philosophy not a religion, but it has many of the functions of a religion. Two or more of these are often combined to be practiced in the same temple. Every person's mixture is a little different, especially among the more educated. These different religions have mutually contradictory elements, but members of Asian cultures do not generally expect reality to be coherent, and they happily choose to apply each one where it seems appropriate. In some cases, however, one influence has a much stronger presence. For example, the working and rural class tend to be strongly animistic, having a spirituality dominated by many gods and ancestor worship; though they are not alone in this, as even some wealthy, educated, urban populations display strong influence from these traditions.

As Christians, we believe that the purported spirits of ancestors are in fact demons impersonating ancestors, holding people captive in a web of fear, greed, and emotion. The fear is based on demons' ability to cause sounds, movements, disease, and events, as well as the sheer terror of the supernatural. They promote greed through the promise to give help in obtaining prestige, possessions, and pleasure. They twist emotion by exploiting affection for recently departed relatives, pretending that those people's spirits are now in desperate straits needing the care of the living.

One of the dominant Taiwanese ways of showing love is by giving instructions. Whenever someone has any sort of problem, their friends and family's immediate response is to give many instructions about what that person should have done that would have prevented it, and what to do now to solve it. Also, often, there is nothing that can presently be done to undo the purported cause of the problem, which is scant comfort; in fact, it burdens the person with guilt and embarrassment on top of his or her concern and grief. There seems to be little awareness or reluctance to produce this feeling, only a desire to demonstrate to themselves and everyone around them that they themselves would never make such a mistake. Their highest values are harmony, health, wealth, and happiness, and they believe it is up to the individual to work hard to obtain these values, so they have mastered the practice of finding ways to control the events of their lives. This is also the central function of folk religion: coping with the spiritual realm and manipulating it so as to avoid harm and obtain help. This view often naturally carries over if a Taiwanese person converts to Christianity. If this God is the biggest, then He should do the best at providing what they wish.

It is not uncommon for believers to depart from their new-found faith if some serious difficulty occurs. They are not hesitant to give instructions to God Himself about how to manage things, and become angry if He does not follow their advice. Of course, the Taiwanese do not have a monopoly on this practice, but it is certainly noticeable in their way of thinking about and relating to God.

Another attitude that is still widespread in Taiwan is that the people there do not need "foreign religion" (by which they mean primarily Christianity) because they already have their own moral standards. This is connected, understandably, to the view that the primary function of religion is to tell people to do good and produce a peaceful society. There is no concept of a Creator God who wants and deserves a relationship with us. Their worldview is strictly horizontal, not vertical. Even one of David's fellow physics professors, a professing Christian, expressed this opinion. So, his Christian commitment consisted of a personal choice for Christian principles as one among many equal options on the market. This continues to be the consensus on religion in Taiwanese society. Of course, few profess to entirely follow any given set of standards or even intend to; those individuals are just satisfied that they know about the standards and apply them when other practical considerations do not overrule them. They may openly joke about both ethical principles and laws as being things just there for a person's "reference." A few people among our acquaintances seek to do what they feel is right no matter what. As with those who try to be honest, we must admire them and attribute it to their response to God's work in their hearts.

This attitude toward standards extends to their outlook on laws. With no concept of an authoritative or supreme God to whom we must be accountable, laws are just an aspect of human society. And Chinese society as a whole until the early 20th century was governed by aristocratic dynasties who ruled by making laws for their own profit. Often, laws were not intended to be just, and the governed classes avoided observing burdensome laws as often as they could. Even some of our most committed Christian friends still explicitly expressed this attitude toward laws: "Oh, don't you know laws are just for convenience or to use when you want to get even with someone?"

A growing proportion of the population of Taiwan professes to believe no religion, especially educated people in the cities. In the villages, traditional folk religion is still in strong control. But even those who profess no religion still go to the temple to pray for help when they are in trouble, on the assumption that it cannot hurt to give it a try. But when the try is unsuccessful, they feel no loyalty to that god. The idea of a loving God who knows and does what is best for us, and who does not need to be told how to help us, is hard for the Taiwanese to grasp.

I (David) taught an elective course on science and religion and gave a survey in the first class of each semester. One of the survey questions asked if students had experienced ghostly voices and movements in a folk religion temple or ceremony. In our earlier years there, most students had, but as of 2010 almost no one had had such an experience, and many did not really understand the question. This is a major change in a generation's time. However, until the time we left, some students were still telling us of personal experiences with spirits while alone in their rooms at night. This may reflect a decline in participation in temple ceremonies, rather than decline in demonic activities.

An interesting point in those surveys was that many students marked both a belief in ghosts and spirits and atheism as their "religious outlook." I asked another physics professor about this apparent discrepancy, and he explained that in Taiwan "atheist" means you do not believe in one supreme God but believe in many small gods. By contrast, Western atheists are naturalistic materialists, disbelieving in any gods or the spiritual realm in general. Interestingly, in the Roman Empire one of the crimes for which Christians were executed was atheism: they believed in one supreme God but not "small" gods (including the emperor). Clearly then, some knowledge of cultural context is necessary to understand what is meant by "atheism."

When we moved to Taiwan, the major problem for young people from non-Christian homes who wanted to become a Christian was that their family would put strong pressure on them (especially on the oldest son) to participate in the ancestor-worship ceremonies, particularly during Chinese New Year. Everyone understood that Christians are not allowed to worship other gods, including ancestors, and in fact this is their primary objection to Christianity. Other than this, Christianity has a generally good image as a system of ethical standards, and parents have no objection to their children adopting such standards; in fact, they may encourage it. But many families object when Christian faith becomes exclusive to the extent of displacing all other principles, especially the worship of gods, ghosts, and ancestors. The traditional folk concept is that spirits of the dead are still all around us and interacting with us, able to help and harm us, and we also can supply their needs; indeed, we are filially obligated to do so. Parents whose children convert to Christianity may weep about who will care for their spirits after they died. As a result, some students who became Christians were disowned by their parents. Christianity causes widespread offense because of its unfilial disregard of duties to care for an ancestors' spirits' needs. By 2010, a generation later, very few students experienced this pressure if they wished to become Christians, and the consensus among non-Christians was that they would not put any such pressure on their children if the children wanted to become Christians. This has been a major reduction in one obstacle to Taiwanese young people trusting Christ. No doubt, this remains more of a factor for people from the villages and countryside that have not had as thorough an exposure to Western values.

Christians in Taiwan—both believing nationals and foreigners working with the Taiwanese—never have succeeded in producing an acceptable consensus on how to express gratitude and remembrance of ancestors short of actually worshiping them, though sincere attempts have been made to reach such a consensus. When we first came to Taiwan, students who became Christians generally treated their parents much better than they did before, keeping in touch with their parents, doing their best to study well, and showing concern for their parents' problems and needs. Often, they showed much more respect than their non-Christian siblings. Despite these extraordinary efforts, if they did not worship the ancestors, they were still criticized as unfilial. But, again, this distinction has become less common over the years.

Christian funerals are carried out in glaring contrast to traditional funerals. Taiwanese towns have a large funeral area, with many auditoriums of various sizes for holding funerals. Traditional funerals have professional mourners and small brass bands, and, in recent years, loudspeakers blasting the sound for the world to hear. The hired workers weep and wail, bemoaning the late departed and proclaiming the survivors' grief that they will never again see those who are gone. Meanwhile, in the auditorium next door, a Christian funeral is underway, with banners of appreciation for the deceased, and victorious songs and a sermon of assurance that he or she is with the Lord and we who remain will see them again if we too are believers. There is grief, but it is grief at a period of separation, not forever. They grieve, but not as those who have no hope. We were surprised that the traditional funeral practitioners did not protest having such an obvious contrast and insist that the Christians go elsewhere. Many Christian funerals, however, are held in churches. There are a few Christian cemeteries (generally Christian sections of public cemeteries). One comment we did hear about funerals is that it is not appropriately respectful to the deceased to express so much joy in Christian funerals. We have heard it said that it is unfair that the Christians' heaven is so much better than the heavens of other religions!

I (David) was appointed Physics Department chairman for three years, from 1987-90. One day I walked into a laboratory classroom where several teaching assistants were talking. Apparently, they had just been swapping ghost stories, because they asked me "Chairman, are you afraid of ghosts?" I said I was not, and they immediately responded that I should be because the Bible talks about evil spirits. I pointed out that they asked if I was afraid of them, not whether I believe they exist. I do believe they exist, but I belong to Jesus and He is bigger than the spirits. I have a "big brother" on my side. They had never thought of that idea.

We have had occasion to pray with some new believers, and they begin by telling God who they are, as is the custom when visiting a Taiwanese temple to pray to the god there. So, we learned to tell them that God already knows their name and they do not need to tell Him.

We knew a person who said that a cockroach led him to faith in Jesus. One day he saw a cockroach crawl across the eye of the idol in their house. He reasoned that if the idol could not even protect itself against being insulted by a cockroach, then the god it represented was not dependable enough to really help meet his needs.

An explicit principle advocated by Taiwanese society is that adults should not compliment children on their accomplishments, for fear that will make them proud; we should only point out where they fall short and can improve. This is supposed to encourage them to make progress, but it mostly produces very discouraged children. Yet for many generations, parents have treated their children this way. Only a few families have dared abandon this practice. The typical goal is to be number one in your class, which makes one child successful and the rest all failures. Everyone is told that if you work hard enough you can be number one, which is obviously impossible. There can only be one number one. There seems to be little comprehension of the different aptitudes of different people. "Smart" only means academic learning ability. Other skills are not equally valued. Taiwanese society produces a few geniuses and many others living with an invisible "Failure" label printed on their forehead. Many young people rebel against this impossible standard, but it still seems like a prevalent attitude in society.

Another factor in this pattern of criticism is that folk religion practitioners have a habit of insulting their children in public for fear that if they praise their children the gods and ghosts will harm the children. When our daughter Jeannie was in grade school, she took lessons from our neighbor, a Taiwanese mother. Jeannie often came home crying about the harsh criticism she received. Then, one day, she came home very happy, announcing that she realized that "Lin Mama scolds me because she loves me!" This is the attitude that some young people have adopted toward their parents and teachers, and we admire their patience in accepting this. But many rebel against such a display of "care."

All of this influences the Taiwanese concept of God, leading them to assume God places high expectations on us that very few if any can achieve, and that He watches us waiting to point out our faults. Many Taiwanese people feel that Christianity is a "good religion," but "I'm not good enough to be a Christian." Taiwanese society has minimal understanding of the Protestant conception of Biblical grace. Even Chinese believers struggle to grasp the key concept of grace. Unable to grasp that God forgives them, they struggle to forgive others who offend them.

Many Taiwanese, including Christians, live with a serious anger problem that occasionally erupts. They regret this tendency but cannot overcome it. They even have a term, *qibaole*, which means they have "eaten" so much anger that they are full of it, to the extent that they withdraw and do not even eat physically for days. Finally, the anger either dissipates or the person emotionally erupts. They are unable to express it to anyone and work through it in a healthy way. We believe that a major factor in this is a lack of understanding of receiving and giving grace, forgiving and being forgiven. In many families, children are taught not to express their negative emotions, so they have learned to bottle up those feelings and as adults are truly incapable of talking about their anger. Many withdraw, while others eventually lash out.

The culture has no clear procedure for forgiveness. Taiwanese people are hindered from forgiving because they equate it with condoning the wrong, when they know that is false. This is not even logical; the definition of forgiveness is dealing with a wrong, so if we say there was no wrong, what is there to forgive? We are not sure we ever succeeded in explaining the Biblical concept of releasing your right and obligation to execute justice, leaving it up to God to carry that responsibility.

I (Judy) once tried to mend a relationship with an offended friend. In my American way, I tried to arrange a time to have tea together and discuss the situation. My friend said, "Why would I want to waste my time doing that?" But suddenly, after many months, she put on a special party for me. I knew I had been forgiven in a Taiwanese way. Once they are ready to let the offense go, the culture does not have a place for talking about it or asking forgiveness. It simply disappears. They seek reconciliation by doing something kind to the person who offended them. If, however, they do not ever want to let go of the offense, they simply keep their distance from the offender forever.

When the situation with this friend and her group who were all upset with me first began, I knew nothing about it until a missionary friend came to me saying this group had sought her out to be a go-between. When there is a desire for reconciliation, the proper channel is a third person, not direct contact with the offender.

When we first went to Taiwan, we asked students why they chose the subject they did for their major in university. We phrased it in terms of what they liked about it, and why they were interested in it. They just looked at us blankly. We came to realize that the idea of personally choosing a field of study was not a significant principle in Taiwanese society. There was little consideration of personal interests and aptitudes. Students studied what their parents wanted them to study, which was no doubt what had the best prospects of a steady and lucrative job. The top possibilities were law and medicine. Next came engineering and accounting. I (Judy) had a group of first-year girls who wanted to have a Bible study with me. They were all majoring in social work because they felt interested in it. But within a semester all had switched to accounting, all at their parents' insistence, because the job prospects in social work were very poor. The girls had dared follow something they felt interested in. They hated accounting. Fortunately, social work has become a field with major employment opportunities since then, but not in time to help those girls—apart from the group leader who has gone on to do social work abroad many years later.

Taiwanese society explicitly values harmony above honesty, and thus advocates the use of "well-intentioned lies," or what we would call "white lies." Their concern for relational harmony is commendable, but we believe that this practice is counterproductive, generating basic distrust between everyone. This produces the opposite of that highly desired harmony. We have met occasional individuals who have figured this out and decided to be scrupulously honest, apart from any basis in Biblical teaching. But they are just that: lone individuals, still swimming against the current.

Apart from outright distrust, Taiwanese people often think that others do not really mean exactly what they say, assuming everyone is lying whenever that seems convenient. They are masters of speaking indirectly, a habit that makes shades of truth very difficult to separate. In some situations, this helps parties avoid unnecessary confrontation, but it generates endless confusion. People are so busy guessing what the person means that they do not hear what the person really says. They are confident in their assumptions about what the speaker is thinking, but in fact are often wrong. This transfers to their reaction to God's Word, not taking seriously His statements of commandment and consequences. They also love to find hidden meanings in the Bible and are easily influenced by teachers who profess to see the "real" meanings and applications of Bible passages.

Yet, we from the West can learn from this concern for harmony. We tend toward the opposite extreme, with insufficient concern for harmony, blurting out the truth whether it is helpful or not, and calling that "honesty." In their contacts with Westerners, many Taiwanese have felt horrified at the damage that can be caused by such tactless speaking, and feel confirmed in maintaining their indirect approach to conflict to promote harmonious relationships.

This subject is also related to the fact that Taiwanese society is collectivist and honor/shame based, while the West is individualist and law/guilt based. While we will not go into that as a part of these reflections, it is a part of the cultural difference which undeniably influences their beliefs and behaviors and our outlook and reaction.

When we first began living in Taiwan in 1976, we asked if there were any books on family life written by Christians printed in the Chinese language. The reply was that Taiwanese people have strong families and do not need any help. Within ten years that perception had completely changed, and many people were very aware that families were in serious trouble, both in marriages and in parent-child relationships. Government and education sectors devoted considerable resources to this problem. Books on family life began to appear, from both Christian and non-Christian perspectives, translated from other languages or written by Chinese/Taiwanese authors. This has become a significant part of the witness of churches and Christian organizations. Focus on the Family opened a Taiwan-based branch, and several Taiwanese Christian family counseling ministries were started. When Christian television began to be broadcast in Taiwan, speakers on family life were an important part of their programming. In more recent years, these ministries have extended into Mainland China as well, though with limitations to their explicit Christian content.

In years gone by, special needs children in Taiwan were hidden away by their families. It was a matter of saving face for their parents, because the society believed that the problems of special needs children were the result of parents having done something wrong in their previous existence. Parents carried a great burden of guilt and tried to find a way to make up whatever they had done to warrant receiving their special needs children. Parents felt that they caused their children's problems, and thus owed it to their children to try to minimize their suffering. This came in addition to whatever concept there was of parents building up their own debit account in the cycle of existence.

In recent years, Christians have introduced the view that these children are God's creation, greatly treasured by Him, and given as a gift to bless their families in some way. Our friend, Wang Mama, has a special needs daughter. God has used her family to spread the good news all over Taiwan and Southeast Asia that these little ones are not a curse but a blessing. More churches are following Wang Mama's example and establishing Sunday Schools for special needs children. Her yearly camps for special needs children and their families are held in Taiwan, Malaysia, and Hong Kong. In response, many families hungry for this God and His message have come to believe in Him.

We are grateful to have had the opportunity to live and work among the Taiwanese and to share observations from our perspective about some of the unique cultural challenges they face. The culture is in rapid transition. We hope and pray this transition will move in a direction that improves the daily life of the people and points them toward the spiritual truth they are seeking.

# 6. My Thoughts on Chinese Spirituality[11]

## By Josephine Qiu

When I hear the words "Chinese Spirituality," as a Chinese, the first thing that comes into my mind is Buddhism, because Chinese people love to offer things in sacrifice. The last generation, the one my parents belong to, is kind of superstitious. For example, when I was born, my mother went to the fortune teller to ask what was absent from my future life. It is believed that the five elements—metal, wood, water, fire, and earth—are necessary for one's life. The fortune teller said that wood was absent in me, so the characters chosen for my name have a lot of parts connected to "wood" in them.

Additionally, whenever I have some big events coming up, my mom will always go to a pilgrimage site and do something like draw one object from many which serves to tell my fortune, to see if that behavior is appropriate for me. For instance, before I came here to America, she went to a place called *Rao Ping* which is located inside a mountain. Many people go there to have their fortunes told. I was not with her when she went that time, but she got a small yellow object, a talisman, for me, which could keep me safe from any kind of accident that could possibly happen. I carry it around with me now in my bag. And when the Buddhist fortune teller told

---

[11] *Editor's note: This experiential essay is based on a 2017 interview with a woman from the southeast corner of China. She was nearing her mid-20's and had been living in the United States for about two years at the time of the interview. She reviewed the manuscript and said that it still accurately reflects her current thinking, while adding a bit of additional information from the interluding years to further support her ideas. I appreciate her time and honest, insightful sharing. – K.P.*

her it was appropriate for me to go abroad, then she agreed. But if the fortune teller had said it was a bad idea, then Mom would be a little bit worried about me here.

For people from my hometown and for most Cantonese people, I think this association with Chinese spirituality and Buddhism is very true and natural. Even people from Hong Kong show evidence of this because in Hong Kong there is a place called *Huang Da Xian* where people go. I have heard there is also another version of *Huang Da Xian* in New York, in Chinatown. And people go there for fortune telling all the time, when there are some big events happening in their lives. Some people go there regularly—every month, I think—to perform regular services like worship and offerings which will keep them safe from all kinds of unexpected accidents in life.

My hometown is not that big, but it is very crowded. Before our college entrance exam, most parents will visit the temple of Confucius because they think Confucius will have an influence on our studies, since he represents education. So, there is a blending of Buddhism and Confucianism in our minds. The two are not in conflict with each other as Westerners might expect because we see all the gods as being part of a hierarchy. There is a god who oversees all the gods, and then below that he will appoint each god to take care of each area of responsibility, such as safety, education, war, money, and marriage.

I think Buddha is the highest god, and Confucius is under him, appointed to take care of education. One of our most famous Chinese stories is *Xi You Ji*, The Journey to the West, also known as *The Adventures of the Monkey King*. There is also a kind of hierarchy in that story. Buddha, the mightiest god in heaven, appointed a god who was called *Yu Huang Da Di* as the second most powerful god below Buddha. Whenever there is something that *Yu Huang Da Di* could not handle, Buddha would appear. In that story, whenever the Monkey King did something to heaven and made a mess of things and *Yu Huang Da Di* could not handle it, then Buddha appeared to take care of everything. When Buddha appeared, he trapped the monkey inside of a mountain.

It is quite easy for most of us, as Chinese, to keep this straight because there is a very strict hierarchy. We learn about it when we are young so we know it well.

And I think it also comes from real life—the story of the Monkey King is from our imagination, but it comes from real life, from the old traditional hierarchy, the old teaching from before, and from the old emperors. This has been passed down to us over thousands of years.

We learn about it both at home and at school. The historical part is covered in our history classes. But our parents also tell us about those things, just not in very specific detail. As young children, we only have a general image of how strict the hierarchy was in ancient times. But after we enter primary school, the teacher shows us everything in more detail. Even though Buddhism is especially followed in my home area, I think people from all over China will know about this because it is part of Chinese history.

Growing up, my religious life and the situation in my home was more open compared to other Chinese people because I had Christian people inside my house. I went to church every Sunday when my grandma was alive, when I was in primary school. My mom used to be a Christian, but after she married my father, who kind of believed in Buddhism, my mom had to change her religion to Buddhism. There were not many changes to our family dynamics as a result. I do not think my grandma was very strict about the boundary between Christianity and Buddhism. She did not mind living in an area surrounded by a strong Buddhist influence, but she still insisted in her own religious beliefs and traditions. I would say she was very devout but still tolerant of people who believed other things.

I did not see my mom's life before she became a Buddhist, but after she married my father, I think based on what she has said, life became a little bit more complicated. She had not done the Buddhist requirements of worship before, but how she needed to prepare a lot of things for Buddhist offerings every year. According to tradition, the god would come to visit us once a year. We had to prepare pigs, ducks, chickens, and some snacks to prepare an elaborate offering for the god inside our house. After that, we needed to send the god away, so we would have another ceremony. This happens once every year.

My mom usually goes to the temple two times a month, on the first of every month and the fifteenth of every month. These are her obligatory dates according to the lunar calendar. She goes to a temple near to our house. There are a lot of temples around us, so she just picked one that is the most popular and is said to be the most accurate. She gives offerings there in addition to the large annual ceremony at our house. We also set off fireworks. Our largest fireworks display is held within a month or two of Chinese New Year.

Readers may have heard of the kitchen god. It will come as no surprise that the kitchen god and offerings to him are always located in the kitchen area. We need to feed the kitchen god very regularly, by burning some incense. We need to feed him once or twice a month—I cannot remember exactly.

Even though I grew up with a Christian grandma and a Buddhist father, the other major world religions have always felt far-removed from me. I just learned about some of them from TV, but the impression they gave me is that they are mysterious and a little bit terrifying. Because they feel mysterious and we do not understand them clearly, we feel like we are not going to draw too close to people who believe in those other faiths. In my personal experience, we are more willing to learn about Christianity and Catholicism than other world religions.

It is hard for me to put into words, but I guess it has to do with some sense of spiritual lightness and darkness. When I think of Hinduism or Islam, it feels to me like they are from the darker side. But when I think of our own Buddhism, or Christianity and Catholicism, it is like something from heaven, from the sun. If I go in or near a place where people practice Hinduism or Islam, I feel a real sense of darkness. But when I go into a Buddhist temple or a church, I feel very light.

In addition, Hinduism has a practice called meditation. That is also a very mysterious thing. And some Chinese also try Hindu meditation because they are under a lot of pressure. According to them, meditation can help them change the chemistry inside their body. That makes me feel uncomfortable because it is *so* mysterious. I was reading a book, I cannot remember the name of it, but they said that when you reach a really high level of meditation, you are very close to their god. And you can even see your own body organs. That is terrifying.

As far as I know, there *is* a type of meditation in Buddhism, but in China it is mostly practiced by monks, not by average people. The monks have their own textbooks and all kinds of strange areas which originated from somewhere called *Tian Zhu*, an ancient area that is now also part of China, but in the story of the Monkey King it was the home of Buddha. So, the characters needed to walk all the way from their home to *Tian Zhu*. And when the monks are calling on Buddha, they will do something very similar to what many people think of as meditation.

I would also like to mention that every monk has six or eight dots on their head which are caused by incense. Before they enter the monastery, they need to go through a ceremony and the oldest monk will burn their head after shaving off the hair. They will burn their head six or eight times, making a symmetrical line on the head. Most of the formal monks still have that.

I have not read any of the old Buddhist writings. I cannot understand them because they are written in another language. As far as I know, those writings do not really have a meaning, but they are like a spell that the monks use to call to Buddha. It is a kind of chanting where they say the words over and over. I have not read from other writings such as the Qur'an either, but I have read some from the Bible. From the Bible, I learned about how humans were created and how everything was formed. But in the Buddhist teachings, they do not really have something to explain the origins of things and people. Even the mighty monkey was just formed from a rock. It simply broke through the rock somehow and came into existence.

So, Chinese Buddhists do not really have a story about origins. And the old Buddhist teachings do not really tell us about how the other gods were born or formed. Even the ancient Greeks and Romans had stories to explain where their gods and humans came from, but we have no idea. We only know there was once a big giant named *Pan Gu*. He broke through something to form the sky, earth, ground—to form all kinds of plants. After that, we know that all kinds of gods just came into existence, but we have no idea where they came from.

I find that my ideas about different kinds of spiritualty have changed a lot. When I was very little, I thought those kinds of things were possible, were created by people, were from nowhere. We could not trace the origin of those stories. As I have grown up, I have come to believe that there must be a reason why these beliefs are passed on from one generation to the next, all the way down to us today. And I feel like some of the mysterious things are accurate. Just because we cannot understand something does not mean it is false or fake.

Still, even though we cannot understand something, we can believe it is true. For example, when my mom went to the fortune teller, she received a type of poem which was supposed to tell her how my life would be in America. The poem told her I would meet someone in America, and after I came back to China, I would not find a job there but instead would return to America. All those things happened. It is mysterious and there is no other apparent reason for it. We could not explain it, but it came true. It is not scientific but sometimes it is still true, and that is what is scary about it.

In modern China, I have seen a blend of old and new, of spiritual mystery and science. I went to Hong Kong in December 2018, and I stopped by Huang Da Xian to have my fortune told. When I got a poem after drawing from a number of possibilities, I took it to the fortune teller. I noticed that when they asked me when my birthdate was, they referred to a book for my decoded fortune. They also have a book for explaining what the poem is trying to tell us, and many people believe the poem conveys a message from God to us. So, I have noticed that fortune telling has evolved to be based upon a systematic pool of knowledge.

If God really exists, I think he would be someone to help me go through everything. Not to do all the things for me like what is described in Buddhism, but to help me go through the difficulties in life. He could give me some spiritual strength. So, that is what I like about Christianity. It does not just tell us to go through all the miserable experiences and then we can reach heaven. Instead, it gives us strength from the inside and then helps us go through all kinds of difficulties. The Chinese or Buddhist part just tells us to suffer before we go to heaven. If you do not persevere through the suffering, you will go to hell, where you will continue to suffer. It is like double the amount of suffering, and this is the part I do not like about our traditional beliefs.

Some people ask whether God wants people to suffer. From the story *Journey to the West* we are told people must go through 81 difficulties before they can reach heaven. There, they could get some books with information and spread that information to the whole world, to save the world. That is similar to the general idea of Buddhism. To some extent, suffering is the very heart of Buddhism.

After a person dies, I believe that the spirit of the person will remain in our room, area, or region after they die. They turn into ghosts or some type of spiritual substances. I do not think they are able to hurt us, so I am not afraid of them. But I believe in their existence. The body of the dead person goes into a grave or is cremated but their spirit wanders or travels for a certain period and then goes somewhere new, but I do not know what that new area is. Maybe a parallel space where they can stay.

Reincarnation is also a popular belief among some Chinese Buddhists. What they tell you is that if you suffer and do good things in this life, the next life will be better. Maybe you will be born into a rich family or a royal family. I think that is a kind of good belief, because if people hold this belief in this life, they will persist in doing good things. But we have no way of knowing if it is true.

Some people may think that the only kind of useful beliefs are the beliefs that are absolutely true. But I do not agree. I think if you have a belief deep in your heart, it will give you more strength or motivation, no matter whether what you believe in is true or not.

Chinese Buddhists may also tell you that if you do bad things in this life, you will be put into hell, and you will not be able to be a human in your next life. You will suffer for a long time in hell, until all the criminal things and all your guilt from the previous life are burned out of you. And then you will leave hell and return to the world again.

This may cause some confusion for non-Chinese who visit temples in China. Sometimes the walls depict pictures of Buddhist heaven and hell, and those pictures do not fit into the standard, classic sense of reincarnation. How can we believe in both? Hell, especially, may be more like a place where people just stay for a time between one life and the next. Those pictures may display a god in heaven and another god in hell, and each of them will judge people. Those gods are very scary looking. And one of the gods has two subordinates to help him. One has a horse's face and the other has an ox's head, but they both have human bodies. They are very dark, strange, and scary creatures.

I once saw a picture of a god from the ancient Middle East that had a head like a bull but an open belly where fire could be put for sacrifices. When I saw that statue, I did not like it. Later, my friend told me that kind of statue was used to offer child sacrifices, and I felt horrible. The pictures of the god's subordinates in the temple made me feel terrible too.

Some of my non-Chinese friends talk a lot about good and bad or right and wrong. When I was young, I thought there were absolute rights and wrongs. But as I have grown older, I do not think "right" and "wrong" are so clear. If you do not hurt others, it is not really a matter of righteousness or falseness. But, if you hurt others, it is definitely wrong.

Even if I make a personal choice that hurts me in the end, it is not technically wrong because I did not hurt other people and so it usually has nothing to do with others. That is not really a big deal in the bigger picture because it is my choice. I do not think anyone has a right to judge a person's choice as being "right" or "wrong." If I think there is a chance that I would hurt someone else by making a certain decision, I usually choose the option that will not hurt the other person.

However, we cannot always foresee the future or probable results. Sometimes we still end up choosing to do things that hurt others. When that happens to me, I believe it is my duty to try to make it up to them if possible. If I cannot make it up to them, I will bear it in mind for a certain length of time and keep reminding myself not to do it again. But some damage will already have been done, so while I must bear it, I would feel miserable. Yet, I feel it is also my personal choice to learn to let go of the offense, not to hang on to it too long, and not to do it again in the future. When I say I should make it up, I think the meaning of that depends on what the offended person would prefer or need. For example, if it were my parents, they do not need money from me. But they may need something else from me, so I would try to figure out what they want or need and then try to give that to them.

I do not expect my thoughts about spiritualty and my spiritual life to remain the same in the future. As my experience accumulates, I recognize the way that I look at things will likely be very different after five or ten years. For example, in the future, perhaps five or ten years from now, I will probably be able to accept things that I do not want to accept now.

That is the main difference we can observe between individual Chinese, I think. Some of the Chinese around me now see or experience more things, and they become numb. It is like they do not have any special feeling toward the things that happen around them. I do not want to be or become that way. So, I want to keep thinking about all this and avoid their response. I guess the key to avoiding that is to reach as high as I can, to try to experience more. For instance, I can achieve higher education or avoid spending time with people who take that other approach. I think keeping an open mind and always continuing to learn will help me to avoid becoming closed off and numb.

That is why I do not want to form a family so early. Some of my classmates are already married and have their own children—two or three children at my age. I do not like that because they become numb to the world and only care about their family. They do not care about bigger and deeper things happening outside. Between their family activities, social media, TV, and not joining in challenging activities, they do not improve themselves. They do not go out and meet other people. Their life becomes so closed and they are so focused on small, personal things instead of being open to new ideas. It is like they are thinking, "Those things are too far away from me, and I do not care about them." I do not like that kind of attitude.

As I reflect, I see another reason for me to believe in the existence of spiritual beings and substances is because in both the Western and Eastern worlds, we all have some kinds of stories about those spiritual things, like ghost stories. So that is another reason for me not to just write off all spiritual things as superstition. People will not imagine something from nothing. It must be based on something that was true or seen or experienced at some point. Maybe they cannot explain it, so they come up with all kinds of stories. It is tricky to know which stories are spiritually true and which are not. Even though the Western world did not overlap with the Eastern world much in ancient times, they still have similar stories. So that is why I think we should pay attention to what the stories say and consider what really exists.

On the campus of Shenzhen University, there is a big *ba gua* located in a central area of the university grounds. A *Ba Gua* is an area where people are trying to seek spiritual balance, or where there is a very clear presence of both the light and the dark together [like the balance of black and white or yin and yang in Taoism]. We believe that this spiritual balance in the area can affect future generations. A university normally should not have such a spiritual place inside, but in this case it does exist. For the last four or five generations, there have been a lot of people trying to escape from Mainland China to Hong Kong. On that spot, they were shot, and a lot of people died in that area during that time. And that area is now where Shenzhen University is located. A lot of strange things have happened there in the recent past. This is why that kind of *ba gua* came into existence.

It is hard to explain because it is all very mysterious. Some people will even bring in an expert before moving into a new house to study which way the porch is facing and where the kitchen should be located. The expert will often recommend that the family put something on the porch to block the living area from direct contact with the outside area to protect the family spiritually. It is all very complicated.

Additionally, most people will choose their tomb location and marker before they die. Many rich people in China will still spend a lot of money building their tomb because they believe that the location and design of the tomb will influence the well-being of the next generations.

It all may seem strange to non-Chinese, especially if a Chinese person believes in reincarnation or they believe that their ghost is outside somewhere and not in the tomb while only their body or ashes will be buried there. But we must understand that the Chinese people who believe in the importance of this are not really thinking about their own spirit, which will probably be off somewhere else anyway. They are acting for the sake of their children and grandchildren, believing that the choices and plans they make about their final arrangements will help bring the next generations more good luck and less trouble.

There are really rich people in my hometown spending tens of thousands of dollars just to create their tomb before they die. Even for common people who are not so rich, they are very careful when choosing their own tomb, and they normally prearrange everything. There is even a saying in China now that some people "cannot afford to die!" It is awful, but true! People can chuckle about the outrageousness of it now, but it is hard for people to deal with a mysterious thing. If I cannot afford to die and I think that is going to bring a lot of bad luck upon my family, it is a horrible feeling, a real burden.

The final thing I want to share is an observation from living in America. I think some uniform faith and spiritual belief is what has made America such a strong country. And the faith of many Americans helps them to keep their country strong. But in China, it is different. Since we were ruled by the Communist Party, the Party has become our god. It tries to take the place of a god for us. But I think people will really be lost if they try to believe in the Party that way. Because I think God is a spirit and one person or group of people cannot have the same kind of spiritual power as a god. Those are two very different things. When the People's Republic of China was created by Chairman Mao, people regarded him as God, but during the Cultural Revolution, people suffered from the mistakes that Chairman Mao—as a human—made. Suddenly their belief in their only God broke down and the next generation has been lost about what to believe in.

I am happy for this chance to offer some observations about Chinese culture and spirituality. By sharing my ideas frankly, I hope readers will have a clearer picture of an average Chinese person's experience and inner thinking. I cannot speak for everyone, of course, so I hope my ideas will help non-Chinese friends feel more comfortable when they speak to Chinese acquaintances.

# 7. Understanding and Ministering to Hui Chinese[12]

## By Kaylene Powell

Over the past two millennia, some people groups have naturally seemed, for a variety of reasons, to be less receptive to the good news of Jesus Christ. Likewise, certain people groups have been more constrained by geographic remoteness or legal restrictions and have therefore received little or no active witness from local or outside sources. One of these broader groups is the Muslim peoples of China. In fact, for some individuals, the very idea of *Chinese* and *Muslim* describing the same human being is about as logical as labeling someone as both *French* and *Buddhist.* The two identifiers simply do not seem to fit together. During a friendly conversation, an African Muslim refugee transplanted to Illinois scoffed when I suggested the idea. "Muslims? In *China*? No, they are not like us. The Chinese belong to a different religion!"

In truth, there are a great many Muslims in China, and they can be divided into several different minority peoples. Much could be written about the Uigurs of

---

[12] *Editor's note: I conducted extensive research on the Hui people and their worldview in a period between my early and later years as an educator in the Chinese mainland, after having befriended and worked closely alongside some members of that minority group. Near the end of my time in China, I moved to a Hui urban neighborhood. There, I was able to see some of the historical and theoretical insights I had discovered lived out in daily life more clearly. I hope this piece will encourage a broader discussion of the spiritual beliefs of China's 55 different officially recognized minority groups, several of which are Muslim, and how these beliefs are sometimes misunderstood in Chinese society. I offer these insights in a spirit of humility and love for members of all groups under the Chinese umbrella: the majority Han as well as the Hui and other ethnic minorities. - K.P.*

Xinjiang Autonomous Region or other, smaller Muslim groups, but the focus of this article will be on a group known as the Hui (pronounced "hway"). Followers of Jesus—whether non-Chinese believers or members of the Han Chinese majority—must have a deeper understanding of the history and the mindset of the Hui if they are to have any competence in ministering to Hui friends and neighbors. By gaining valuable background knowledge and considering how it applies practically in relationship-building, such a person can lay a better foundation for sharing the Gospel with Hui acquaintances from their earliest days of interaction. This article contains a summary of such background knowledge and points of application.

## Origins of the Hui

How did Islam first appear in China and how did there come to be different groups of Chinese Muslims? This is a point of some controversy because it seems there are few or no written sources of Chinese-Muslim history that date back more than four hundred years. Because of this, some scholars argue that the accuracy of the oral history of Islam's roots in China is built "on very slender foundations" (Mason, 1929, p. 43). However, enough evidence from both recent written sources and historical oral sources can be triangulated to reach some sort of reasonable consensus. The first Muslim delegation came by sea, sent from the Caliph Uthman, arriving in China (probably in Guangdong) in A.D. 651. As this group came for trading and ambassadorial purposes, they "were not concerned with propagating their faith among the Chinese" (Mason, 1929, p. 77). Roughly a hundred years later, sizeable numbers of Muslims started to enter Chinese territory from the west by way of Central Asia. Many of these were Muslim soldiers who eventually settled permanently in western China (Mason, 1929). Though it appears that members of Muslim armies played a role in bringing Islam to China, in general, the religion was introduced much more by traders and diplomats than by any sort of political force (Hollian-Elliot, 2006).

Early Muslim traders applied for and were granted permission to enter and later settle in China by Tang and Song emperors over the next few centuries. While some came by sea and established Muslim communities on the east coast, many more came along major trade routes like the Silk Road and took up residence in the central and western parts of China, including within the regional capital city of

Chang'an (modern-day Xi'an). Many of these early traders were single men, and they wanted to marry local Chinese women. According to Aldrich (2010), after receiving official permission from the emperor, they could do so, and their wives were expected to convert to Islam. The biracial offspring of these initial marriages became the earliest Chinese Muslims (Hollian-Elliot, 2006). Han (majority) Chinese initially began to call those early traders and their new families "Hui" (a Chinese term which means *to go back* or *to return*) because many of the first traders did not plan to stay in China long-term but hoped to return to their homelands one day. Eventually, however, most of the traders who had come across Central Asia remained for one reason or another, assimilating culturally in many ways with their Han neighbors (Hollian-Elliot, 2006). These people became distinct from other Muslims living in China because they were at least partially Chinese by blood while still maintaining Muslim beliefs and certain customs. Other groups such the Uigurs have rarely intermarried with the Han and are therefore considered "Chinese" in the sense that they have lived within the political jurisdiction of the Chinese state. In early centuries, Han Chinese began to label all Muslims (both Chinese and Arab) as "Da-shih" but later abandoned that term to use the names "Hui" or "huihui" as the standard, distinctive label for Chinese Muslims by the beginning of the Yuan dynasty in the late 13$^{th}$ century (Israeli, 2002). While the Han would still use "Hui" to refer to all Muslim minorities living under Chinese rule for centuries to come, in this chapter, the term "Hui" will refer to the largest ethnically Chinese Muslim minority in modern China.

The early Hui merchants generally sought to go about their business peacefully and avoid conflict with Han officials, so they followed religious traditions quietly and refrained from overtly proselytizing others for their faith. Despite this, the number of Hui continued to grow steadily because of "natural family growth, adoption of Chinese orphans, and occasional conversions." Further immigration of and intermarriage by additional traders, religious leaders, diplomats, and soldiers from Arabia and Central Asia also accelerated the population increase (Hollian-Elliot, 2006). A new facet of "Islam's multi-racial community" began to take shape, and over time this new people group would greatly affect the communities in which they lived (Ruthven, 2006). As time passed, the Hui became distinct from other Muslim minorities because they spread out to live in cities and areas all over China. Unlike Tibetans and other minorities who were generally tied to one geographical area and therefore more easily controlled by ruling dynasties, the Hui were not as easily subjected to minority-related restrictions (Israeli, 2002). In fact, throughout Chinese history, Han administrators saw the Hui people as a distinct minority because of their religious beliefs and related customs, but those administrators were still often hopeful that the Hui would eventually become "Chinese" in every sense of the word (Israeli, 2002).

By the time of the Ming Dynasty, the Hui were firmly established as a sizeable and distinct minority because the Ming were so bent on the Sinicization of all peoples residing in China that only the minorities who had formed or maintained their own distinct communities and cultural molds by that point survived the extreme pressure for cultural assimilation (Israeli, 2002). Aldrich (2010) notes that the Hui were set apart by several characteristics from the other, now officially recognized, Muslim minorities such as the Uigurs, Kazakhs, Dongxiang, Kirghiz, Salars, Tajiks, Uzbeks, Bao'an, and Tatars . The Hui were partly Han by blood, while members of several other groups rarely intermarried with the Han and were generally "Chinese" because of designated political boundaries, and they lived in all areas of China instead of being mainly restricted to one area. In addition, throughout the course of their history, they have communicated in the local Chinese dialects of their various regions. While they have revered the Arabic language and the Qur'an revealed in that language, relatively few Hui, both in the past and today, have become well-versed in Arabic (Israeli, 2002). This factor, in addition to periodic times throughout history when Hui Chinese were cut off from members of the larger Muslim community, led to the need for a unique language besides Mandarin that would meet the needs of the Hui (Aldrich, 2010). They invented two new systems to assist in the understanding of Arabic texts. The first, *xiaojing,* used the Arabic alphabet to write Chinese characters, similar to the way the *pinyin* system aids today's students in learning to read characters. The second was called *hui hua* ("Muslim speech") and was basically a way of transliterating Arabic words into Chinese-sounding equivalents using similar sounding Chinese characters. Thus, for example, *salam* became *sai liang mu* (Aldrich, 2010).

Besides their own specialized vocabulary, another characteristic of the Hui that greatly influenced Chinese culture and history was their dietary restrictions. They followed many of the standard Islamic dietary such as abstinence from pork and alcohol. When the Ming rulers were coming to power, a new method for roasting whole pigs became popular in southern China. The communities of the north, especially in Shandong Province adapted the cooking method to use ducks in place of pigs out of sensitivity to their Hui members. As a result, in the 1400's, a dish (*Beijing kao ya*, commonly known as "Peking Duck") was created that would become one of the most delicious and widely renowned delicacies in all of China (Aldrich, 2010). Over time, the Han and various travelers who visited China discovered how delicious Muslim-Chinese food was, and Hui restaurants became famous for both their delicious dishes and their high standards of cleanliness.

Another distinct characteristic of the Hui was their attitude toward education. Even before many Han were receiving a broad education in more subjects than those required for passing the Civil Service exam, as early as the 16th century Hui communities developed a standard curriculum of madras education so that their children could receive both academic and religious instruction (Aldrich, 2010). Perhaps more significant was their unique appreciation for educating both male and female students. As early as the mid-fifteenth century, girls were allowed to receive an education in Hui communities, and within a hundred years a new curriculum had been designed specifically to meet the educational needs of female students (Aldrich, 2010). This was at least three hundred years before Han girls would have significant educational opportunities, mostly at foreign mission schools. As the Han strove with various degrees of personal devotion to following the teachings of Confucius, they could readily see differences in the way their Hui neighbors lived and were challenged by their unique attitudes and customs. As a 15th century Han author observed:

> [Muslims] have fixed sums of money which they give each month
> to keep alive the poor of their areas. They aid equally those who
> come from elsewhere. Our scholars profess the religion of the Sage

but do not care about others' life or death. [The Muslims, on the other hand,] make little of funerals, keep fasts and consider that not feeding others is to kill themselves. (Aldrich, 2010, p. 205)

Yet, it is also crucial to remember that while the Hui were set apart in some ways, they were also "Chinese" in other ways. Over the course of time, the Hui had to adapt themselves to the majority culture in order to continue residing harmoniously beside Han neighbors and communities of other minority peoples. This "superficial acculturation" led to the Hui behaving as "Muslim indoors, Chinese outdoors." For example, this attitude could be seen in mosques that were built in the styles of pagodas (Ruthven, 2006), the adoption of non-Arabic names, such as *Ma* to replace Muhammad (Hollian-Elliot, 2006), the practice of placing a household altar containing the Qur'an and incense where Han families would traditionally set a household shrine (Aldrich, 2010), and the adoption of Han clothing styles. For the sake of seeking imperial favor, the Hui made various concessions such as ceasing to adorn the main entrance of a mosque for a Caliph's grand entrance, placing plaques that declared reverence to the emperor inside their prayer halls, and wearing the prescribed queues (long hair braids) but tucking their queues inside their white caps while performing *salat* during the time of the Qing Dynasty (Aldrich, 2010).

Before moving on, we should note early missionary attitudes toward and efforts among the Hui. A work commissioned by the 1910 World Missionary Conference in Edinburgh and produced by the China Inland Mission sought to educate people of that generation about the origins of and then-current attitude of the "Mohammedans" of China. However, while the thick volume was well-intended and included some very insightful observations, it tended to group all Chinese Muslims together without appreciating the diversity among different minority groups (Broomhall, 1910). The Committee on Work for Moslems (a subgroup of the China Continuation Committee) produced some resources over a century ago to assist those trying to bring the Gospel to the Hui and other Muslim minorities (e.g. Mason, *List of Chinese-Moslem Terms*). A few early Protestant missionaries worked with Salar and Dongxiang minorities, though very harsh living and ministry conditions kept more from living with those peoples long-term. A number of other workers found it fairly easy to reach the Dongan, as that group spoke more Chinese while the Salar and Dongxiang spoke Arabic-based dialects (Covell, 1995). The Hui, however, seemed virtually invisible to most missionaries. As one scholar explains:

> Not that they looked exactly like the dominant non-Muslim Chinese . . . they tended to be larger in build and have a longer face, deeper eyes, and a thicker beard than other Chinese. Their Islamic faith . . . set them apart from other Chinese. Infrequently, their communities were dispersed among the non-Muslim Chinese. More usually, when separate, they were almost an impenetrable enclave. Therefore, from the missionary view, they faded into the dominant Chinese Confucian and Buddhist background. They [who represent roughly 60% of the whole Chinese Muslim population] were the hidden Muslims of China and largely neglected in the missionary outreach. (Covell, 1995, pp. 174-175)

## Conflict Between Han and Hui

Though there were numerous favorable and sympathetic decrees from Han emperors towards their Hui subjects (Aldrich, 2010) and many concessions have been granted to Muslim minorities in modern times (Hollian-Elliot, 2006), interethnic relations have often been less than ideal. Much could be written about the historic and current tensions between the Han and the Hui; what follows is a very basic summary of the roots of this ethno-religious conflict. While the Han and the Hui initially shared some fundamental values, Han rulers were eager to maintain control over all the subjects within their realm, including Muslims (Hollian-Elliot, 2006). The Han harbored many misconceptions about the Muslim faith and way of life that have plagued Han-Hui relations ever since (Aldrich, 2010). At the core of this poor relationship are long-standing stereotypes: the Han have seen themselves as culturally superior to all minorities and outsiders (Israeli, 2002) while Chinese Muslims have viewed the Han as a corrupt and irreligious people (Hollian-Elliot, 2006).

Why have Han rulers and authorities sometimes been paranoid about the customs and attitudes of the Hui? Some of the most fundamental themes of Islam flatly conflict with the idea of submission to an authoritarian non-Islamic state. One obvious problem is the fact that devout Muslims will submit to no one but *Allah*; this has been hard for Han followers of Confucian philosophy and emperor or dictator worship to grasp. *Hajj*, the annual Muslim pilgrimage to Mecca, was historically seen by Chinese leaders as a repudiation of loyalty to the authority of the Son of Heaven (the emperor) and even today is only permitted for passable applicants who are closely monitored along the way by Communist Party officials (Aldrich, 2010). Thus, the Hui have often had restrictions imposed upon their overall freedom of worship, for Muslim presence in China has always posed a challenge, and at times even a threat, to the Chinese establishment (Israeli, 2002).

For their part, the Hui have often been offended by the behaviors and beliefs of their Han neighbors. The Hui dislike Han burial customs and the newer tradition of cremation, and they do not appreciate the historical Han fear of ghosts, despite their own traditions regarding the *jinn* (Aldrich, 2010). They believe that ancestor veneration—such a vital part of Han tradition—is a form of idolatry (Israeli, 2002), and they are deeply offended by prayers offered to or bowing before statues of Buddha (Aldrich, 2010). The Hui also reject the heavy consumption of pork and alcoholic beverages that is a socially significant part of Han culture.

On the other hand, the Han have harbored and perpetuated many myths and misconceptions about the Hui. At times, some very righteous Hui were revered in almost god-like status by members of the Han community—something that could sit very poorly indeed in the mind of a devout Muslim (Aldrich, 2010). In addition, according to a Hui convert to Christianity, the Han have spread stories that the Hui do not eat pork because they actually worship a pig-god, which is obviously a deeply offensive piece of slander to Muslims. Success in economic and business ventures has long been a source of contempt of the Hui in the minds of some Han (Aldrich, 2010), so a stereotype of selfishness and greed has often been projected onto members of the Hui community by their Han neighbors (Israeli, 2002). The Hui have often responded to these and other troubling points by withdrawing and interacting as little as possible with the Han living around them, "reclaiming their ethnic identity" by perpetuating their history, customs, and beliefs to new generations through myth preservation and storytelling (Israeli, 2002).

When looking at Han political authorities, it is important to mention the long tradition of sometimes violent uprisings and protests on the part of various Muslim minorities (mainly Uigurs) that have caused government officials to be generally suspicious of all Chinese Muslims (Hollian-Elliot, 2006). Equally disturbing to the officials has been the challenge of understanding and distinguishing between what they call the "Old" and "New" sects of Islam in China—the "Old" referring primarily to the Hanafi school and the "New" referring to various other Islamic sects that have gained stronger followings in recent decades (Israeli, 2002). Han officials have used both mundane and brutal methods of dealing with such unrest and uncertainties in the past. Several famous incidents from the Cultural Revolution such as the "Shadian Incident," can be cited as examples of the more extreme responses. In the Shadian district in August 1975, a thousand Hui, including many children and elderly people, were massacred during a week of intense attack by the People's Liberation Army, and around 4,400 Hui houses were destroyed (Israeli, 2002; Aldrich, 2010).

Perhaps the saddest part of the Han-Hui conflict in the mind of Christians may be the ethnic misconceptions and divisions that hold Han believers back from befriending and sharing the Gospel with this minority spread throughout their own country. Both the Han Christians living in their own ancestral areas and those who have been displaced to locations in Western China for a variety of reasons have contact with the Hui in daily life. If they were able to befriend Hui neighbors, salespeople, and co-workers, many spiritual seeds could be planted. However, the factors described previously have led the Hui to withdraw into their own communities and often appear unreachable. Therefore, the hearts of Han believers will need to be specifically burdened and broken for the lost state of the Hui who live near them if those Han are to be moved to pursue the Hui with the relentless love of Christ. Likewise, Han believers will have to assume a posture of humility and learn far more about Hui beliefs and culture if they are to communicate effectively with the Hui for the eventual purpose of meaningful evangelism and discipleship (see discussion by Covell, 1995).

## Modern Situation and Mindset of the Hui

The Han made up 92 percent of the whole Chinese population in 2000, while combined minority groups made up the other 8 percent. Of that 8 percent (roughly 106 million people at that time), about one-fifth are Muslim. The Uigurs represent the largest overall Muslim minority and the Hui the largest ethnically-Chinese Muslim minority. In 2000, the number of Hui totaled just over 9 million (Hollian-Elliot, 2006), though other, reliable statistics have estimated their numbers to be as high as 15 million (Israeli, 2002). The largest concentration of Hui live in the special autonomous region set aside for them by the Communist leaders, a small province called Ningxia which is located in north-central China, on the western edge of China's more populated areas. Other sizeable Hui communities are scattered throughout the rest of the country. While the Hui generally adhere to the Hanafi Sunni school of Islam, how conservative or liberal a Hui person is depends a great deal on where they live. As a rule, the further west someone travels, the more likely they are to encounter conservative, devout Hui believers; conversely, the Hui living in cities along the east coast are often more liberal and relaxed in their religious observances (Hollian-Elliot, 2006; Aldrich, 2010).

Geography is not the only thing that generally distinguishes sub-groups within the modern Hui people; another key factor is differences between generations. Overall, the older Hui tend to be more devout in their religious customs, such as attending mosque or fasting, than the younger generations. Throughout their history, Hui community leaders have often struggled with how to educate the youth under their jurisdiction. The trends of apathy towards Qur'an study and overall secularization cause many Hui parents to worry in much the same way that Muslim parents around the world worry about the coming generations (Miller, 1995). Some have questioned whether or not today's Hui children can receive an orthodox education when most or all of their exposure to the Qur'an is based on Chinese translations or interpretations of the Islamic Scriptures (Israeli, 2002).

In terms of social customs, at birth the Hui usually perform the rite of circumcision (Israeli, 2002). As noted earlier, it is very rare for non-Hui Muslims, such as the Uigurs, to intermarry with the Han; people who choose to do so may be expelled from their local *umma*. The Hui are somewhat accepting of intermarriage between their children and Han neighbors, though it is still much more common for a Hui to marry another Hui. If a Hui wants to marry a Han, older generations of Hui still desire that the Han prospect convert to Islam and go through ritual cleansing to remove impurities from the body before marriage (Aldrich, 2010). Modern day Hui still prefer to follow prescribed cleansing and preparation rituals and bury the bodies of their deceased loved ones instead of cremating them, which has become the Han standard. When Han of previous eras buried their dead in coffins, they often viewed Islamic burials without caskets as showing a lack of filial piety (Aldrich, 2010). Many modern-day Han feel disgruntled when the Hui are granted special burial rights by the central government, seeing this as a form of favoritism.

The origins of the Hui and the history of their relationship with the Han majority have done a great deal to shape the reception of the Hui in modern times. While the level of religious piety and the personal attitudes of individual Hui families and communities will vary from area to area, some general trends may be noted. First and foremost, there is a dichotomy between separateness and inclusiveness in the minds of the Hui as they think about whether or not they are "Chinese." In a way, the special customs and behaviors of the Hui have led the Han to view the Hui as "non-Chinese" (Israeli, 2002). But how do the Hui classify their own identity?

First of all, they do not expect special treatment just because they are from an ethnic minority and they take great pride in how their people have contributed to Chinese society, both historically and in the present-day (Aldrich, 2010). My discussions with a Hui Christian indicated that on the one hand, modern-day Hui (especially the younger generation) accept their place in Chinese society and consider themselves a part of the Chinese people. On the other hand, the Hui continue to retain many of their old customs and eagerly desire to pass those customs and beliefs on to their children and grandchildren. They are also willing and even happy to share their special traditions with non-Hui friends and acquaintances, unashamedly displaying those things that make their people distinct. While holding on to their own traditions, they do celebrate many of the same traditional Chinese festivals as their Han neighbors—but sometimes with appropriate adaptations made to the Han customs. For example, the Hui will eat *yue bing* (mooncakes) on Mid-Autumn Day, but unlike the Han, the Hui must produce and consume separate mooncakes which contain no lard (Aldrich, 2010).

The Hui typically do not decorate the doors of their houses with Chinese characters. They tend to cater to shops and restaurants that are run by Muslims and produce *halal* items. They often refer to themselves as followers of *Qing Zhen Si* (the pure and true religion) and center their communities around the local mosque instead of smaller family units so revered by the Han in their traditional ancestral rites. Local groups of Hui are often completely independent of each other. While worship services are held every Friday, many Hui attend mosque only on special occasions. Most Hui acknowledge the five pillars of Islam but do not pray five times a day. Although special mosques for women have been built in some cities, generally, modern Hui women are excluded from mosque prayer services. Except in very conservative areas, Hui women do not usually cover their heads (Covell, 1995).

All of this has created a sort of "dual identity" in the minds of the Hui. To honor their living family members and their ancestors means to affirm both their Chinese connection and their Arab roots (Aldrich, 2010). In some ways, they blend right in with the Han communities they live beside, but in other ways, they love to perpetuate myths and customs that are uniquely theirs in order to preserve their own identity (Aldrich, 2010; Israeli, 2002). One particularly difficult question for modern Hui is how to live under Communist rule. Surprisingly, a sizeable number of Hui have joined the Communist Party—a practice which requires an official denial of the existence of God—and some have even become high Party officials. Hui Party members typically make a distinction between actually believing in a religious system and simply going through the outward rituals of one's inherited religion. Thus, especially during the month of Ramadan, it is not unusual to see many Hui Party members attending services at their local mosque (Aldrich, 2010). Whether or not the Hui become members of the Party, they still have to wrestle with a balance of submitting to the regulations imposed upon them by the Party leadership while also following their consciences in matters of fulfilling various religious obligations (Aldrich, 2010).

While the Han, both in the past and present, have tended to group all Chinese Muslims together, the Hui see themselves as distinct from other Muslim minorities in China. This has an ambiguous impact on their receptivity to Christianity. For some Hui, receiving Christ can be just one more part of their identity that makes them non-Han; for others, conversion to Christianity would be just one more sign of submitting to something foreign to their traditional ethnic code (Covell, 1995). Yet they also recognize that because they are not living in an Islamic country, they have to choose whether they will engage in *jihad* against non-Muslim authorities or continue to submit and make some cultural concessions. Some Chinese Muslims dream of an Islamic state in China but know it is impossible because of the de-centralized Muslim population (Israeli, 2002). Most, however, simply hope to live their lives and practice their religion peacefully in the local communities where their families are now established (Aldrich, 2010).

## Applications for Ministry

For any non-Chinese Christians who encounter Hui Chinese in or outside of mainland China and any Han believers who welcome the calling to reach out to their Hui neighbors, many challenges may arise. The most prominent of these challenges are to understand the root issues of the Hui worldview as well as their sense of ethnic isolation, and the confusion and generational tension resulting from a mixture of traditional education with secularization and atheistic conditioning among young Hui. How may Han Christians and non-Chinese Christians respond to these hurdles so that more effective relationship-building and evangelization can take place? The following section contains some proposed answers.

First, both the Han believer and the foreign believer must choose to assume a posture of humility and take on the attitude of a learner. Our learning must include the history of the Hui people, their general attitudes and practices, and the roots of conflict between the Han and the Hui. We need a foundation in the main beliefs of Islam, Confucianism, and Buddhism, as well as the history of Christianity, Christian-

Muslim relations, and the spread of Christianity in China. This foundation will help us understand how the mindset of both the Hui and the Han developed and be able to better discern the reasons for resistance to the Gospel among the Hui. Likewise, we may start to see which *similar* and which *distinctive* approaches we can use in sharing the Good News with our Hui neighbors and our non-Christian Han friends. This learner-attitude is based on the expectation that we will be intentional about pursuing relationships with the Hui we meet and interact with in our everyday lives. When we meet and befriend a Hui individual or family, we must demonstrate open hearts that are willing to learn *from* them. It is not enough to learn *about* the Hui by reading books and articles; we must gain an emic perspective about their lives by building deep relationships with them, gaining further understanding of their culture in their own words.

Additionally, we must assume a humble learning posture in our willingness to communicate with the Hui using their own native languages. While many Hui fluently speak the local dialects of their Han neighbors in the specific areas of China where they reside, they also use some Arabic and mixed (*hui hua*) terminology in their everyday speech. In areas such as Ningxia where there are high concentrations of Hui living together in relative isolation, they speak unique dialects of Chinese to which all non-Hui must work hard to adapt. In the past, it was recommended that those going to work among Chinese Muslims learn Arabic as well as Chinese before entering the country (Broomhall, 1910). For the cross-cultural worker today, learning some Chinese before arriving in China can provide a definite advantage, but unless one is planning to work specifically with the most educated Hui *imams*, any working knowledge of Arabic beyond very fundamental Islamic words is unnecessary. Both the Han believer and the foreign believer are encouraged to start with a solid, ongoing acquisition of standard Mandarin, then apply themselves to the learning of any local dialect once they settle in a given location.

As we learn more about the worldview and lives of our Hui neighbors and friends, we must observe both those things that make them distinct as a people and the things they have in common with their Han neighbors. One essential theme of Chinese culture and history is the concept of suffering. This is a topic on which Hui and Han can closely relate, as both people groups went through times of shared, indiscriminate suffering in past centuries *and* in more recent times (Aldrich, 2010). It is equally important to note that both groups have a very deep appreciation for the past and see what happened to their people in the past as being linked to what happens to them in the present. Focusing on areas of commonality might prove useful for at least two reasons: universal life themes can provide a supple basis for planting seeds of truth, and a focus on similarities may both motivate Han believers to reach out to the Hui in their midst and also open the hearts of the Hui toward friendships with the Han.

In modern China, a unique opportunity presents itself to those Han believers and cross-cultural workers who work as educators. Schools and universities are some of the most common and natural settings in which the Han and the Hui interact on a daily basis. For the non-Hui educator, working in an ethnically mixed classroom or office can present special challenges and seem intimidating, but the prospects for promoting inter-ethnic understanding and demonstrating the love of Christ to *both* groups are equally great and exciting. When planning and presenting lessons, such educators should open doors of communication so that they and their students can hear the "other" side of various cultural points. For example, the instructor might ask both Han students *and* Hui students to give an explanation for why they practice certain customs or hold certain opinions. If teachers are more conscious of doing this, there are several advantages: they will promote meaningful communication between their students, learn much about the lives and hearts of the people they are ministering to, demonstrate that students are equally valuable to the teacher and to God, and begin to eradicate long-held stereotypes that have often hurt Han-Hui relations due to deeply entrenched ignorance. In other words, Christ-following educators in modern Chinese schools have the awesome responsibility of being conduits of love: helping to build bridges horizontally, between people groups, and vertically, between people and God.

For non-Chinese believers who live or work in the mainland, several useful points bear emphasizing. They need to consider carefully if and how they will celebrate both Hui and Han festivals with Chinese friends. If they celebrate major holidays, they need to be aware of what signals they may be sending to members of the host culture by taking part in some holiday-related practices, and they must also use sensitivity if they plan holiday celebrations that include an ethnically-mixed group of attendees (Aldrich, 2010). They should be prepared for how Hui friends and neighbors may interact with them or view them, especially when foreigners first move into a community. The Hui may ask newly arrived foreigners in verbal or non-verbal ways if they are Muslim (Aldrich, 2010); for example, some Hui may lift an index finger in the air as an unspoken way of asking a foreigner if they are also Muslim (a practice some might liken to the ancient Christian practice of drawing a fish in the dirt). In response, Christians should be both direct but also warm and polite in explaining where they stand spiritually. Female workers can make the most of every opportunity to provide Hui women with various forms of education and develop relationships with whole families as a means of sharing the Good News; these methods have been well-received historically throughout the Muslim world, and in this regard, Hui Muslims are not necessarily different (Aldrich, 2010).

Even though there are special issues and challenges that arise when ministering specifically among the Hui, some basic principles and observations from general ministry to Muslims are noteworthy. First, according to the summary of a report by the 1980 Pattaya Consultation:

> As soon as we begin to listen to Muslims and try to share the Gospel, we begin to realize how difficult it is to express ourselves in a way that Muslims understand. The painfulness of this experience ought to drive us back to the Bible, in order to learn new ways of understanding our faith and relating it to the Muslim mind.
> (Chapman, 2003, p. 323)

Believers must fundamentally look to God's Word as their source of ultimate Truth, their greatest source of strength, and their most powerful resource for ministry. They will not do anyone any favors by focusing on the Qur'an as a basis for evangelism; historically, this has only muddied the waters and led to very few conversions—and many watered-down conversions at that (Covell, 1995). Having a thorough knowledge of and confidence in interpretation of their own Christian

Scriptures can be an impressive thing in the eyes of many Muslims and may help Muslims see Christians as more competent and trustworthy when conducting faith-based discussions (Miller, 1995).

Secondly, the role of prayer and the reality of spiritual warfare cannot and should not be ignored. The work of foreign missionaries in Ningxia began in the 1880s; more than a hundred years later, the only significant numbers of known converts were amongst the Han that had migrated (either by mandate or by choice) to the area over the previous century (Covell, 1995). Work in Muslim territories is hard, arduous, and not for the faint of heart or for those who are not devoted to prayer. Both Han and foreign believers who engage in ministry among the Hui must develop regular, deep practices of prayer and must also, if possible, be involved with a local community who will pray for the ministry situation. An important question that is beyond the scope of this chapter is whether church planting among Hui Muslim Background Believers should lead to Hui-only congregations *or* mixed Hui-Han congregations.

It is always important to bear the specific context in mind; different Muslim communities, families, and individuals will display varying levels of devotion to orthodox teachings and "folk" Islam traditions. A believer must pay attention to the unique differences of each context and every relationship in order to adjust methods appropriately while still presenting fundamental truths from the Word (Chapman, 2003). For example, the question of mixed-gender Bible studies would probably not be much of an issue in many Hui communities (Swartley, 2008). Sometimes, Muslims will feel more comfortable talking about their home culture than their faith (Swartley, 2008). It is good to start building relationships around topics that are comfortable for them and pray for God's Spirit to open more doors as friendships progress. Finally, it is essential to view evangelism as a process—sometimes a *long* process! Believers need to remember that it often takes a long time to lead a Muslim to Christ, and once they come to Christ, they need very high levels of discipleship and support in their new faith (Swartley, 2008).

## Conclusion

When Han and non-Chinese believers are better informed concerning the origins of and worldview of the Hui, they will be better equipped and more effective in the task of reaching the Hui for Christ. Though there has been little known historical success in evangelizing the Hui, with better preparation and a refreshed unity of purpose and passion to go to great lengths for the sake of saving the lost, future efforts can yield more fruitful results. For nothing is impossible with God.

## References

Aldrich, M.A. (2010). *The perfumed palace: Islam's journey from Mecca to Peking.* Berkshire, UK: Garnet Publishing Limited.

Broomhall, M. (1910). *Islam in China: A neglected problem.* London: Morgan & Scott, Ltd.

Chapman, C. (2003). *Cross and crescent: Responding to the challenge of Islam.* Downers Grove, IL: InterVarsity Press.

Covell, R. R. (1995). *The liberating gospel in China.* Grand Rapids, MI: Baker Books.

Hollian-Elliot, S. (2006). *Muslims in China.* Philadelphia: Mason Crest Publishers.

Israeli, R. (2002). *Islam in China: Religion, ethnicity, culture, and politics.* Lanham, MD: Lexington Books.

Mason, I. (1919). *List of Chinese-Moslem terms.* Shanghai, China: China Continuation Committee.

Mason, I. (1929). The Mohammedans of China: When and how they first came. *The Journal of the North China Branch of the Royal Asiatic Society, 60*, 42-78.

Miller, R. E. (1995). *Muslim friends: Their faith and feeling.* St. Louis, MO: Concordia Publishing House.

Ruthven, M. (2006). *Islam in the World* (3rd ed.). Oxford, UK: Oxford University Press.

Swartley, K. E. (Ed.). (2008). *Encountering the world of Islam.* Atlanta, GA: Authentic Media.

# 8. What is "Chinese" Theology? Honor and Shame in Chinese Spirituality[13]

## By Jackson Wu

Asking "why?" is one of the fastest ways foreigners in China become confused and frustrated. People in China all seem to agree about what Chinese should do. In a country as large and old as China, some underlying rationale must exist. Something orders the seeming randomness. But outsiders quickly find that no one, not even Chinese people, can quite agree on *why* Chinese do some of the things they do. That is simply the way things are done.

Perhaps then, an even bigger challenge is answering the question, "What is Chinese spirituality?" One is more likely to speak fluent Mandarin than get a room of people to agree on the meaning of "spirituality," a word difficult to define with precision.

But as with Chinese culture in general, when discussing Chinese spirituality--things are not as they seem. Debates about "spirituality" drift into a discussion of the meaning of "Chinese." What makes something "Chinese"? Must a characteristic be unique to China? Must some idea or practice come from a Chinese person? Does something become Chinese when most people accept it as "Chinese"?

What about Chinese Christianity? Someone might even think the phrase is a contradiction. Countless Chinese people are quick to explain, "Chinese is a Western

---

[13] *Editor's note: The following thought-provoking contribution to this project comes from an expert on the influence of honor/shame within cultures and our understanding of theology. In addition to extensive writing, he has served as a church planter and taught theology and missiology for Chinese pastors in East Asia. - K.P.*

religion." For much of the 20th century, Chinese citizens often heard the mantra "One more Christian, one less Chinese."[14] In conversation, I find people often surprised to hear that Christianity did not originate in the West but in Israel, the Ancient Near East. In many respects, an ancient Jewish worldview is more like contemporary Chinese culture than it is to the modern West. The vast number of Chinese Christians in China and around the world demonstrate that Christianity can put on Chinese clothing just as it looked "Western" for much of two millennia.

To be clear, we should not dichotomize "Western" from "Chinese." Whatever adjective one puts in front of "theology," if it is *Christian* theology, it derives from the Bible and so will share numerous points of emphasis. Readers should therefore not infer that "Western" is a pejorative label. Theology that is "Western" simply refers to a theology expressed in the prominent ways of thinking (e.g., thought categories) found in Western culture.

Because the subject of Chinese Christian spirituality is vast, we need first to give attention on a narrow but foundational aspect of the topic. By any estimation, the Bible is critical to any discussion of *Christian* spirituality. How Chinese read the Bible and relate its meaning to Chinese culture will invariably shape Chinese Christian spirituality.

Therefore, in this essay, we will consider the question "what is 'Chinese' theology? Christians' theological perspective will substantially influence their practice. We will explore the meaning of "Chinese." What is "Chinese" and who decides? Although these questions seem broad, our focus will specifically concern Chinese theology. What is *Chinese* theology and who are its representatives? And what is the role of "foreigners" and/or non-Chinese people?[15]

---

[14] This well-known phrase is noted many places. Cf. Promfret, 2006; Yang, 2003.

[15] In China, the verbal distinction between "Chinese" (*zhong guo ren*) and "foreigner" (*wai guo ren*) is commonplace and is not offensive as some Westerners might expect. A complication emerges, however, when we consider people with a Chinese ethnic heritage yet who were born or raised outside of China. Many on the Mainland will simply call these people "Chinese" (*zhong guo ren*), although the latter more precisely might be called *hua ren* (i.e., overseas Chinese). A *hua ren* is a "foreigner" if (s)he is not a Chinese citizen; yet will frequently be called "Chinese" (*zhong guo ren*). Mainland Chinese do not typically distinguish verbally between "Chinese citizen" and "ethnic Chinese" since *hua ren* is almost exclusively used to refer to non-mainland Chinese; thus, it is not normally applied to Mainlanders. In this essay, I will try to be clear where potential ambiguity exists. In general, the phrase the term "foreigner" will apply to non-citizens of China. When referring to *hua ren*, I will primarily use "ethnic Chinese."

We begin by asking "who" determines what counts as "Chinese" theology. The second section will suggest a potential way forward by exploring the characteristics of anything that might be called a "Chinese" theology. Although this essay is modest in scope, I will attempt to integrate research from academic disciplines. I hope an interdisciplinary approach will equip us to consider these questions with humility and balance. In so doing, we can avoid the natural temptation to content ourselves with answers that suit our personal experience and agenda.

## Who Defines "Chinese" Theology?

The question seems nonsensical to many people. Of course, they say, Chinese people write and develop Chinese theology. I wish it were that simple or even true. I am often asked how Chinese Christians theologize and how is a Chinese pastor's theology different than that found in the West. The answer is surprising and disappointing. Listening to an average sermon in a typical Chinese church sounds a lot like listening to a sermon in America. While variety exists, in China and America, little distinguishes the content, emphasis, method of delivery, metaphors, and, too often, application.

This observation in fact is not surprising but natural. Certainly, missionaries have increasingly come to China in the past few centuries; that is only part of the explanation. There is another reason for the relatively similar theologies. Scholars often characterize Chinese culture as collectivist and honor-shame oriented. Like all generalizations, these labels are true to different degrees depending on the place and person. Nevertheless, Chinese people generally have a high regard for authority and hierarchy. This respect is no doubt rooted in China's Confucian past.

What does this mean for theology in Chinese churches? As respecters of tradition and teachers, Chinese believers are less inclined than others to challenge convention and creatively adapt established norms. They are prone to uphold and defend the instruction passed on to them from Western missionaries. Confucian cultures are far more likely to emphasize the importance of conforming to groups and historical teaching. Consequently, many Chinese Christians simply reiterate a traditional, Westernized theology.

Theology is truth about God expressed from a cultural and situational perspective. In other words, all theology is contextualized.[16] No one's theology exhausts biblical truth. When people typically talk about "theology," they typically discuss topics historically raised in *Western* theology by theologians seeking to address concerns found in Western cultures. Theologians have worldview lenses that filter both what they observe and overlook. Reading the Bible from a Western or Eastern perspective will produce theologies that are more Western or Eastern.

We cannot assume, however, that everyone living in a Western or Eastern society will have a stereotypical Western or Eastern worldview. Countless influences shape how we think and feel about the world. These might include family background, life experiences, and circle of friends. As we all can attest, a person can even think and behave in contradictory ways depending on the situation, people around us, stress, social pressures, and clarity of conviction. A hard-nosed, uncompromising drill sergeant could be a playful dad to toddlers when he comes home. Logically minded scientists can suddenly string together various emotive arguments to refute social and religious ideas that they find disagreeable.

With these observations in mind, we next consider who might be considered a "Chinese" theologian. What makes theology "Chinese?"

## Who are "Chinese" Theologians?

Which Chinese thinkers best represent Chinese theology? To consider potential candidates, we will look at four groups of Chinese theologians. One should not assume the theologies within these groups are homogenous. But even this oversimplification will demonstrate my previous claim. Being Chinese and a theologian does not necessarily imply one has anything that can be distinctly called "Chinese theology." In fact, one could argue that many Chinese theologians are quintessential *Western* theologians.

We first consider theologians who teach "Sino-theology" and are often called "cultural Christians" (*wenhua jidutu*) (e.g., Yang & Yeung, 2006; Lai & Lam,

---

[16] Early articulators of this idea include Bevans, 2002; and Bosch, 1991.

2010; Lai, 2001).[17] These writers are academics more than practitioners. Sino-theologians do not necessarily profess personal faith in Christ or Christian teachings. They consistently emphasize the importance of using Mandarin for developing a distinctive Chinese theology. Their writings are filled with references to philosophy, linguistics, and Chinese works. One sees almost no biblical exegesis, very little engagement with systematic theology, yet we find frequent surveys of select historical theologians. Consequently, Lai Pan Chiu (2010) even questions, "Is Sino-Christian theology to be recognized as a Christian theology at all?"

A second group of theologians are found in China's officially sanctioned Three-Self Patriot Movement (TSPM) church. A major objective of TSPM theologians is to harmonize the church with the goals of the state. Deng Fucun (2010) Vice-President of the TSPM of the Chinese Christian Church, rejects "[Western] conservative theological thinking" that "places church above the country." Furthermore, he says, "No faith belief or church rules should go beyond the statements in [the Apostles' Creed and the Nicene Creed]. Neither systematic theology nor doctrinal theology should contradict them" (p. 303). Complaining about justification by faith, Bishop Ding Guangxun[18] claims,

> It is overemphasized in China, as if it is the all in all of Christian faith. The idea is that anyone who believes will go to heaven after death, and those who do not believe will go to hell. This is an idea that denies morality. By extension, Hitler and Mussolini, as Christians, would be in heaven, while Confucius, Laozi and Zhou Enlai, non-believers, would be in hell. This is the only logical conclusion according to this idea. (Ding, 2004, pp. 124-125)

In another source he comments, "After all, the God who is worthy of our worship and praise is not so small as to be concerned with a few million Chinese who profess to believe in him . . . He does not mind terribly much if many, for good reasons, do not recognize his existence" (Ding, 1980, p. 124).

---

[17] Also, see the Institute of Sino-Christian Studies. Online: www.iscs.org.hk.
[18] His family name is transliterated as either "Ting" or "Ding."

Anecdotally, I once asked a friend about the theological training he received while attending the TSPM's premier seminary in Nanjing. He is now a house church pastor. He explained that students rarely studied the Bible itself. Rather, they spent approximately half their class time studying historical theologians; the other half on Chinese culture. He also confirmed with the what can be seen when reading TSPM writers: TSPM theologians are strongly influenced by thinkers like Paul Tillich and Karl Barth. We could just as well add Karl Marx and Karl Rahner to that list.

Leaders within Chinese house churches represent a third possible source of Chinese theology. Numerous challenges face anyone who attempts to characterize the theology of house church pastors. Many such leaders simply do not write or publish theology.[19] The growth of Reformed theology is well attested (cf. Peng, 2015; Baugus, 2014; Chow, 2014; Fällman, 2013). Likewise, various shades of Pentecostal theology exist (cf. Menzies, 2015; Chan, 2005).

We can find devotional materials easily online. If one visits Chinese training centers or surveys theological resources available online, he will find that most theological texts are translated from Western writers. Historically, other influential theologians, like Watchman Nee and Wang Ming Dao, were highly influenced by fundamentalist theology. Evangelism is a major impetus for theological reflection (e.g., John Sung).

Finally, we turn to a fourth group--overseas Chinese (*hua ren*). This broad category includes ethnic Chinese from Taiwan, Hong Kong, Singapore, Malaysia and many Western countries. Once again, one struggles to find a consistent pattern that marks a "Chinese" theology. Taiwanese theologian C. S. Song not only rejects the universalization of Western theology, which he regards as oppressive; he even dismisses the Bible as an "absolute norm" (Song, 1974; cf. Wu, 1994). For Song, theology emerges from one's situation (Wu, 2013). Malaysian theologian K. K. Yeo has written several dense volumes in the effort to construct a distinctive Chinese theology (e.g., Yeo, 2008; Yeo, 2002; Yeo, 1998). He wants Chinese theology to set people free from Western "imperialism," which is "guilty of neglecting social reform,

---

[19] Cf. ChinaSource. (2016). Why Don't Chinese Pastors Write Books?

and are only interested in saving pagan souls" (Yeo, 1998, p. 241).[20] He denies that justification by faith concerns salvation (Yeo, 1998).[21] When interpreting the Bible, his key principle for theologizing is "being faithful to be being Chinese" (Yeo, 2008, p. 425).

By contrast, Chinese evangelical theologians do not veer far from historical Western theology. For example, John Calvin significantly influences the teaching of Jonathan Chao and Stephen Tang, who leads the Reformed Evangelical Church of Indonesia. Singaporean Simon Chan attempts to delineate Asian theology yet does so within the conventional categories of systematic theology. "What passes as Asian theology tends to be confined to a limited number of themes and theologians;" Chan suggests, "A more adequate way of organizing an Asian theology is to center it in the doctrine of the triune God as the divine family" (Chan, 2014, pp. 23, 42). He regards Pentecostal Christianity as the solution for developing a genuinely Asian theology. Australian Dan Wu's 2016 study on shame in Ezekiel explores a traditionally Eastern theme within biblical studies.

What can we conclude from our survey of Chinese theologians? Regardless of one's theological persuasion or ambitions, we find no definite pattern that distinguishes "Chinese" theology. Among some theologians, it appears being "Chinese" is defined largely in contrast to "Western" theology. These writers are prone to "eisegesis," whereby an interpreter reads his or her culture into the biblical text. However, when the Bible serves merely as a launching point for one's theology, it increasingly veers from what can be deemed "Christian."

What about Chinese theologians who emphasize the importance of the Bible, systematic theology, and biblical interpretation? The influence of Western theology on these writers is apparent. Were one to overlook their names, readers would not be able to distinguish the approach and conclusion of these scholars from Western theologians. By and large, they begin with the same categories, take up the same debates, use similar methods, and highlight conventional themes found in the work of non-Chinese writers.

---

[20] Yeo (2008) equates "religious imperialism" with "proselytism," which he says, "is akin to the Roman ideology of conquest."

[21] For Yeo, salvation is a sociological-relational term. Cf. Yeo, (2008).

Put simply, we should distinguish between the work of Chinese who do theology and Chinese theology itself. Having an ethnic Chinese background does not mean one theologizes in a distinctly Chinese way. It is possible that a non-ethnic Chinese person can contribute to Chinese theology if he or she had a "Chinese" perspective. This observation again raises the question, "What then constitutes a Chinese theology?"

## Toward a "Chinese" Theology

What basic elements should characterize Chinese theology? Scholars suggest many possible answers. We have seen that ethnicity and place of birth are insufficient conditions.[22] Another option is to distinguish Chinese theology by the specific issues it addresses. For example, one might use ancient Chinese cosmology, ancestor worship, the Chinese New Year, socialism, or other topics relevant to Chinese culture. Certainly, we expect Chinese theologians to reflect on these matters; however, orienting Chinese theology in this way is problematic.

Defining Chinese theology in this way does so in a manner quite unlike conventional views of Western theology. That is, "Western" theologians ideally have tried to begin with the biblical text itself. Their conclusions are then systematized and applied to their context. By orienting "Chinese theology" around such culturally specific topics, we effectively reverse the order. One puts the systematic horse before the biblical cart. Additionally, this suggestion not only conceives of Chinese theology too narrowly; Western theology implicitly retains its pride of place among cultural theologies.

So how might we move forward? An integrated approach is most promising. A composite picture of "Chinese" culture emerges when we survey research from multiple disciplines. I can already hear warnings that we avoid anything that smacks of "Orientalism" and reinforces outdated stereotypes. All stereotypes and composite descriptions of culture are susceptible to the same criticism. People are individuals who cannot be pigeonholed into rigid cultural boxes. Nevertheless, we are all

---

[22] It remains debatable whether they are even necessary conditions. Nothing thus far suggests any necessity of ethnic background.

influenced by our communities and the various cultures and subcultures around us. Many stereotypes exist for a reason; to some degree, they are generally true of a certain group of people. This is why we can speak of "Western" culture, since a large number of people, to some degree, share many common behaviors and traits.

A consistent set of characteristics mark Chinese culture. A multitude of studies give ample evidence of this conclusion. Some of the desired ideals of East Asian society include: past-time orientation, respect for hierarchy, interdependence, group orientation (collectivism), the concept of "face," modesty, and harmony with others.[23] We find agreement among theologians and missiologists. For instance, Enoch Wan (2003) states, "The message of the Gospel within the Chinese cultural context should be characterized by the emphasis on honor, relationship, and harmony, which are at the core of traditional Chinese cultural values." Tan Hann Tzuu (2012) says a contextualized Gospel for Chinese culture will emphasize relationship (*guanxi*), harmony, and filial piety. Other writers similarly highlight the importance of honor and shame (Wu, 2013; Chan, 2014; Richards & O'Brien, 2012; Louie, 2012).

Despite vast theological differences, a closer examination also shows subtle agreement among writers with respect to the needs of Chinese Christianity. They envision Chinese theology as something practical and oriented towards shaping moral character. It will be concerned with community life, especially the family, which is a model for the broader society. The very word "country" (*guo jia*) combines the characters for kingdom and family. Furthermore, a Chinese theology will emphasize the importance of authority, responsibility to others, and respect for tradition. It will likely be more narrative than systematized, more proverbial and not merely propositional.

---

[23] This specific list is compiled in Zhu, 2008. It is an exceptional summary of the vast scholarly literature concerning Chinese culture. A few sample works include Hwang, 2012; Li, Wang, & Fischer, 2004; Sun, 2008; Lei, 2005; Nisbett, 2003; Kipnis, 1997. An overview of major facets of Chinese culture can also be found in Wu, 2013. At a popular level, see Zhang & Baker, 2008.

## Christian Theology with Chinese Characteristics

All theology is contextualized because all theology, if done well, is influenced by multiple contexts. These include historical context, biblical-canonical context, and the interpreter's context.[24] Therefore, Chinese theology, like American theology, African theology, and Indian theology, will incorporate insights from across academic disciplines. Because the Bible was written for all nations, Christian theology is not the possession of a privileged culture. By implication, those who construct Chinese theology cannot assume *a priori* either that Chinese culture alone has sufficient resources to interpret Christian Scripture or that some other culture cannot contribute to Chinese theology.[25] Accordingly, a robust Chinese theology will not merely make someone more Chinese; it will help us become more well-rounded as humans.[26]

As *Christian* theology, Chinese theology should engage people's worldview, not merely select topics and circumstances. It does not *merely* deal with the superficial issues and habits that emerge with the flux of any culture. Therefore, in this section, we will highlight a few key areas that reflect the underlying worldview assumptions common throughout Chinese culture and history.[27] Ultimately, we attempt to find common ground between what is "Chinese" and what is biblical. This will be the starting place for constructing Chinese theology.

Scholars frequently describe both China and ancient biblical contexts as "honor and shame" cultures (cf. Malina, 1993; deSilva, 2000; Moxnes, 2010). In truth, honor and shame are present in all cultures; yet, people in traditional societies tend to be especially sensitive to honor-shame dynamics.[28] What is an "honor-shame" perspective? In broadest terms, "shame" is the fear, pain, or state of being regarded

---

[24] The interpreter's context inevitably filters what (s)he reads but it should not force cultural definitions onto the biblical text that are foreign to its historical and/or literary context. See Wu, 2015.

[25] For instance, nothing inherent to Chinese culture disallows the use of a "grammatical-historical method," which some people claim to be a "Western" method of interpretation.

[26] This statement could be made about any culturally clothed theology.

[27] I intentionally use the phrase "Chinese culture and history" to include the vast swath of Chinese culture. Chinese culture is not monolithic now or in any age. For example, Chinese people today in urban areas will be more Western and individualistic than traditional Chinese. We cannot limit our description of "Chinese" to any one era or sphere of culture.

[28] An "honor and shame" culture is often contrasted with a guilt-oriented cultures and fear-power cultures. We should not sharply separate these cultural perspectives since every society and subculture has characteristics of all three worldview paradigms.

unworthy of acceptance in a social or public context (e.g., relationships). It is the negative valuation of one's worth, whether felt or imputed to another. "Honor" refers to positive recognition given to or received from a group or individual based upon some type of excellence or norm. A person acquires honor by following norms, whether originating from a group or an individual. Honor and shame can have both moral and amoral (i.e., descriptive) connotations.

Honor and shame can be achieved and ascribed to people. For example, successful students and athletes achieve honor by earning high scores. A criminal can achieve shame by breaking a law. On the other hand, people are ascribed honor or shame by virtue of their position, relationship to others, or even *natural* characteristics such as gender or skin color. Citizens show respect to leaders of a country due to their office. Likewise, children honor teachers and parents to some degree simply because they have positions of authority.

An honor-shame worldview is characterized by at least four overlapping concerns: reputation, relationship, role (or rank), and ritual.[29] Those in honor-shame cultures are acutely aware of the importance of one's reputation. In Chinese culture, "face" is a term typically used to mark one's reputation and is the measure of his or her social status. A person's reputation (or "face") serves as one's "social currency" (Chang & Holt, 1994). For many Chinese people, "face" is "more important than life itself" (Zhang & Baker, 2008).

For the sake of properly contextualizing Chinese theology, we would be wise to note that the concept of "face" can convey various connotations (cf. Ho, 1976).[30] The two most common words, *mianzi* and *lian*, have much overlap; yet, many have observed subtle distinctions, which might be utilized for theological benefit. *Mianzi* is the more general term and concerns whether someone conforms to or exceeds social expectations; it does not necessarily refer to moral character. As Hu (1944) states, it describes a person's reputation stemming from "high position, wealth, power, ability, through cleverly establishing social ties to a number of prominent people;" however,

---

[29] Due to space limitations, the following is a general overview of honor and shame. Readers are encouraged to see a more in-depth discussion in Wu, 2013.

[30] Hwang says this distinction relates to Mandarin, not Cantonese. See Hwang, 2012.

everyone has *mianzi*, since it is "dependent at all times on his external environment" (Hu, 1944, pp. 45, 58, 61).

By contrast, anyone can have *lian* so long as they demonstrate a basic sense of shame or character (cf. Hu, 1944). Cheng says:

> [*Lian*] can never be lost or broken without suffering a disgrace in the eyes of others or oneself; it is therefore identified with the sense of honor, integrity, and shame of a person. Everyone is expected to protect his [*lian*] at all times, though not everyone is expected to have [*mianzi*] or have it all the time. (Cheng, 1986, pp. 334-335)

The significance of *lian* is most evident if we imagine telling a coworker "*ni bu yao lian*" (You do not want *lian*). To make this statement would be insulting and essentially say that the coworker is immoral and shameless.

Second, our reputation is inextricably linked to relationships (*guanxi*). Andrew Kipnis (1997) says, "one's relationships in fact constitute oneself" (p. 8). *Guanxi* regulates and reflects one's social and material obligations (Kipnis, 1997).[31] Peter Verhezen (2008) calls *guanxi* a person's "social capital." However, Westerners sometimes have a one-sided view of *guanxi*, regarding it negatively as the corrupt use of relationships. One's moral obligations arise from his or her network of relationships. With *guanxi*, interdependence and mutual responsibility are emphasized over individual rights and personal prerogative (Hwang, 2012). Furthermore, "The personal dimension of *guanxi* stresses the significance of trust, which implies that moral obligation is more important than legal contract" (Lei, 2005, p. 83).

The most important relationships are found in the family. In fact, one writer calls family China's "real religion" (Smith, 1990). Because parents and ancestors give a person life, (s)he is obligated to honor them, showing filial piety. Family is so important to Chinese people that the state has long used it as a metaphor for the Chinese nation. Dilin Liu (2002) explains, "since state is considered one's extended family, loyalty to one's local and national governments is tantamount to loyalty to one's family and ancestors" (p. 60; cf. Rappa & Tan, 2003). In daily life, a younger

---

[31] A helpful, brief summary is found in Vanhonacker, 2004.

person will even greet an elder as "Uncle" (*shu shu*) or "Aunt" (*Ayi*), even if they have no blood relationship.

Within traditional Chinese philosophy, righteousness (*yi*) is rooted in relationship. Accordingly, to do what is righteous is to act appropriately within a given relationship or situation. A righteous person seeks reconciliation and social harmony rather than the shame and punishment of another (cf. Yu, 2006; Yeo, 2008; Hwang, 2012; Cheng, 2007, "Justice and Peace"). Looking ahead, this understanding of *guanxi* and *yi* can help us develop Chinese theology.

We certainly should not force any Chinese concept into the biblical text. Nevertheless, a Chinese perspective can balance the Western propensity to emphasize the individual at the expense of a group (e.g., the church, family) and law at the expense of honor-shame. A Chinese theology could expose conventional blind spots and contribute to ongoing theological debates. For instance, we can better grasp the biblical idea of covenants, not merely as abstract laws, but as the formalizing of a relationship that binds two parties together and changes people's identity.

Third, relationship-oriented cultures are more hierarchical than egalitarian, laying stress upon a person's role or rank. As people play their roles within the larger community, society and family flourish. Conformity brings harmony whereas competition divides (cf. Stover, 1974; Fingarette, 1966). Leaders are obligated to take care of those under their care, who in turn try to protect the honor their leader and group. Although China has a long history of laws, a law has no inherent authority. In China, a law's authority stems from its being an extension of a ruler. Traditionally, "Law is only an instrument to govern the state; its source of authority comes from the authority of the king" (Liang, 1989, p. 142). A law might be good or bad, depending on how it is used by those with power (Liang, 1989).

Finally, honor-shame cultures have a high regard for ritual or tradition. In traditional Chinese culture, *li* ("ritual") refers to "cultural patterns that are deemed proper or decent" (Yeo, 2008, pp. 191–95). Tradition carries implicit authority. On the one hand, this respect for the past tempers the excessive adulation of novelty. On the other hand, it becomes foolishness when it masks pride and prevents needed change. Stories and proverbial idioms are common ways people pass along tradition.

Naturally, traditional societies grasp the social significance of symbols. A *ketou* is an ancient Chinese way an inferior showed deference by lying prostrate before a superior. Thus, Kipnis describes how people in Fengjia attempted to influence their social identity. He writes, "Residents who wished to construct themselves as non-peasants tried to avoid situations that required bows and *ketou*" (Kipnis, 1997, p. 174).

Reading the Bible from an honor-shame perspective has countless implications for Chinese theology. Many are as significant as they are subtle. Honor and shame do not act like premises in a theological syllogism; rather, they serve as lenses that reveal shades of meaning. They shine light on potential subtlety and applications. For example, Western theologians have long warned against the dangers of "legalism," whereby someone tries to earn salvation from God through good works. However, legalism at its root is an honor-shame problem. Brene Brown (2013) comments,

> We get sucked into perfection for one very simple reason: We believe perfection will protect us. Perfectionism is the belief that if we live perfect, look perfect, and act perfect, we can minimize or avoid the pain of blame, judgment, and shame.

In short, what people call "legalism" is an attempt to protect oneself from exclusion and shame. An atheist in his own way could behave like a so-called "legalist" yet without having Martin Luther's anxiety about whether a holy God will accept his good works.

## Toward a Chinese Theology

This final section will show how reading the Bible from a Chinese perspective leads to a Chinese theology. I explore elsewhere what a Chinese biblical theology might look like (Wu, 2015). I have also given more detailed, scholarly attention to specific issue such as the doctrine of salvation (J. Wu, 2016; Wu, 2013). In what follows, we will suggest how Chinese theology might address an array of biblical teachings. I merely introduce these ideas; readers are encouraged to examine each topic in greater depth.

Chinese theology will be centered on the glory of God. Rather than being a mere mantra, Chinese believers are well equipped to see the significance of this theme. A person's most basic obligation is to honor one's king and father. For God's children, worship is a pervasive part of daily life. It cannot be compartmentalized to a place or narrow window of time. In this way, we feel the weight of Paul's words when he says, "So, whether you eat or drink, or whatever you do, do all to the glory of God" (1 Cor 10:31).[32]

Theology that is Chinese is ever-mindful that biblical writers consistently try to spur an "honor-shame reversal." That is, they seek to overturn the prevailing norms for determining what is worthy of honor or shame. Hebrews, 1 Peter, and the Gospel of John provide obvious examples. The writer of Hebrews appeals to many Old Testament saints in Hebrews 11 to motivate readers to follow Christ's example, who "despised the shame" of the cross, (12:2) then was "crowned with glory and honor" (2:9), and so brought "many sons to glory" (2:10). David deSilva (2010) summarizes the strategy of Peter's letter:

> He insulates his audience against their neighbors' attempts to shame them by explaining why the judgment of outsiders is fundamentally flawed and not a reliable indicator of a person's true worth. He further insulates them by reinterpreting their experience of shaming and rejection in such a way that continued resistance and endurance emerges as a noble response. (p. 164)

John's creative play on words has a similar effect. John 9 repeatedly emphasizes the threat of being an outsider who is "cast out." After the blind man is finally cast out by the Pharisees, Jesus shares a parable in John 10 about sheep whom the shepherd "brings out" (10:4). John uses the same word, ἐκβάλλω, repeated in the previous chapter and elsewhere (e.g., 9:22, 34-35; cf. 12:42-43; 16:2). Jesus essentially restates his promise from John 6:37, "All that the Father gives me will come to me, and whoever comes to me I will never cast out."

Chinese Bibles routinely use "crime" (*zui*) to translate the word "sin." This translation is highly problematic because it drastically limits the meaning of sin. The

---

[32] All Scripture citations come from the English Standard Version (ESV) unless otherwise noted.

original biblical words do not inherently have a legal denotation. A legal metaphor is one of many adequate metaphors to convey wrongdoing in the world. This is one reason the Bible often uses a separate word--"transgression." The Western propensity to interpret the Bible through a Western, legal lens is now encoded in Chinese Bibles. As a result, the essence of "sin" is framed in a way that misleads Chinese Christians, causing them to overlook or minimize a plethora of other metaphors for "sin," evil or wrongdoing.

A few noteworthy passages in Romans help make the point. In Rom. 1, Paul does not use law-language to describe "unrighteousness" before God (1:18). Instead, people "did not honor him as God" and "exchanged the glory of the immortal God for images resembling mortal man and birds and animals and creeping things" (1:21, 23). Consequently, "God gave them up in the lusts of their hearts to impurity, to the dishonoring of their bodies among themselves" (1:25).

Furthermore, what is the primary problem in Rom. 2:23-24 with those who boast in the Law? The main verb of the sentence is "dishonor," not "breaking the law." In fact, the latter is a prepositional phrase; it merely explains how the Jews dishonored God. Law breaking is just one way among others that people might dishonor God, since Gentiles do not have the Mosaic Law (2:12, 14). Verse 24 begins with a "for" (γάρ) and so provides confirmation. Quoting Isaiah 52:5, Paul writes, "The name of God is blasphemed among the Gentiles because of you." Finally, perhaps the most famous verse about sin in the Bible might be Rom 3:23, where Paul succinctly summarizes, "for all have sinned and fall short of the glory of God."

Multiple passages throughout the Bible use honor and shame to characterize salvation. Since humans become shameful in God's eyes, we naturally expect the solution to concern honor and glory. Indeed, Jesus prays to the Father, "The glory that you have given me I have given to them, that they may be one even as we are one" (John 17:22). He uses honor to invite followers when he says, "If anyone serves me, the Father will honor him" (John 12:26). Elsewhere, salvation is depicted as glorification (cf. Rom. 2:10; 8:18-21; Heb. 2:10). When we receive glory from God through Christ, how can people continue to seek face from others via people pleasing?

Even faith is explained using honor and shame. Christ asks the Jewish leaders, "How can you believe, when you receive glory from one another and do not seek the glory that comes from the only God?" (John 5:44). Not surprisingly, we find a similar understanding in Romans, where Paul elaborates extensively about justification by faith. Concerning the one who is truly justified, he writes, "a Jew is one inwardly, and circumcision is a matter of the heart, by the Spirit, not by the letter. His praise is not from man but from God" (Rom. 2:29). The person who is "justified by faith" "boasts in the hope of the glory of God. Not only that, but we boast in our sufferings . . . and hope does not put us to shame" (Rom. 5:1–5).[33]

We can interpret many biblical doctrines through the lens of honor and shame. The Bible is replete with familial imagery when describing God's people. Those in the church are brothers and sisters under one Father (1 Cor. 8:6; Eph. 2:18; 4:6). As members of Abraham's family, ethnocentrism, nationalism and other social divisions must be set aside (Gal. 3:26-29). China's long dynastic history provides a helpful backdrop to explain the nature of faith as "allegiance," not mere intellectual assent (cf. Bates, 2017). Much more could be said about the church (e.g., Wu, 2011).

## Conclusion

The potential for a distinct Chinese theology is immense. This should not surprise us since Chinese culture and the historical context of the Bible, although not identical, share many similarities. This observation has implications for how we go about developing Chinese theology. One does not need to eisegete Chinese culture forcibly into the Bible any more than theologians have needed to force Western culture into the Bible.

Since Scripture is inspired for all nations, people from across the spectrum of cultures have the opportunity to understand the Bible. Every cultural perspective has its advantages and disadvantages. No cultural lens is complete. This explains why the task of developing Chinese theology is urgent. What contributions and insights might be possible when we read the Bible with Chinese eyes?

---

[33] The ESV uses "rejoice in" to translate καυχάομαι (5:2, 3, 11), which is translated as "boast" in 2:17, 23 (cf. 1 Cor 1:29, 31; 3:21). Thus, Paul uses a single word within the same context. The translation decision hides Paul's wordplay.

But who has "Chinese eyes?" To answer this, we asked the question "Who defines Chinese theology?" We considered several theologians with Chinese backgrounds. A diversity of theological perspectives can be found in Mainland China as well as among ethnic Chinese in the diaspora. Naturally, Chinese theologians are highly influenced by Western thinkers. Judging from their work, some Chinese scholars might even be called "Western" theologians. It is quite difficult to discern common features that both characterize most Chinese theologians and distinguish them from non-Chinese writers. Although counterintuitive, we conclude that a Chinese background theologian does not necessarily have "Chinese" theology. Even non-ethnic Chinese people can help develop Chinese theology.

We considered a subtle, more interdisciplinary approach. Scholars from various fields portray a Chinese worldview in similar ways. No generalization describes every individual Chinese person; yet, certain trends do exist. I described China as an "honor and shame" culture. This admittedly broad label encompasses several key aspects that affect a Chinese person's worldview. These include a concern for reputation, relationships, one's role (or rank) in society, and an appreciation for ritual (or tradition).

Finally, I suggested a few ways that honor and shame help us develop a Chinese theology. We briefly saw how a Chinese perspective can shed light on the meaning and significance of several doctrines, such as sin, salvation, and faith, among others. Chinese theology need not contradict traditional Western theology.

Any Christian theology, whatever its cultural bent, should complement the true insights gained by theologians throughout the world and in history. The Bible is foundational to anything worthy of being called "Christian" theology. As we read the Bible from a Chinese perspective, a Chinese theology will emerge that contributes to a more robust Christian theology. In this way, we seek to give "face" to Christ, who is "crowned with glory and honor."

## References

Bates, M. W. (2017). *Salvation by allegiance alone: Rethinking faith, works, and the gospel of Jesus the King.* Grand Rapids, MI: Baker.

Baugus, B. (2014). *China's reforming churches: Mission, polity, and ministry in the next Christendom*. Grand Rapids, MI: Reformation Heritage.

Bevans, S. (2002). *Models of contextual theology*. Maryknoll, NY: Orbis Books.

Bosch, D. (1991). *Transforming mission: Paradigm shifts in theology of mission*. Maryknoll, NY: Orbis Books.

Brown, B. (2010, November 1). *Want to be happy? Stop trying to be perfect*. CNN. cnn.com/2010/LIVING/11/01/give.up.perfection/index.html.

Chan, S. (2005). Wither Pentecostalism. In Allan Anderson & Edmond Tang, eds. (pp. 575-586). *Asian and Pentecostal: The charismatic face of Christianity in Asia*. Costa Mesa: Regnum.

Chan, S. (2014). *Grassroots Asian theology*. Downers Grove, IL: IVP.

Cheng, C. Y. (1986). The concept of face and its Confucian roots. *Journal of Chinese Philosophy 13*, 329-348. doi: 10.1111/j.1540-6253.1986.tb00102.x

Cheng, C. Y. (2007). Justice and peace in Kant and Confucius. *JCP 34*(3), 345-357.

ChinaSource. (2016 Dec 27). *Why don't Chinese pastors write books?* Translated by China Christian Daily. chinasource.org/resource-library/chinese-church-voices/why-dont-chinese-pastors-write-books. Translated from Anonymous Chinese pastor. (2016 Dec 27). "中国牧者不爱写书的几个原因." *Christian Times*. http://www.gospeltimes.cn/index.php/article/index/id/37236.

Chow, A. (2014). Calvinist public theology in urban China today. *International Journal of Public Theology 8*(2), 158-175.

Covell, R. (1986). *Confucius, the Buddha, and Christ: A history of the gospel in Chinese*. Maryknoll, NY: Orbis Books.

Deng, F.. (2010). The basis for the reconstruction of Chinese theological thinking. In M. Ruokanen & P. Huang, (Eds.), *Christianity and Chinese Culture* (pp. 297-308). Grand Rapids, MI: Eerdmans.

deSilva, D. (2000). *Honor, patronage, kinship & purity: Unlocking New Testament culture*. Downers Grove, IL.: IVP.

deSilva, D. A. (2010). "Turning shame into honor: The pastoral strategy of 1 Peter." In Wayne L. Alloway Jr, Robert Jewett, & John G. Lacey, eds. (159-186). *The shame factor: How shame shapes society.* Eugene, OR: Wipf & Stock.

Ding, G. X. (1980 Summer). Religious policy and theological reorientation in China. *China Notes, 18*(3), 124.

Fällman, F. (2013). Calvin, culture and Christ? Developments of faith among Chinese intellectuals. In F. Khek Gee Lim, (Ed.). *Christianity in contemporary China: Socio-cultural perspectives* (pp. 152-168). New York: Routledge.

Fingarette, H. (1966). Human community as holy rite: An interpretation of Confucius' Analects. *HTR 59*(1), 54-55.

Ho, D. Y. F. (1976). On the concept of face. *American Journal of Sociology 81*(4), 866-884.

Hu, H. C. (1944). The Chinese concepts of "face." *American Anthropologist 46*(1), 45-64.

Hui, C. C., & Holt, G. R. (1994). A Chinese perspective on face as interrelational concern. In Stella Ting-Toomey, ed. (95-131). *The challenge of facework: Cross-cultural and interpersonal issues.* Albany, NY: State University of New York Press.

Huilin, Y. & Yeung, D. H. N., (Eds.). (2006). *Sino-Christian studies in China.* Newcastle, UK: Cambridge Scholars.

Hwang, K. K. (2012). *Foundations of Chinese psychology: Confucian social relations.* New York: Springer.

Kipnis, A. (1997). *Producing Guanxi: Sentiment, self, and subculture in a north China village.* Durham, NC: Duke University.

Lai, P. C. & Lam, J., (Eds.). (2010). *Sino-Christian theology.* New York: Peter Lang.

Lai, P. C. (2001). Chinese culture and the development of Chinese Christian theology. *Studies in World Christianity, 7*(2), 219-240.

Lai, P. C. (2010). Sino-Christian theology, Bible, and Christian tradition. In J. Lam and P. Lai, (Eds.) *Sino-Christian theology* (pp. 161-178). New York: Peter Lang.

Lei, D. (2005 Spring). Guanxi and its influence on Chinese business practices. *Harvard China Review*, 81-84.

Li, J., Wang, L. Q., & Fischer, K.W. (2004). The mericas s y of Chinese shame concepts? *Cognition & Emotion, 18*(6), 767-797.

Liang, Z. P. (1989). Explicating "law": A comparative perspective of Chinese and Western legal culture. *Journal of Chinese Law, 3*(1), 55-92.

Liu, D. L. (2002). *Metaphor, culture, and worldview: The case of American English and the Chinese language.* Lanham, MD: University Press of America.

Louie, S. (2012). *Asian honor: Overcoming the culture of silence.* Bloomington, IN: Westbow.

Malina, B. (1993). *The New Testament world: Insights from cultural anthropology.* Louisville, KY: Westminster.

Menzies, R. (2015 Jan). Pentecostal theology and the Chinese church. *China Source.* Online: chinasource.org/resource-library/from-the-west-courtyard/ mericas s -theology-and-the-chinese-church.

Moxnes, H. (2010). Honor and shame. In R. L. Rohrbaugh, (Ed.). *The social sciences and New Testament interpretation* (pp. 167-176). Grand Rapids, MI: Baker.

Nisbett, R. (2003). *The geography of thought: How Asians and Westerners think differently . . . and why.* New York: Simon & Schuster.

Peng, P. (2015 June 26). Reformed theology: A Christian thought movement to a church movement. *China Source.* Translated by Ma Li. Online: chinasource.org/resource-library/articles/reformed-theology.

Promfret, J. (2006). *Chinese lessons: Five classmates and the story of the new China.* New York: Henry Holt & Co.

Rappa, A. L. & Tan, S. H. (2003). Political implications of Confucian familism. *Asian Philosophy, 13*(2/3), 87-102.

Richards, R. E. & O'Brien, B.J. (2012). *Misreading scripture with Western eyes.* Downers Grove, IL: IVP.

Smith, H. (1990 Summer). Chinese Religion in World Perspective. *Dialogue and Alliance 4*(2), 4-14.

Song, C. S. (1974). The new China and salvation history: A methodological enquiry. *South East Asia Journal of Theology 15*(2), 55-56.

Stover, L. (1974). *The cultural ecology of Chinese civilization: Peasants and elites in the last of the Agrarian states.* New York: New American Library.

Sun, C. T. L. (2008). *Themes in Chinese psychology.* Singapore: Cengage Learning.

Tan, H. T. (2012). *The Chinese way: Contextualizing the gospel for the Chinese.* Self-Published.

Ting, K. H. (2004). *God is love: Collected writings of Bishop K. H. Ting.* Colorado Springs, CO: David C. Cook.

Vanhonacker, W. (2004 June). Guanxi networks in China. *The China Business Review,* 48-53.

Verhezen, P. (2008). Guanxi: Networks or nepotism? In Laszlo Zsolnai, ed. (89-106). *Europe-Asia dialogue on business spirituality.* Apeldoom, Netherlands: Garant.

Wan, E. (2003 Oct). Practical contextualization: A case study of evangelizing contemporary Chinese. *Global Missiology 1*(1), n.p. [cited 27 Dec 2011]. Online: http://ojs.global missiology.org/index.php/ merica/issue/view/27.

Wu, D. (2016). *Honor, shame, and guilt: Social-scientific approaches to the book of Ezekiel.* Winona Lake, IN: Eisenbrauns.

Wu, J. (2011). Authority in a collectivist church: Identifying crucial concerns for a Chinese ecclesiology. *Global Missiology 1*(9), n.p.

Wu, J. (2013). *Saving God's face: A Chinese contextualization of salvation through honor and shame.* Pasadena, CA.: WCUIP.

Wu, J. (2015). *One gospel for all nations: A practical approach to Biblical contextualization.* Pasadena, CA: WCL.

Wu, J. (2016). How Christ saves God's face . . . and ours: A soteriology of honor and shame. *Missiology 44*(4), 375-387.

Wu, J. (1994). C. S. Song. In D. Michaud (Ed.). *Boston Collaborative Encyclopedia of Western Theology* [BCEWT]. http://people.bu.edu/wwildman/bce/song.htm.

Yang, D. L. (2003). Theological and cultural reflections on the relationship between church and society in China. *Chinese Theological Review*, 64-75.

Yeo, K. K. (1998). *What has Jerusalem to do with Beijing: Biblical interpretation from a Chinese perspective.* Harrisburg, PA: Trinity Press.

Yeo, K. K. (2002). *Chairman Mao meets the Apostle Paul: Christianity, Communism, and the hope of China.* Ada, MI: Brazos Press.

Yeo, K. K. (2008). *Musing with Confucius and Paul: Toward a Chinese Christian theology.* Eugene, OR: Cascade.

Yu, J. Y. (2006). Yi: Practical wisdom in Confucius's Analects. *JCP 33*(3), 335-348.

Zhang, H. H. and Baker, G. (2008). *Think like Chinese.* Annandale, NSW: Federation Press.

Zhu, B. (2008). *Chinese cultural values and Chinese language pedagogy.* Master's thesis, Ohio State University, Columbus, OH.

# Part 2

# Moving Mist: Historical and Modern Development of Chinese Spirituality

# 9. Neither Wheat nor Tares: The Problem of Sowing Seeds in Fields Deep with Traditional Chinese Spirituality and Chinese Nationalism[34]

## By Nathan Faries

### Introduction: The Failure of Christian Missions in China

Let me begin by asking the indulgence of my readers. The title and subtitle above should already suggest to you that I will not pull any punches in this essay. I am striving to be as honest as I can without causing offense. Please allow me to be somewhat blunt and provocative in the pages ahead in order that I might make what I believe to be important points about "Chinese spirituality" and its relationship with foreign Christian missions.

China has never been fertile ground for the seeds of Christian faith. The first two missionary eras came to nothing. Christianity originally came to China in the Tang Dynasty (618-907) and then again in the Yuan Dynasty (1271-1368), and it disappeared each time as those empires failed. The third era of Christian missions likewise endured for approximately the length of one dynasty, the Qing (1644-1912),

---

[34] *Editor's note: Dr. Faries currently teaches at Bates College in Maine and is well-versed in many areas of Chinese culture, including language, literature, and religion—areas from which he has drawn to produce other, previous published writings. Readers may find some of the ideas of this essay iconoclastic. Indeed, in editing it, I found myself pausing to reconsider my own views at several points. I trust his powerful writing will help readers refine their own understanding and perhaps clear the way for more understanding and respectful engagement between Chinese and Western friends. - K.P.*

the final dynasty of imperial China, before the foreign missionaries were again forced out of the country and China was considered "lost" under the new Communist regime. The first Protestant missions began in that third era, the late-Qing nineteenth century, and work was slow enough that millennialist triumphalism ("We are ushering in a new age of Christian culture!") faded toward Social Gospel work ("We are planting the seeds of the Christian faith by loving people with the love of God and doing good works in His name") as the century turned. Missionary frustration at times elicited cringeworthy comparisons of the Chinese people to the stubborn, "stiff-necked" Jewish people of the Old Testament. Some missionaries laid blame on the impenetrability of the Chinese language which they said must have been invented by the devil himself to foil the good work of spreading the Gospel.

The Christian missionary invasion ended in a kind of defeat, but there is nothing new and no shame in being rebuffed by the power of Chinese culture. The Mongols and the Manchu people both "conquered" China before the Protestant missionaries came. These invaders of earlier times, even as they took their hard-won place on China's imperial throne, inevitably succumbed and adapted to that exalted position. They always sat on the *Chinese* throne. Just as China never became Christendom, China never became Mongolia or Manchuria. When those rulers in the natural course of events passed the reins unwillingly to their successors, China itself remained and scarcely admits now that it was ever ruled by foreign powers or that it is capable of noticing even a ripple of change. Jonathan Spence's *To Change China* is just one famous volume that describes this commonplace observation about Chinese power overwhelming foreign cultures without ever needing to win on the battlefield (Spence, 1980). Though the Christian missionaries left behind institutions—hospitals, schools, charities—when they returned home, they left behind relatively few Chinese Christians in 1949 when China was "lost" to the Communists. Four million, significantly less than one percent of the population, is a high estimate, and just a few hundred thousand of those could be claimed by the Protestants who had toiled in the field and tithed from home so assiduously for the most recent hundred years.

Foreign missionaries are once again present in China today, but they are reduced to sneaking about like amateur spooks, smuggling Bibles back into the country that printed them in the first place, using code words for God, and, through behavior that links religious faith with political subversion, endangering any Christians or new converts who enter their circle. Chinese Christianity has now existed in mainland China continuously since the early seventeenth century, but what has become of the Jesuit dream of a Chinese Emperor Constantine and the Protestant dream of a massive grassroots Christian movement filling the Chinese countryside with churches? These dreams continue to be narrated as reality and defended by Catholics and Protestants alike, but they are so far merely aspirational stories. Predictions of a Chairman Constantine ascending miraculously and clandestinely through Communist Party ranks, hopes that frequent gifts of Bibles and other Christian literature to Chinese leaders by visiting evangelists will someday bear fruit, and wild claims about "the fastest-growing church in the history of the world" continue to constitute an overblown rhetoric detailing the "success" of overseas missions in China.

In sharp contrast to the despondency of the early Maoist days, Western reporting on Chinese Christianity today, secular and religious alike, is inevitably tinged with a reinvented triumphalist narrative of both religious and political revolution. Most any headline will do to illustrate the point. The examples below will inevitably seem outdated to readers of this printed book, but they are actually representative and perennial narratives of the sort available since at least the 1980s, and I invite readers to do their own online search for articles on "Christianity in China" in any given year and scan the top results. In 2016, Pascal-Emmanuel Gobry wrote the following in *The Week* under the banner "Can Christianity Save China?": "At this point it is no longer a question of if China will become a Christian nation, but when." A few paragraphs later, the augured Chinese Christian culture is already set to rescue China from its oft-prophesied inevitable collapse under the weight of its aging population and endemic corruption: "Christianity could be China's only chance to survive." These are heady predictions from a religion that failed to save the Christianized Roman Empire, from a faith that has itself so far survived to less than half the age of the Chinese culture it intends to rescue. We might also question the assumptions underpinning the story: Is preserving economies and political structures, cultures and empires, what Christianity is really all about? If, presumably, Chinese culture has ruined China, what precisely needs to be discarded and replaced by Christian culture in order to save what is left of "China?" Is Gobry's account a story of Chinese Christian spirituality or is it about the American liberal democracy, rule-of-law, and free-market capitalism that many American Christians like to equate with their religious faith? Finally, if Christianity really spreads through China as quickly as such writers predict, and if the faith continues to decline in the West as some of the same writers prophesy, might we not rather describe the situation as Chinese culture rescuing Christianity? Even the more-sober reporting in a 2017 *Atlantic* article by Ian Johnson, a publication and a writer without overt religious commitments or a clear vision of a Christianized future China, sets up the Chinese Christian position as a showdown between members of a religious "revolution" in the unregistered Chinese Christian churches and the oppressive Communist government that might push back with force at any moment (Johnson, 2017). For both Gobry and Johnson, Christian evangelism is situated as a plot point in a certain brand of optimistic socio-political narrative.

The current overly sanguine appraisal of the Christian numbers in China and the ostensible marriage of Chinese Christianity to the eventual triumph of American political systems in China seem to be primarily based on foreign self-regard. They are based on a faith, not in God, but in the essential contribution of foreign agency to the conversion of China. When China was strictly closed to foreign missionaries and diplomats, it seemed to be lost; now that it is more open to America,[35] now that we have an embassy and now that we can sneak in a few missionaries under cover of ESL programs and business dealings, we imagine there is hope once again. And how are we wont to explain all that evangelistic progress that was made in the three decades (1949-1979) without us? Well, that must be the power of persecution and of course the fruit of all those seeds planted by the earlier missionaries, we say. The harvest, *our* harvest, is finally ripe, and foreign missionaries must now return to China to gather it in.

---

[35] Waley-Cohen (2000) reminds us that the very myth of Communist China's isolation is itself a self-centered American construct.

On the contrary, if there has been any substantial growth of Christianity in China in the last seventy years since foreign missions ended for the third time, compared with the torpid pace in the century of sacrificial foreign missionary labor before 1949, the credit seems to belong to China itself, not to outsiders. The conditions for the growth of Christianity in China were not as desperate as they seemed from the outside during the 1950s and 1960s; because Communist power seemed absolute, because church growth was invisible to us, because we were not part of the picture, many peremptorily assumed there was nothing to see. When we consider that China was given up for "lost" by the missionaries after their expulsion following 1949, and when we consider what a surprise it was for foreigners in the 1970s and 1980s that the church had not died, but was actually thriving, we must confess that the Chinese Christian Church itself under the leadership of the Chinese Communist Party (CCP) achieved a measure of success on their own for which foreign missionaries had stopped hoping. China is not exactly being Christianized in China's CCP-led Reform Era (1979-present), but the Christian Church in China is healthy and growing now. This. In spite of some of the questionable work of foreign missionaries (smuggling legal Bibles across borders using methods that subvert Chinese political authority, teaching Chinese converts that the registered churches in China are false puppets of the government) and because of some of the good policies of the Communist government (supporting many religious endeavors, including the building of churches, the printing of Bibles, and the funding of charitable organizations).

## The Trouble with Parables and Looking Through the Lenses of Culture

The parable of the sower and other Gospel "seed" passages are sometimes used to comfort the frustrated missionary who naturally needs, as we all do, reassurance that our lives have not been lived in vain and that apparent failure will be transformed into success in God's good time. The current success of the Gospel in China too often becomes a narrative of our success, of missionary success, of Anglo-American success. In reality, the success continues to be modest. In reality, where the Spirit is working for Christian success in China, it continues to work in mysterious ways, not always according to outsider Christian narratives and expectations. In reality, the barriers to the Gospel and to foreign evangelism in China have not changed much over the past two centuries. The salient barriers are not primarily rules set up by an authoritarian Communist government. Some of the most notable barriers are the blinders we put on ourselves as we try to understand the Chinese mission field.

Three fundamental interpretive tensions are built into the traditional missionary application of the parable of the sower to a foreign mission "field" like China. (Note how the metaphorical connection to this key parable is built into our missionary rhetoric.) These three equivocal aspects of the narrative are an important part of the foreign missionary problem in China, which is partly a problem of our own limited perspective: first, the only good soil in the parable is empty soil; second, the only competition for the desired crop is thorns; and third, the story's farmer is sowing seed on his own land in the proper season. By contrast, the spiritual soil of China is not choked with rocks or thorns or burnt by the sun. The soil is good, rich soil; it is simply someone else's field, and a healthy crop is already growing there. The foreign Christian missionary is dismayed that the crop does not look enough like the grain he himself wants to plant. On the other hand, the owner of the field, traditional Chinese spiritual culture, for his part cannot figure out what this uninvited foreign farmer is trying to accomplish in the midst of a flourishing plot of land so late in the season.

The metaphor found in John 10, that of other sheep who are not of this pasture, but who will listen to the voice of the shepherd, might be a more productive line of thought for missionaries in China. However, foreign Christians still need to reckon carefully what it means to move "sheep" from one pen to another. Under what circumstances can we be certain that the sheep are being rescued, and under what circumstances might we suspect they are simply being stolen from another perfectly good shepherd? How big is any individual missionary's Christian "pen"? Who is "in" for them, and who is "out"? "Sheep-stealing" is a well-rehearsed interdenominational missionary complaint, and the concept should be considered on the broader inter-religious and intercultural planes as well. Jesus and St. Paul challenge us from the earliest days of the Church to consider the fundamental questions: What are the essential elements of the faith, and what are elements of our culture that should not be confused with religion? Foreign missionaries must consider these questions carefully and constantly with both humble self-reflection and rigorous understanding of the "pasture" or "field" in which they set out to do their work.

I realize this concept is not new to my readers, but rather a fact that missionaries and missiologists live out and theorize about in profound ways every day. I write this to encourage these good people to do better what they already strive to do, and I write so that some may better understand the special challenges of a particular region of the world. It has been my observation that, for various reasons, sometimes involving historical ignorance and prejudice and a kind of conservative Christian anxiety about the "demonic" or occult associations in Eastern philosophy, many foreign Christians have shunned serious study of Chinese spiritual thought and long misunderstood Chinese national sentiment.

If we want to understand what stands in the way of our Chinese peers embracing Christian religious claims, spirituality and nationalism are essential points of departure. For better and worse, these spheres are not discrete and separable fields, for Chinese or for Americans. On the one hand, this fact should give us common ground for mutual understanding; on the other hand, the ways in which our nationalism and spirituality intersect can lead to divergent and unrealistic expectations of each side for the other. Each side feels strongly that we should agree on both spirituality and politics, and in the end, we agree on neither. Can a Chinese Christian support the Chinese Communist government? Is a Chinese government-supported church necessarily corrupted by its political sponsorship? Are unregistered Chinese churches necessarily unpatriotic and secretly allied with American political goals? Much in the same way the waters of American nationalism and religiosity grow muddied and lead some to write articles about how Christian culture will overspread China and save it from its current flawed political systems, Chinese nationalism and concepts of spirituality are likewise intimately tied together.

Whether we are speaking of the United States or of China, the forces of nationalism and spirituality tend to have a symbiotic, mutually supporting relationship, rather than a cannibalistic or parasitic relationship. In the absence of direct political persecution by the state, religious citizens generally find ways to reconcile and connect their spiritual and their civil loyalties. Even in the presence of direct persecution, one's loyalty to nation simply becomes more complicated. The concept of "nation" for the persecuted individual might split away from the current governing regime, for example, and attach itself to other concepts like traditional culture or geography or idealized narratives of nation. One's home is not easily discarded in favor of loyalty to another nation, even if citizens of that other nation introduced them to a higher religious loyalty. A serious faithful American Christian is likely to think their faith makes them a better citizen of the United States, and a Chinese Christian is unlikely to think of themselves as a religious "counter-revolutionary" trying to overthrow Communism or to consider themselves less Chinese in their relationship to Chinese culture or the Chinese government simply because of their faith in a Christian God. On the contrary, a Chinese Christian, in choosing to ally themselves with a non-indigenous belief system and possibly putting themselves in the way of some difficult conversations with family and friends, is likely to become more conscious of and more attentive to their own practice of and commitment to certain aspects of their Chinese cultural identity. American Christians, by contrast, growing up as some might say in a "Christian nation," are apt to take the conflation of culture and faith for granted and may require more intentional self-reflection to help them attend to their intellectual blind spots.

How Chinese nationalism and Chinese Christian spirituality collaborate in various ways is something I have explored before in my book *The "Inscrutably Chinese" Church* (Faries, 2010). Chinese Christians have many strategies for understanding how their religious and national identities fit together. I suggest that various narrative structures, the stories we tell about ourselves and our nations, are helpful in oiling the machinery of compromise. In this essay, I want to confront what is probably a more salient question and the cause of so much missionary frustration: not "what are the strategies Chinese Christians employ to reconcile apparent conflicts in identity," but rather, "why do so many Chinese people who have learned about Christianity fail to find a fruitful connection to it?" What are some of the features of

Chinese thought that keep the vast majority of Chinese from making that leap of faith?

## Seeing Through to the Unseen Worlds: Traditional Chinese Spirituality

Chinese concepts of spirituality can be traced all the way back to the beginnings of written history. The earliest extant Chinese texts, dating to around 1200 B.C., are divination texts: requests for important information from the unseen worlds (the cause of a mysterious disease, advice on the best course of action in a fraught military campaign) and written assurances that proper sacrifices will be made in gratitude for answers or to ensure that further supernatural help from the other world will be forthcoming. This sort of religious conversation with the otherwise silent and invisible spirit world should sound familiar in its basic structures—prayer and sacrifice, human interpretation of apparent responses—to readers versed in the Biblical texts of ancient Jewish culture or even popular practice in contemporary Christian culture. I will return later to this theme of cultural similarity. My goal is not to bolster any facile claim that there is no essential religious difference between cultures, but rather to help the reader understand why many Chinese skeptics are prone to deny any *important* difference and why exclusivist Christian claims are so difficult for many Chinese and other non-religious around the world to countenance. Christians (and Muslims and Jews and many others for that matter) do need to take seriously the fact that the burden to prove their way is the *only* or the *best* way to happiness here and eternal happiness hereafter rests heavily on their own shoulders. Believers in exclusivist doctrines need to consider candidly the plethora of religious choice in our newly interconnected world and recognize the existence of entire regions like China where the need to make such a decision for one faith and against all others has always been a foreign concept.

Not vastly different from the basic praxis of Western Christian spirituality, China's cultural spirituality is founded from its prehistory on proper ritualized behavior in the everyday world and ritualized communication with the realm of deities and the spirits of the departed. Over the course of three millennia, important Chinese thinkers like Confucius and Laozi built upon this foundation and it was powerfully influenced by imported Buddhist concepts of the universe heavily localized for the Chinese context. Chinese spirituality is rich in ideas and history. Taking into account significant regional differences, every Chinese person is steeped from their birth in some local recipe of this same religio-philosophical stew of Confucian, Daoist, Buddhist, and prehistoric Chinese traditional beliefs and practices. In several key moments of historical inter-religious tension, Chinese thinkers have produced trenchant critiques of their opponents and defenses of their own doctrines.

However, in sharp contrast to Western Christian spirituality, China's religious environment is largely lacking in systematic theology, apologetics, or a missionary impulse. Chinese peers in conversations about religion are likely to find many points of similarity between Christianity and traditional Chinese spirituality; they will be less prone to point out sharp distinctions. They are liable to say often, "Chinese people do that too." For better or worse, many Chinese peers do not have the instinct that many Christians feel to distinguish one religion from another and to rank them in a hierarchy of proximity to ultimate truth. Chinese religious culture has generally developed better tools of philosophical synthesis as opposed to apologia. Communist authoritarianism is the least of a foreign missionary's concerns in China. The stage was already set thousands of years ago for the profound intercultural spiritual misunderstandings missionaries still encounter today.

## 5,000 Years of Continuous Chinese Nationalism

Like Chinese spirituality, Chinese nationalism is also an ancient reality. Though a thorough understanding of the contemporary scene is important, nationalism (like spiritual skepticism and synthesis) does not begin in the age of Communist propaganda. Evidence of China's sense of itself as a proud and exceptional culture distinct from the less civilized cultures on the outskirts—an attitude we might call "culturalism"—can be found in ancient times, at least in the writings of literary elites like Confucius and his ilk (see Frank Dikotter's *The Discourse of Race in Modern China*, 2015). The vestiges of this pride compose a part of today's Chinese sense of self: witness China's relentless adherence to the myth of its "5,000 years of continuous history" and a very real belief, not entirely unfounded, that China's Asian neighbors are latecomers—derivative cultures that should continue to play their traditional role as dependent tributary states. China is a proud nation, and with good cause. We should also understand that the contemporary version of Chinese nationalism so important to understanding Chinese thought today is in many ways a new thing emerging from the "century of humiliation" (1839-1949) at the hands of imperialist Western powers. If culturalism is based on perceived superiority over outside cultures, the new nationalism confronts for the first time the complicating factor of outside cultures failing to recognize that cultural superiority, the apparent and never-before-necessary call to defend and prove a superiority which had always been self-evident.

What then are the components of today's nationalism? First, Chinese nationalism today is in part a new defensive nationalism wed awkwardly to the longstanding nationalism of internal confidence. A second shift in Chinese nationalism has taken place over the ages: if ancient Chinese culturalism was possibly concentrated among the literate ruling classes, nationalism today is a widespread attitude thanks to the rise of mass media, a shared experience of violated national integrity by foreign powers in the nineteenth century, and a shared satisfaction in the restoration of that integrity in the twentieth. Third, today's Chinese nationalism insists on certain traditional geographical claims ("this territory is and always has been rightfully ours"), certain cultural and textual traditions (the endurance and resilience of China's philosophies and political ideals, the superiority of Chinese poetry), and on a national sense of justified aggrievement and of just restitution ("we were temporarily the 'sick man of Asia,' but now the Chinese dragon awakes," to mix two commonly cited metaphors). Finally, Chinese nationalism depends on a Chinese concept of insiders and outsiders, a concept which is both ancient and has also been transformed by the appearance of the new world order in which China for the first time in history had serious reason to doubt its power and its ability to persist on the world stage. Chinese nationalism depends on a specific vision of the world as a place of "us and them," a division of the world into friends and enemies; Christianity, unfortunately, too often found itself and willingly positioned itself among the enemies. For a long time, Christians were no more enlightened than the Chinese or others around the world in holding to their own racialist and culturalist biases, and they were often too ready to cooperate with their nations' imperialist strategies in their zeal to spread their faith and their culture. This is the lasting legacy that foreign missionaries confront when they travel to China. This history may seem faded and barely relevant in the light of current missionary strategies and good intentions; however, it has not been forgotten by the missionaries' powerfully nationalist Chinese audiences.

## How Far Can Christianity Compromise with Chinese Cultural and National Claims?

Christians still too often approach China with a nineteenth century style condescension and lack of deference, precisely the attitude that gave rise to contemporary Chinese nationalism and that continues to rankle Chinese citizens today. Christians need to be aware of this history and consider carefully the consequences of stubbornly holding onto uncompromising points of view. Some of us were raised in churches where "compromise" was used as a synonym for sin and falling away from God; each reader and each missionary needs to parse this word and their understanding of the rigidity of Christian orthodoxy with as much wisdom they can. We need to consider carefully each aspect of doctrine and opportunity for cultural accommodation, judge accurately the cost of inflexibility (and the cost of compromise), and discern with wisdom what precisely constitutes our "mere Christianity."

How many potential Chinese converts will be willing to cross this or that Christian line in the sand and stand with that brand of Christianity against their nation or their culture? Is this a necessary or appropriate choice to ask Chinese friends and acquaintances to make? Is this a core feature of Christianity to which we must demand adherence by new Chinese believers? In what ways are we sometimes requiring these momentous choices of Chinese Christians without even knowing or acknowledging we are doing so?

I am speaking here most directly to the case of foreign missionaries within China and perhaps American Christians talking with first-generation Chinese immigrants in the U.S.; that is, talking with Chinese people who hold immediate ties to nationalistic Chinese identity. The cases of long-term overseas Chinese and Chinese Americans, for example, have their own infinite set of nuances (see Fenggang

Yang's *Chinese Christians in America* (1999) for an excellent account of many of those experiences), but those communities and the individuals that comprise them can also share many of the challenges and barriers to faith common to anyone who grows up with some degree of Chinese cultural identity.

    I am being intentionally provocative for good reason, because I believe this to be of fundamental importance. If Christians intend to be faithful to their God, to themselves, and to the peers with whom they communicate their faith, they need to consider carefully the inherently paradoxical nature of Christian missionary work and be fully aware of potential inconsistencies in their own faith claims. Many well-intentioned Christians will undoubtedly protest in response to my previous paragraph that they respect Chinese culture and would never set up a false dichotomy between the Christian faith and the core cultural beliefs of the national mission field. I fear this belief can be both sincere and unwittingly disingenuous. Americans, and American Christians among them, too easily talk about how much they love foreign cultures without first devoting themselves to acquiring a real knowledge of that culture; often Christians may actually mean not that they love the foreign culture itself, but that they love the people of that culture with a Christian love that, yes, will eventually require an interrogation of the original culture. It is that original culture, after all, that has already kept potential converts and their nation as a whole from Christian salvation for so long. Christians may too often "love" foreign cultures in a sentimental or patronizing way that does not take into account the powerful, maybe unbreakable, and valid hold that culture can have on a person or the ways in which the Christian faith may need to be part of a compromise solution if it is to take hold in the target culture in any enduring way.

    To take one famous example, ever since the seventeenth century, the Catholic Church has engaged in open debate about Chinese rituals of ancestor veneration: Are those behaviors religious actions analogous to spiritualism, the worship of idols or ghosts, of demonic powers? Are those loyalties and the practices that accompany them—practices that represent essential and ancient cultural loyalties to almost all Chinese people—in necessary conflict with Chinese Christian loyalty to God? I cannot presume to weigh in on the true answer to the theological question; I can simply state that in the years after the Vatican pronounced against Chinese rites, a very real barrier was set up between Chinese people and the Catholic faith in China. In addition to the cultural and spiritual barriers for individual decision-makers, as a matter of Chinese state policy, Catholic missionaries became persona non grata for most of the eighteenth century. The Vatican has since softened its position in a number of statements on the compatibility of Chinese culture and Catholic practice. Though the Church has long had other problems with the current Chinese regime, the Catholics decided they could and needed to compromise with Chinese cultural practice in this particular area. I will not speak for absolute truth or the mind of God, but I can applaud the Jesuits' serious study of Chinese culture and this instance of an open discussion regarding important theological questions. Perhaps we may respect both the original difficult, principled, negative decision by the Vatican and also the eventual more-accommodating pronouncements that allowed for significant, though not total, freedom for Chinese Christians trying to live out their loyalties to a variety of cultural demands.

By contrast, when Christian missionaries enter the field with good hearts and real love, but with little knowledge or serious consideration of cultural difference, there is a danger that whatever strangeness they encounter might by default be placed on the "thorny ground," the "heresy" or "sin," list; after all, if we believe ourselves to be truly saved, then the most certain way to ensure someone else is truly saved is to make them conform to our ways. This missionary problem in this sense is closely analogous to the glib phrase "loving the sinner and hating the sin," a slogan that purports to solve a serious religious paradox, but actually does nothing of the kind. Just as in the situation of Christians "loving" a foreign culture—what Christians might really mean is they love China enough to demand it conform to the universal truths of their God, and perhaps these Christians are overly certain about their list of universal truths and insufficiently aware of how much their own cultural background influences their list and departs from "mere Christianity." "Loving the sinner and hating the sin" may contingently reconcile a logical contradiction for the Christian who professes it, but it does nothing for the "sinner" to whom they are referring, who cannot feel the love intended by the saying, whether that sinner is a pagan on the mission field or a non-conformer at home. What does it mean to "love the sinner and hate the sin" if, their "sin" is an inescapable aspect of their identity? Likewise, what if a Chinese person's "sin" is burning paper money at their grandmother's grave? What if to disallow this action is asking that person to deny their love for their ancestors and their connection to a belief system that gives them hope in this life and the next? Perhaps Christianity can offer them a different sort of hopeful mental understanding of the afterlife, but perhaps Christianity does not offer a similar ritual that allows them to feel connected to their late grandmother. And of course, an even more serious missionary problem arises: perhaps the Christian faith creates more uncertainty and anxiety than Chinese tradition does about the eternal fate of that beloved relative.

This inevitably brings us back to the thorny perennial questions evangelists of all kinds in all places must deal with: What are the essentials of the faith that must be communicated? What are the beliefs and the behaviors that must be accepted and lived out? Where are the flexible joints in the Christian faith, and where are the unyielding dogmas? In the Chinese case, what are foreign missionaries supposed to do when they find some aspect of their own belief system is incompatible with Chineseness as that identity is understood or experienced by most Chinese today? Who will bend? Who will compromise? How do we conduct a conversation with Chinese on these questions?

Where Christianity is finding success in China today, it is apparently discovering various kinds of cultural flexibility. The Chinese Christian does not need to look or think or act precisely like the American Christian or the Nigerian Christian. If such cultural and political adaptation were impossible, China's registered churches would all be false to the faith and the unregistered churches would all be false to their Chinese roots. (I believe some foreign missionaries still believe this is in fact the case.) Where Christianity is failing to "find good soil" in China—in all those frustrating missionary conversations that seem to go nowhere, in all those abortive backsliding partial conversions—we cannot simply blame the Chinese spiritual "soil," but also need to consider our theories and methods of cultivation. Christians and their non-believing Chinese acquaintances are hitting a wall of obdurate cultural intransigence, a rigidity on both sides. The "stiff-necked" Chinese meet the "stiff-necked" Christians.

As I have suggested, we are dealing with two highly incompatible brands of cultural stubbornness. The very pliability of Chinese spirituality, Chinese openness to religious belief, the richness of that soil, actually becomes a significant barrier to China's widespread cultural acceptance of the obstinately exclusivist doctrines of the Christian faith. In general, the more inflexible and conservative the brand of Christian spirituality, the more traditional Chinese spirituality either pushes back against the missionary or is pushed out of the Chinese Christian convert.

This is probably a good time to return to the caveats with which I opened this essay. I continue to speak bluntly and paint with broad strokes. I think I am correct, and I am trying to be truthful and helpful in what I say, but do not take my word alone, or anyone else's, about Chinese people and their spirituality as gospel truth. A corollary to this point is that, in one sense, we should not believe in the concept of "the Chinese people" at all, not in the false sense of China as a massive undifferentiated monolith. Essays of that sort traffic in generalizations, and this essay is no exception. I have already been talking about "Chinese people" or what "a typical Chinese person" thinks or "Chinese spirituality" as if there were not nearly a billion-and-a-half individual minds and souls each thinking about the ultimate unseen realities with a billion-and-a-half different shades and nuances. There is little to be done about this reality. We need to organize and group people together in some ways and for some purposes. I, like all the others who write in this genre, simply believe a great many of the current generalizations my readers have heard about China are faulty, and I hope to break those down in order to set more accurate and useful generalizations in their place. Take from this whatever is useful and discard the rest. I hope some of this general information is helpful, but in any personal dialogue about religion, there are always two unique individual human subjects—not two broad cultural caricatures—who remain radically at the center.

Use your own experience to judge what is true and what is useful in these matters. If you do this simple and necessary act, if you look to your own experience and to the obvious facts palpable in the world around you, you will already be well on your way to living life and thinking about "spirituality" in a particularly Chinese manner. And this is, after all, the main goal and theme of this essay and this book, to help you see clearly where you stand outside Chinese culture and from there to take a step in the direction of the inside.

## Where Spirituality and Nationalism Meet

What, then, are the faulty generalizations, and what truer knowledge about China can we substitute in their place? What sort of broader cultural guidance might help us negotiate these complex person-to-person intercultural discussions of weighty philosophical and religious matters? We have spoken briefly about the sources and major trends of Chinese spirituality, but how is it practiced in China today? What exactly is this pliable and assimilative traditional Chinese spirituality, and how does it cooperate with traditional and contemporary Chinese nationalism?

The phrase "Chinese spirituality" may call forth Shangri-la visions of inner peace and healing through meditation, mystical powers in the martial arts, or a wise old man with eyes closed and holding smoking incense sticks between his palms bowing before a golden Buddha. These are the stereotypes that I grew up with and the tropes that popular culture continues to recycle, and those are some of the images I am hoping to complicate and nudge toward truth. Chinese people enjoy many of those fantastic fictional narratives as well—the stories are not merely Western stereotypes. And beyond the media representations, in real life there are many millions of Chinese who practice one or more religions with some level of rigor or devotion, many millions who indeed actively and intentionally use spiritual practices to seek inner peace, enlightenment, empowerment, including probably 60-80 million Chinese Christians. However, the vast majority of Chinese citizens are either self-professing atheists and/or they practice religion in a "cultural" or syncretistic manner that outsiders who adhere to exclusivist religions like Christianity or Islam are liable to consider "nominal" faith. It is these dominant latter forms of Chinese religious thought that will be my focus here, and as far as I am able, I will try to help the Western Christian reader see themselves and their evangelistic approaches through the eyes of these "typical" non-Christian Chinese.

In brief, traditional Chinese spirituality is largely incompatible with Western Christian spirituality because it is flexible and syncretistic and because it is married to a proud Chinese nationalism that includes a powerful anti-foreign component. Taking a close look at a Chinese proverb or slogan will serve to elucidate the relationship between these concepts and practices of spirituality and nationalism. To return to this matter of truth-seeking in these controversial matters, a popular Chinese saying, especially prominent in the recent decades of the post-Mao era of "reform and opening up" (starting in late 1978) is 实事求是 (*shi shi qiu shi*). This is normally translated as "seek truth from facts." I believe to the Chinese ear, the phrase has the tenor of a relatively recent government slogan and may be associated in many minds with fundamental Marxist material pragmatism, for example, Communist endeavors such as Mao Zedong's pre-revolution Socialism-inspired tours of the Chinese countryside and the reports he would write detailing rural economic life. He was gathering data about his country in order to better envision a path forward: seeking truth from facts. The phrase is certainly linked in the Chinese mind to Deng Xiaoping's pseudo-capitalist programs of economic reform. To outsider ears, in the U.S. for example, with our history of anti-Communist suspicion and Cold War tensions, such four-character phrases bear the rhythms of and associations with authoritarian propaganda, empty phrases used to shout down opposing viewpoints and obscure corrupt or impractical systems of power. We are liable to view these slogans cynically as Communist-sounding phrases that paper over truths rather than seeking them out.

If we want to see China clearly and see ourselves from a Chinese perspective, attempting to hear these slogans with Chinese ears is a good place to start. The fact of contemporary Chinese nationalism means that in general the Chinese view their government and their systems—and they hear government pronouncements very differently—from how outsiders see and hear the same things. Even when a Chinese friend might share a foreigner's cynical or critical attitude about the Chinese Communist Party or some of its policies, they might not choose to express this opinion in the same way the foreigner might express it or they may not share their full cynicism in the foreigner's presence. This is common sense and common courtesy, of course, which nationalistic Americans should themselves understand quite well, but to get inside the nationalism of someone else, a Chinese nationalism that in some sense may embrace what Americans habitually view as China's oppressive government, is a radical thought experiment for many foreigners.

In general, if we wish to understand the "insider" perspective on China, we need to recognize and moderate our foreign cynicism about the legitimacy of the Chinese Communist Party; we need to see plainly and question our own assumptions that the "oppressed Chinese people" are necessarily dismissive of official government messages and eager for "real democracy" to arrive. We need to recognize these attitudes and temper them with common Chinese positions in the debate: "How can we argue with the astounding economic results the Party has achieved?" "Every nation needs to balance the demands of stability and the demands of freedom, and stability is particularly important in times of radical transition."

Anytime we are in conversation with a Chinese acquaintance and catch ourselves thinking that this person secretly needs what my country or my church has to offer, we need to remind ourselves that they are not approaching the conversation with the same attitude. Whether our ways may actually benefit that person metaphysically or politically is an open question, but this is not an attitude to which Chinese friends will readily accede. We should not conclude that Chinese nationalism is blindly supportive of the Communist Party; we simply must not believe that the Chinese people are closeted American nationalists or, the dangerous corollary to this assumption, the Chinese people are secretly monotheists just one regime change away from both Democracy and Christendom. Whether we are talking about the Chinese people's strident calls for reform in the spring of 1989 or current domestic protests over human rights issues, Chinese desire for improvement in their own society does not diminish their interest in Chinese sovereignty and self-determination; it does not reflect a covert longing for China to become a U.S.-style republic. Chinese people are naturally wary of inordinate American political or economic influence seeping into their country. In my recent downtime reading of *The Daily Show: An Oral History*, I ran across this simple, brief quote that hits the proper note of complexity on this question. The book at one point describes the international appeal of *The Daily Show* by citing the case of a Chinese fan illegally downloading, subtitling, and posting episodes on social media: "We're not interested in your politics," the Chinese viewer is quoted as saying. "We're interested in the style of the show and the idea that you can use jokes to tell the truth" (Stewart, 2016). Christians would do well to remember that there is not a constant tide of warm feeling toward the U.S. government among the Chinese people; there is no widespread envy of American political structures or American forms of capitalism. It is too easy to imagine the Communist Party and its propaganda is the only thing standing in the way of the Chinese people embracing America and our ways, including our religion. In truth, the Chinese people do not need the Communist Party to teach them patriotism.

Chinese people love their nation and are intensely proud of their culture, and this is a point where spirituality and nationalism meet. Chinese civilization is profound enough and rich enough that the love of nation has become part and parcel of Chinese spirituality. Again, we are not talking about masses of people bowing before the idol of a strong tyrant or blindly believing nationalistic propaganda. North Korea in its intense and tragic isolation might still be preserving this kind of fantastic Communist dystopia to some degree, though recent news casts doubt on the level of information containment even there. China is far from that most extreme case.

Laurence Thompson describes the Chinese case in his classic *Chinese Religion: An Introduction*. Thompson in this text does not simply rehearse the long histories of China's three or four discrete major religious and philosophical schools of thought. Instead he addresses the challenge that every teacher of religion in China has faced: the fact that these schools of thought—traditional Chinese religious practice, Confucianism, Daoism, Buddhism—cannot really be talked about in isolation from one another; they are rarely or barely independent entities in the Chinese mind (Thompson, 1995). And to take what might be mistaken for mere syncretism a step further, Thompson suggests that China itself, or Chinese identity itself, constitutes a kind of spirituality that inevitably absorbs and combines these philosophies. "Chinese religion" is not about the religions that inhabit the geographical boundaries of China. When we say "Chinese religion," the word "Chinese" plays a similar role to the word

"Christian" in the phrase "Christian religion." And this should remind us of the challenge—perhaps impossibility—of conquering China, whether you are a Khan, a King, or a Christian.

Chinese people come from a historically self-contained and self-satisfied state. They are proud and nationalistic, and they are not looking to the West, to Christians or the Christian religion, for answers. They already have what they need. We might say, in essence, if you are a Christian American, that Chinese nationals are very much like you. They simply believe in a different nation and a different faith, and their faith is not a missionary faith; it is a national, in their minds perhaps even genetic, faith. One is either Chinese or not Chinese, just as one is either Jew or Gentile, Christian or non-Christian. One is either inside or outside. However, let us be clear that outsiders are not necessarily enemies; though outsiders to the Chinese may be inferior or unfortunate, they are not necessarily bound for eternal punishment as is the perspective of many Christians. This confluence of sameness and difference—these kinds of sameness and these kinds of difference—create a perfect storm of conversational improbability if the purpose of the conversation is actually the religious conversion of the interlocutor. Outsiders are nearly as unlikely to talk a Chinese person into being a Christian as a Chinese person is to talk a foreigner into being Chinese. Chinese people are likely to be polite in such conversations, but they may also be patronizingly curious about how American Christians could think so highly of themselves, of their young nation, and how they could be so certain of their religious beliefs. To paint the world again with an overly broad brush, Chinese people are not in need. They may at times feel and fear some emptiness or metaphysical futility about existence, but the holes in their personal lives or their cultural fabric are not unequivocally God-shaped. They are not looking to the U.S. or to the Christian Church for help.

How does an outsider talk to someone like this? I do not intend this question as a rhetorical complaint about "those stubborn Chinese people who should come around to our way of thinking." That is the missionary thinking from a century-and-a-half ago. I mean that question—"How does an outsider talk to someone like this?"—in the most direct and serious sense, as a question deserving an answer. I am asking us to consider honestly how we should relate to a person who is happy to continue a friendship with us, but who is statistically unlikely ever to accept the basic truths that define a Christian's identity and existence. How might the difficult conversations play out? How is the relationship to be lived out? Do these dilemmas reveal the hubris of nationalistic Chinese culture or narrow chauvinism in nationalistic American modes of religious thought and practice? To some degree readers need to rely on themselves and their knowledge of the unique dynamics of a particular unique relationship. However, I hope the information and guidance in the remainder of this essay will do some of the work of pointing the way toward some strategies for honest and fruitful intercultural communication.

### How, Then, Are We to Live? Seeking Truth from Facts

Let us return now to the Chinese saying 实事求是, seek truth from facts, and to the matter of training the foreign ears to hear more like a generalized Chinese audience. The Chinese audience for this phrase, unlike the American audience, has not experienced decades of ingrained fear of Communism, and they will hear several more facets in 实事求是 that foreigners may not hear. Some analysis of these several points should give readers a basic understanding of how a "typical" Chinese worldview differs from a "typical" American worldview, particularly on questions of nationalism and spirituality. At the risk of saying something that is far too obvious to the readership of a book like this, this kind of "walk a mile" empathy is a good first step toward positive intercultural relationships and possibly fruitful missionary work.

First of all, the association of 实事求是—of anything really—with Communism and with Chairman Mao for the general American audience is immediately negative. For most Chinese people, on the other hand, Chairman Mao is not the simplistic caricature of a tyrant now comically immortalized on every imaginable item of Cultural Revolution kitsch. He is, rather, a flawed and complex leader who loved China and achieved the one thing the previous century of weak emperors, corrupt warlords, and inept Presidents could not: he made China whole and strong. For the first time in a hundred years or more, Mao Zedong made China independent and capable of pushing back against foreign bullying. Kicking out the foreign missionaries was a key piece of that triumph. The slogan's connection to Deng Xiaoping and the economic reforms of the 1980s and '90s is likewise not a sign of Communist hypocrisy, but a point of pride and evidence that "Socialism with Chinese Characteristics" is not feckless dogmatism, but a flexible system of thought that can self-correct and can build on the framework laid by Mao and the other founders to return China to its rightful and inevitable elevated place on the world stage, fully realized in economic terms as well as political and military terms. We are mistaken when we assume that the Communist Party is some kind of foreign intruder in Modern Chinese culture, a kind of artificial growth that might be cut out surgically. Communism, like Buddhism and like the Mongol and the Manchu invaders, had to adapt and integrate when it entered Chinese culture. Communism is in many ways a continuation of what has always been in China. China's history after the 1949 victory of Mao Zedong has surely been full of cataclysmic upheaval, but 5,000 years of "Chinese spirituality" has not been significantly altered by seven decades of Communism.

Along those lines, Chinese ears might also perceive plainly—or subtly understand—that the "Communist" phrase 实事求是, seek truth from facts, resonates with traditional Chinese philosophy. We might call this Confucian thought, or Daoism, or Buddhism; we might call it simply prehistoric Chinese thought. We can even call it by the relatively recent name of Chinese Marxism, but a good deal of the cultural and spiritual content is unchanged: Chinese tradition teaches that if we want matters in life to proceed smoothly, we need to understand the natural movements of the universe and position our lives and actions in line with those movements. We want a good harvest, so we let the earth and the heavens tell us when to plant the rice. We want our children to treat us with respect, so we treat our own elders with respect. We want others to be generous toward us, and we know what to do to pave that road. The laws of the universe are not all that mysterious if we know how to interpret the world around us. The "facts" that lead to "truth" are to be found everywhere, in natural phenomena and tradition and economic indicators. Some of these facts are codified in ancient Chinese texts of ritualized interpersonal behavior, the primers that Confucius and Laozi grew up reading; some are written down later in Confucius' own ethical teachings and his version of the golden rule; and some facts are reinforced later still in Buddhist doctrines regarding the natural karmic justice of the universe. And finally, some facts are recorded in Marxist predictions, which state that exploited peoples will eventually do something to improve their condition. Action and reaction are truths immanent within the Confucian golden rule, within the Buddhist moral economy, and within scientific materialism.

## How, Then, Are We to Talk?

Keeping all these ideas of cross-cultural difference in mind, where are the opportunities and the pitfalls in peer-to-peer cross-cultural communication about matters of ultimate importance? In terms of the intercultural missionary conversation, these ideas mentioned above are potential points of intersection in East/West ethical teaching, but we must always be cautious about mapping comparisons too precisely. Foreign Christians believe many of these same things as their non-Christian Chinese peers: universal natural laws, general revelation of those laws to all humans, some kind of just economy of reward and punishment in the universe.

The conversational rub finally comes in the area of special revelation. Chinese culture has its share of individuals and sects that claim esoteric insights unknown to all the others, but Chinese are generally more modest than Christians in their claims to having special knowledge of truth beyond their senses. This "show me" skepticism is again not a recent arrival with atheist Communism. This brand of humanism goes back at least to Confucius who would often demur when asked about the details of the afterlife or about rituals for deceased ancestors: "We do not yet know how to treat the living," was his famous reply. Granted, we all know that China is full of ritual practice—most commonly prayers and sacrifices to a variety of deities and ancestors—yet we do not find the exclusivist dogmatism of the Christian. As foreign Christians make claims about God's special revelation of exclusive truth to specific (non-Chinese) groups within uniquely inspired texts, they are navigating a minefield. Applying the practical lessons of China's "seek truth from facts" traditions, these foreigners are in danger of appearing credulous and of overstating their certainty on important metaphysical concepts; applying the lessons of Chinese nationalism and the international crises of nineteenth- and twentieth-century Chinese history, these foreigners are in danger of appearing arrogant and imperialistic. And as mentioned earlier, if the conversation turns to ritual sacrifice and the eternal whereabouts of one's ancestors, the foreign missionary is in danger of causing significant anxiety and appearing to demand an overreaching break from the Chinese culture writ large and from the microcosm of that culture which is the individual's family structure.

Christianity to the Chinese person can potentially sound something like this: "You must obey our one Western God alone and follow these rules He revealed to our church, and the consequences of disagreement are the following eternal punishments for you and your family, including all who came before you. Even if you and your family accept our faith, we cannot promise salvation for your ancestors." Chinese religious practice and thought are rife with uncertainties about what comes after death, but it is pragmatic, even hopeful in a secular sense, by comparison with that caricature of Christianity in terms of the agency the individual can feel about the efficacy of their actions in this life. Chinese spirituality is centered squarely in this world, not focused on the next; it is concerned with mundane matters, not the pure or tainted state of one's soul. "How do we care for our parents while they are living?" and "What can those who remain do to care for those who have passed on?" not "Where are my parents going after they die?" If we ask a Chinese person kowtowing and lighting their three sticks of incense at any Chinese temple to tell us what exactly they are praying for, we are unlikely to hear anything about the "salvation of souls," and we are also unlikely to get a clear picture of what they actually believe happens to them after they die. Our nostrils will be full of the sickly-sweet tang of incense, but we will rarely catch a whiff of fear about fire and brimstone. Foreign Christians need to consider carefully how much of that fire they want to introduce to the discussion and what they themselves really believe about the eternal fate of the un-evangelized Chinese ancestors.

On the question of nationalism, foreign missionaries, particularly American missionaries, would do well to deemphasize their own national origin and the Western sources of their individual faith. An attitude of personal humility; an emphasis on the countercultural aspects of the faith (how faith made them, not better Americans, but in some sense citizens of another eternal nation); and a shift of focus to the mutually foreign, geographically central Middle Eastern origins of Christianity—these strategies can help to put the missionary and their Chinese peers on a kind of equal footing with respect to the Christian religion.

As we talk about the "secular humanist" character of Chinese thought, we should not overlook, much less dismiss, the perennial spiritualist beliefs among Chinese in a mirror world of departed souls and other unseen beings full of good or ill intent toward the quotidian realm. These beliefs and the ways in which they can intersect with Christian teaching can lead to other kinds of difficult conversations and, at the extreme, inaugurate dangerous cult-like heresies that both the Chinese government and the Christian missionary would be happy to suppress, though perhaps for different reasons and using different methods. Conversations about deeply held and conflicting supernatural beliefs will be less common among the foreign Christian's more usual circles of Chinese acquaintanceship: educated, urban students and professionals. Even where such beliefs are openly held and more-clearly defined in China, often the economies of the spirit world and the material world are so closely linked as to be difficult to distinguish. This posited spiritual world is not quite so separate and discrete from our world as are the common Christian conceptions of heaven and hell. The Chinese afterlife is more apt to possess a kind of continuity with life before death. A relative's trials in the afterlife might be ameliorated by the living kin offering a sacrifice of a food they enjoyed in life. The opening of a convenience store on the streets of Taipei will be inaugurated by a table of offerings given with prayers, incense, and the noise of drums to some local or household deity, not unlike a gift that might be given to a local politician to smooth a transaction. The products set out on the table, at least according to one shop-owner I talked with recently, go back on his shelves to be consumed again by those who continue to exist in the everyday world.

In these situations, Christians do need to consider what they themselves believe about the nature of this imagined spiritual world and their Chinese peers' interactions with it. Does it take on a demonic nature and require the convert to initiate a break from traditional culture—a demand that should not be made of a

Chinese friend precipitously, particularly by a foreigner—or can it be considered "cultural," playful, or otherwise innocuous?

If excessive demands on these points are made by the foreign missionary on a Chinese peer, many Chinese will wonder why Christians think their beliefs are so different from Chinese traditions, and the "arrogance" of the Christian's exclusivist claims to truth will be challenged with strong "seek truth from facts" logic. Though practically any Christian will speak with great confidence about the realities of heaven and hell and judgment, they will be hard-pressed to give a clear picture of what they actually believe those experiences will look like, apart from some well-rehearsed Biblical metaphors. If the missionary makes a claim about "assurance of salvation," but does not really know how to make a logical case for it, the Chinese friend is likely to push them on the awkward epistemological question: "How do you know?" "Using facts to see the truth" they are liable to wonder and ask very pointedly, "Does Christianity have any clearer answer than Chinese tradition about precisely what sort of experience follows the final breath?" Will there be some brand of justice meted out to the selfish and cruel? Will there be some kind of reward for the humble and charitable? Will our loved ones be there? On these points Chinese tradition is as clear as Christian tradition. Will there be other spiritual beings in the afterlife and maybe a bigger deity or two? Chinese have known this much for thousands of years. Non-Christian Chinese peers are likely to argue that Christians actually know less than Chinese philosophers about how to live in this world and that Christians know only as much or little about the afterlife as China has always known. Convincing the Chinese humanist of the essential fallenness of the human soul and the good-place/bad-place eternally binary nature of the afterlife—so different from the complicated everyday world of the living—will seem neither logical nor merciful to the unbelieving Chinese peer, and this poses a challenging exercise in apologetics worthy of another essay, one written by someone wiser than me.

Christians generally claim to have more special revelation about all things "unseen" than the Chinese humanist does, and, for better or for worse, these claims shape the Christian's life in this world. Chinese claim to have more and better information about things "seen," and they take this knowledge as the essential prerequisite to living a good life in this world; if we live a good life here, the thinking goes, the next world will take care of itself. And so, the "Communist" slogan, 实事求是, is finally just a "Chinese" slogan that describes a pragmatic humanism that has in many ways dominated Chinese thought forever.

### The End of Foreign Missions in China?

I have offered some information, some warnings, and a few conversational strategies for navigating a complex missionary minefield. Inevitably, however, facing a situation in which the foreign identity of the missionary is itself a significant part of the problem, we must consider the possibility of leaving twenty-first-century Christian missions in China to the Chinese themselves. As foreigners, we must commit to learning as much as we can about Chinese culture, traditional and contemporary and we must speak with whatever wisdom we can discern in the moment. If we are convinced in a certain situation we should "witness" to a Chinese friend, we should be prepared for all the difficult questions described above; we should be prepared for disappointment; and if we are disappointed in those conversations, we should be ready to offer a high level of commitment to a friendship that is not merely grounded in evangelistic hopes of converting the other.

Because of all the challenges cited above (and more to follow), I tend to believe we need to let Chinese people do their own evangelism at this point in history. To speak frankly, peer-to-peer Chinese evangelism is the only kind that many Chinese will accept. Back to the topic of the Spirit working in mysterious ways, I suspect the Communists' expulsion of the foreign missionaries after 1949 was probably the best thing ever to happen to Chinese Christianity. The Chinese Communist Party did not and could not abolish Christianity; they could only expel foreign teachers of Christianity. What the Party actually did had a highly subversive effect which the Party apparently did not foresee: they accelerated the pace of Christian localization in China, a process similar to the effect of official imperial acceptance of foreign Buddhism 2,000 years earlier in the Han Dynasty. The Party in effect demanded that the Christian Church in China become a fully Chinese entity, legal and acceptable to the highest levels of government, compatible with traditional

Chinese spiritual thought and ancient and contemporary nationalism. The taint of foreignness was, if not immediately and irrevocably erased, set on the path toward disappearance. The new Chinese government simply and proudly demanded an end to foreign patronage and patronizing. They insisted that foreign Christians perceive Chinese citizens as subjects spiritually equal to the citizens of their own foreign nations. The Communist government effectively stated as we might expect a nation to state after a century of being alternately bullied and pitied by foreign powers, "We do not need you. What standing do you have to tell us what we need or what we should believe?"

Chinese Christians will not speak so haughtily, of course, and will often welcome foreign visitors and teachers to their congregations. Foreigners, however, always need to be humble before Chinese groups, in a proper Christian sense, but also in recognition of China's well-earned pride of culture and history. Foreigners must never play the role of visiting "experts" from the "Mother Church" trying to keep a young church on the right track. We outsiders are no longer necessary to the growth of Christianity in China, if we ever were, and our insistent involvement now carries with it some awkwardness and even brings potentially some level of unnecessary political suspicion on the heads of Chinese Christians who otherwise may worship freely.

What about our Chinese friends abroad, visitors to our foreign cultures who are not under the purview of the suspicious and bureaucratic Communist powers? I am somewhat pessimistic about our level of spiritual influence over these peers as well. American churches—our brands of Christianity—are generally less welcoming or appealing to Chinese visitors and immigrants when compared with America's Chinese Christian congregations. In addition to, and closely tied to, all the barriers described above, there is our Western Christian scandal of denomination. Though it could not be completely true that Chinese Christians themselves have no divisions, Chinese churches do not emphasize or understand denominational difference as Americans do. Among the mainland's registered congregations, a high degree of uniformity is mandated, without being stifling, at least judging by the overflowing services and Bible study classes of Chinese churches. And as we have seen with all other issues (and always acknowledging the dangers of speaking in generalizations) there is something Chinese in this fact; the homogeneity is not merely an unwelcome policy imposed artificially from above. After all, the Communist Party does not make all the rules in Chinese society; the Party is at the mercy of longstanding Chinese cultural norms just as Christians are.

The widespread belief that Chinese Christianity represents a "post-denominational" Christian church has real foundation both within China and abroad. Trying to use a word like "post-denominational" with a Chinese believer will confirm this truth. Chinese believers are "Christians" or they are "Catholics" according to their own terminology. This is an unfortunate historical translation difficulty caused by the divisions between foreign missionaries and the desire of the new Protestant missionaries to distinguish themselves in the Chinese mind from the old Catholic missionaries. This linguistic situation only increases Chinese confusion about the exclusivist nature of Christianity, but these are the only terms Chinese normally use to describe Christian sectarian division. Based on my arguments in this essay, of course, we might argue that "Chinese Protestant Christianity" itself simply constitutes one extremely large Christian denomination of its own, in some ways as exclusivist and closed as any foreign Christian sect. Putting that point aside, the relative unity of Chinese Christianity is impressive. Too many Protestants in the U.S. are fixated on what makes their small congregation the most Christian, the closest to the truth of the Bible and therefore what makes everyone else, to a greater or lesser degree, farther away from God. These conversations are confusing and off-putting to most any visiting seeker, but perhaps particularly to Chinese visitors. One might argue that Chinese Christianity is artificially unified by government control or that the Church in China is simply too young to have faced the key issues that lead to denominational splits; one might argue that division is sadly and inevitably part of China's liberated future. Of course, there must be some truth in these guesses, but I would claim also that Chinese unified "post-denominational" Christianity is one of the natural compromises our "foreign" faith is making and needs to make as it integrates into the long history of Chinese thought. While somehow maintaining a higher degree of religious exclusivity than Buddhism and Daoism have, Chinese Christianity generally resists the extreme competitive and exclusivist splintering of the American churches. Some Chinese Christians predictably make the claim that this is a cultural accommodation that actually heals a wound in Christendom and may help to usher in a new Christian age, another possible example of Chinese culture saving Christianity as opposed to Christianity saving China.

Chinese seekers abroad, I believe, are particularly drawn to Chinese churches for this reason among many others. Chinese people abroad are sometimes more comfortable around other Chinese. Though this might be frustrating for some welcoming and well-meaning predominantly Caucasian congregations, this obvious truth is helpfully explained by theories described in Beverly Daniel Tatum's classic *"Why Are All the Black Kids Sitting Together in the Cafeteria?": And Other Conversations About Race* (Tatum, 2002). The claim, which is intuitive and confirmed anecdotally by personal testimonies I have myself heard, is that living in the United States is inherently stressful for minorities; in addition, depending on where they live, the U.S. can be terribly boring and isolating for overseas Chinese. Chinese visitors would not put it so bluntly, but it is fair to say that they sometimes need a break from majority American culture and from the English language. Chinese churches in the U.S. include many Chinese visitors who are faithful attenders and highly involved in services and events, but who remain on the edge of full or formal conversion. They find some important connection to the community without finding religious faith. Even if they remain undecided about Christian doctrine, these congregants undoubtedly find that Chinese churches fulfill a highly important and culturally specific social function that many American congregations cannot offer them.

Chinese churches offer opportunities for familiar conversation with people who share knowledge of their proud cultural tradition, as opposed to stilted small talk in English with foreigners who "just don't get it." Moreover, Chinese churches offer familiar food at almost every meeting. The question of diet and the social aspect of Chinese food culture is by no means a small matter for Chinese visitors studying or working in the U.S. Most important, perhaps, these churches serve the function of social aid networks, indispensable for anyone new to a foreign culture, but particularly for Chinese whose custom of reliance on such relationships of mutual help runs deeper than most "self-reliant" Americans can appreciate.

American churches are of course full of charitable people who would spend enormous amounts of money, energy, and time to serve fellow Christians and visitors to their congregations—church-run ESL classes can be a great resource and opportunity for charitable witness—but Chinese generally also experience a superficiality in their relationships with American Christians, a standoffishness even in the midst of kindness. This might be understood as natural human difficulty with cultural and linguistic difference, American cultural respect for privacy and self-determination, or through the lens of one of many other complex and innocent causes. The fact remains, however, that the intensity and perceived depth of intracultural Chinese relationships go well beyond that certain style of American interaction that feels lacking to the Chinese. I would speculate, to return to our themes of major cultural difference above, that American Christian interaction might at times emphasize the next world at the cost of intense social exchange in this world. Chinese emphasis on human relationship ethics in this world can unfortunately seem overly transactional, calculating, and lacking in altruism to the American eye; American Christian love or charity can seem to the Chinese eye like another kind of transaction, one performed on the spiritual level to impress a deity or score a conversion, and it may unfortunately feel cold, lacking true concern or connection, on the human level.

## The Imperfect Cross-Cultural Conversation: A Case Study

As an attempt to offer some concluding notes and suggestions for further reflection and to return to the parable from the essay's title, I would encourage readers interested in these issues of religious cross-cultural communication to read some of the conversations between renowned Christian evangelist Luis Palau and Zhao Qizheng, a high-ranking Chinese politician, currently a member of the Chinese People's Political Consultative Conference. I use their published transcripts from *A Friendly Dialogue Between an Atheist and a Christian* in my Religions in China class, and the first four chapters were particularly influential for me as I prepared my thoughts for this essay (Palau & Zhao, 2008). Zhao Qizheng serves as a kind of ideal—

and in many ways typical—Chinese interlocutor for Palau. He is the sort of Chinese citizen whom American scholars and professionals are most likely to meet: highly educated and better-informed about American culture—including Christian narratives, if not religious doctrine—than we are about Chinese culture and religion. I do not endorse this conversation as a model for how to approach this sort of dialogue. On the contrary, I suggest readers learn from Zhao rather than Palau and consider how Palau falls into some of the misunderstandings described above and how a next-generation Christian might improve on his example.

For all his wisdom and life experience, Palau modestly admits he knows little about Chinese culture and religion, yet he repeatedly professes his love for Chinese culture and its people. Zhao, by contrast, has read the Bible, shows real interest and openness to religious understanding, and he is able to state the Christian message concisely in what Palau admits is a "perfect summary of the main points of the Bible" (p. 10). Zhao's side of the conversation indicates human interest in a fellow human, discussion for the sake of relationship, candid expression of his own belief system, and perceptive analysis of why he cannot read the Bible in the same way Palau does. For all his kindness and sincerity, Palau by contrast cannot avoid the black-and-white language of "friends and enemies" when talking about believers and non-believers; Zhao counters that he finds this binary thinking about "us and them" in religious terms to be dangerous. Zhao believes he has enemies in the world, but he considers the real enemies to be those who prosecuted "aggressive wars against China . . . for over a hundred years" (pp. 46-47). The unspoken accusation lingers: those enemies were primarily "Christian" nations, and this sort of condescending, nationalist "Christian" thought that Palau is propagating about heretics and the spiritual poverty of unsaved cultures was part of the justification for such violent disrespect of Chinese sovereignty.

Palau, for all his Christian love, is approaching the conversation with a contemporary version of the same attitudes, as a traditional evangelical apologetics debate, the underlying agenda being to convince and influence. Zhao senses this, naturally, and in one moment of considerate, if slightly awkward, demurral, he puts Palau off: "Aha, I have to be very careful when talking to you. Otherwise you might be leading me to God through your communication" (Palau & Zhao, 2008, p. 17). There is no chance of this, of course, since Palau is completely unable to approach religious questions from a Chinese point of view. When Zhao offers a traditional Chinese philosophical story to account for how Chinese people think about spiritual matters, instead of trying to comprehend the story in Zhao's terms, Palau reinterprets the story in a way that he thinks will support his Christian claims and perhaps demonstrate a "general revelation" claim that the seeds of Christian thought are always present in ancient pagan thought.. Appropriately, the famous Zhuangzi fish story that Zhao (2008) cites is partly about the difficulty or impossibility of understanding the mind of someone outside oneself, someone foreign.

Through this story, Zhao is obliquely criticizing Palau's assumption that he understands the Chinese mind, specifically the official atheism of the Communist Party. Palau assumes atheists all feel lonely at their core, that they all have the God-shaped hole in their souls, if only they can be made to see their own spiritual poverty. Palau insists, "I've talked with many atheists, East and West, and they're very lonely people inside" (Palau & Zhao, 2008, p. 28). Zhao does not see it or feel it or confess it. Part of the communication difficulty here, I would claim, is that Chinese "atheism" is not Western atheism. Atheism as a Western concept is based on the loss of belief in God and the often angry denial of the existence of God exercised in fierce opposition to the perceived hegemony of a predominantly Christian culture. In stark contrast, Chinese atheism should appear to foreign eyes more like a highly spiritual agnosticism, a skepticism about supernatural certainties, but a skepticism living alongside millennia of fully enculturated spiritual thought and practice. Zhao puts Confucius himself under the "atheist" label in this Chinese sense of the word. Unlike some famous militant "evangelical" Western atheist thinkers, the "atheist" Chinese Communist Party officially desires the end of superstitious religious beliefs, but their policies since the end of the Cultural Revolution call into question the seriousness of that desire or any confidence that such a goal can be achieved; the continuance of traditional Chinese cultural practices and even of "superstitious" religious practices among many Party members (including Christian practice by some) is an open secret. Zhao insists that "epistemological materialism does not deny the existence of the spirit," (Palau & Zhao, 2008, p. 36-38) and he links the spiritual lives of individual Chinese to the spiritual civilization, the national spirit of China, the "core values" of the society.

Zhao Qizheng understands, I think, what Luis Palau cannot. Communist atheism and missionary Christianity are not polar opposites. They are not an antithetical pair of foreign warriors entering the field to battle over the soul of China. They are not the binaries in a simple zero-sum game, and they cannot achieve their goals by dealing exclusively one with the other. They are both dealing with the same challenges in the same ancient mission field already thick with the grain of traditional Chinese spirituality and national feeling. They must struggle equally with a terrain they cannot alter. The Chinese Communist Party and the Chinese Christian Church have different loyalties and different goals, but they still must work together and till the same ground. They are both young farmers approaching a Chinese field fully grown; they are applying for employment with the owner of the fields, a farmer who knows his land well. They are not spreading seeds amongst empty fields, and they are not wishing for the failure of the other, though they certainly wish the best for their own crop. They are sitting together with the vast population of China, the owners of this enormous property, and they are making suggestions for the following season, considering strategies and hybrids that will flourish in this place and in this time.

## References

Dikotter, F. (2015). *The discourse of race in modern China* (2$^{nd}$ ed.). London, UK: Hurst.

Faries, N. (2010). *The "inscrutably Chinese" church: How narratives and nationalism continue to divide Christianity.* New York, NY: Lexington.

Gobry, P. (2016, July 14). Can Christianity save China? *The Week*. Retrieved May 9, 2018, from http://theweek.com/articles/635668/ mericas s y-save-china

Johnson, I. (2017, April 23). In China, unregistered churches are driving a religious revolution. *The Atlantic*. Retrieved May 9, 2018, from https://www.theatlantic.com/international/archive/2017/04/china-unregistered-churches-driving-religious-revolution/521544/

Palau, L., & Zhao Q. (2008). *A friendly dialogue between an atheist and a Christian.* Grand Rapids, MI: Zondervan.

Spence, J. (2002). *To change China: Western advisers in China.* London, UK: Penguin.

Stewart, J., & Smith, C. (2016). *The daily show: An oral history.* New York, NY: Grand Central.

Tatum, B. (2003). *"Why are all the black kids sitting together in the cafeteria?" and other conversations about race* (Revised ed.). New York, NY: Basic.

Thompson, L. (1995). *Chinese religion: An introduction.* Belmont, CA: Wadsworth.

Waley-Cohen, J. (2000). *Sextants of Beijing: Global currents in Chinese history.* New York, NY: Norton.

Yang, F. (1999). *Chinese Christians in America: Conversion, assimilation, and adhesive identities.* University Park, PA: Penn State UP.

# 10. A Brief Summary of My Life[36]

## By Ye Weijun[37]

I was born into a family that had no religious faith. My dad and my grandfather were both soldiers, so they have believed in the Communist Party. When I was a young boy, I was very naughty and would often get into fights, but my parents taught me that fighting would not help solve the problem. From then on, I learned to control my emotions.

When I was a child, I had two near-death experiences. The first one happened when I was only six months old. I had a cold, and my grandmother, who was taking care of me at the time, took me to the local hospital to get a shot. The nurse accidentally gave me the wrong shot, and it almost killed me. My mother was very worried and had nightmares. After I recovered, she took me back up into the mountains to live with her and my father even though they were both busy working. The second experience happened when I was eight. I saw my friends swimming in a river. They were all older than I was, but I thought I could do it too, so I jumped into the river. I could not swim, and I started to sink. I felt very comfortable and felt as though I could breathe in the water. All around me, I saw this very bright light. The next thing I remember was lying on the bank of the river. Apparently, a local farmer

---

[36] *Editor's note: This man is ethnically mixed—mostly Han Chinese with some ethnic minority ancestry. Though he was raised for a time in a minority area, he does not speak any of the language of that ethnicity. His family is a good example of one that in recent generations has successfully integrated into collective Han and national-communist ideologies. - K.P.*

[37] *A pseudonym has been used to protect the identity of the contributor.*

had saved me. These experiences really left a deep impression on me and made me think deeply about my life.

When I was eleven I started learning to play the piano. I went on to study music in a conservatory. Sometimes, as a young man, when I was sad or angry, I would go up on the mountain near my home to sit and play my guitar. I would look up at the stars and speak to them, thinking they could hear me.

My family went through the 2008 earthquake that severely affected the southwest part of China. In that disaster, I lost my apartment and music shop as well as my dog and some of my instruments. As we started to recover and rebuild the area, I went on teaching piano and guitar lessons.

Eventually, I met a foreign lady who was teaching English at a nearby school. She wanted to learn to play the cello, so I started giving her lessons once a week. Through her, I soon met other teachers at that school. I also started giving guitar lessons to a young boy and his father. They became my friends, and the father asked me if I wanted to study the Bible with him. I agreed, and we also started reading through a book called "Stranger on the Road to Emmaus."[38]

I had many questions and did not understand who God was or if He really existed, but one illustration that really helped me came from my musical experience. I knew music was real and could touch people's hearts, yet no one can see music or describe exactly what it feels like. I began to think that, in the same way, God was real even though I could not see Him or describe Him. My friend and I kept reading and studying together for several months, and I attended some meetings at the local Three-Self Church[39] with my female cello student.

On April 4, 2012, the day of the Water Releasing Festival in our local area and also China's Tomb Sweeping Day, I talked with again with my Bible study partner, and that day, I decided to trust in Jesus and ask Him to change my life. He did, and now I am a new man! I continue to develop a deeper, stronger faith and am so thankful for the ways He is positively changing my family.

---

[38] This is a book that shares the spiritual journey and testimony of a Chinese intellectual.
[39] The government-registered Protestant church.

# 11. Confucianism, Maoism, and Christianity: Chinese Intellectuals' Difficult Path to Christianity and Why It Emerged in the 1990s[40]

## By Franklin Wang

From grocery stores to presidential elections, China is ubiquitous in American life. Yet many Americans probably do not know that America has had a long relationship with China. For two centuries, America has mostly wished China well and contributed significantly towards China's rebirth as a modern nation and entry into current global system (Pomfret, 2016). American Christian churches have also contributed a lot to God's kingdom in China. A recent publication about the Boxer Incident in 1900 illustrates how much of their own blood American missionaries sacrificed in China (黃錫培, 2010).

On the other hand, Chinese people share reciprocal warm feelings towards "the Beautiful County" (*měiguó*), as the United States is commonly known in China. Even though there are some difficulties, it is clear that the Chinese people feel much closer to the United States compared to other western countries, say other members

---

[40] *Editor's note: Though this paper was first drafted a couple of years ago, the insights it provides remain thought-provoking and meaningful. The reader may approach this essay with their own interpretation of the term "intellectual" to describe an individual. As the author clarified after completing his draft, "In the traditional way of thinking, the so-called six arts of an intellectual include both writing, thinking, physical training, singing, painting and other skills that are not so typically termed academic. In general, I think to be educated means [to be] an intellectual, no matter in what subject." - K.P.*

in the G7. The Chinese public generally views Americans as frank, jolly, and affable. Moreover, Chinese Christians feel deeply indebted for American churches' love towards China, as displayed in two centuries' work and sacrifice. Considering how global churches develop now, we therefore naturally expect that when the most vibrant Christian community in the West and one of the largest and most vital Christian communities in the East work hand in hand in the twenty-first century, great things could happen. Indeed, many are convinced this is what God intends.

However, for such close collaboration to be possible and effective, we need to enhance our mutual understanding greatly. After living almost seven years in the United States, I am keenly aware of how deeply we misunderstand each other and how costly it is (Gu, 2013). In this essay, I want to analyze the unusual influx of well-educated Chinese, or Chinese intellectuals (*zhishi fenzi*), into Chinese churches since the early 1990s. My contention is that one of the reasons Chinese intellectuals were the most difficult section in Chinese society to reach with the Gospel was due to two millennia of entrenchment in Confucianism and a symbiotic relationship with the state (Brockey, 2007; Charbonnier, 2007; Standaert, 2001). As the Communist Party of China (CPC) established the People's Republic of China (PRC), Chinese intellectuals tried to replace Confucianism with Communism and establish a new cooperative relationship with the regime. However, such efforts met a tragic fate due to Mao's personal leadership style and his Machiavellian political movements, culminating in the Culture Revolution. When order was restored and more open, reformist policies were established by Deng Xiaoping, Chinese intellectuals recovered their dashed hope and actively engaged in nation-building led by two strong reform-minded governments from 1982 to 1989.

Given that Deng openly threw his backing to political reform, intellectuals felt increasingly secured in their relationship with the CPC and emboldened to voice out their concerns and demands. Several student movements broke out from 1986 to 1987 but were largely appeased by then CPC general secretary Hu Yaobang. The Tiananmen Square Event in 1989 was both historically inevitable, due to conflict between reform and conservative forces inside of the CPC, and accidental, due to many misjudgments and rash actions on both sides. However, the use of violent force to put down the demonstrations caused great psychological trauma to that generation of Chinese intellectuals, forcing many of them to abandon the desire to reconstitute a symbiotic relationship with the current regime. This single event, coupled with the increasing economic power provided in economic reform and the force of globalization, pulled Chinese intellectuals away from the state. As an exception in two millennia, Chinese intellectuals did not bind themselves with the official ideology or the state due to necessity or desire. Compared to the highly ideological Confucianism, Chinese intellectuals now fell into a "reluctant pragmatism," limiting their efforts in gaining utilitarian goals because other ends were impossible or too costly.

This "reluctant pragmatism" was insufferable for many, who in turn sought viable alternatives, of which Christian faith was one. Some only flirted with Christianity, but many committed. Their influx into Chinese churches has already caused qualitative changes in church composition, leadership, theology, and involvement in society. Looking forward, social forces will continue to favor their pulling away from the state and open doors for evangelistic opportunities among them and associated groups. Chinese churches and their partners, particularly in America, should take this historic opportunity and use it to maximum advantage for God's global kingdom in the twenty-first century.

### Confucianism and Its Symbiotic Relationship with the State

Current Chinese culture is defined by the two-and-a-half millennia dominance of Confucianism. Our history is written by generations of Confucian scholars, our heroes and villains are judged by Confucian values, and the Chinese language has been primarily used to convey Confucian ideas. Of course, any ideology, if applied effectively to a large group of people for a long period, must possess substantial pragmatic value. On the one hand, Confucianism has proved to be one of the most pragmatically effective ideologies in human history. Its continuous dominance in China and East Asia is unparalleled. Confucianism's evident pragmatic success, coupled with its lack of Greek-style metaphysical debates, prompts some observers to label Confucianism as pragmatic. However, judged by its history and teaching, Confucianism is overwhelmingly ideological.

First, while Confucius was alive and teaching, he was not successful at all, and his teaching was only one of the many teachings. Confucianism would not be systematically applied until six centuries after Confucius' death, and even then, its legitimacy was highly contested. Confucius and his acolytes were viewed as hopeless idealists in their lifetime and for many centuries after.

Second, what Confucius sought was the truth or logos (*dao*), the restoration of ancient rites (*zhouli*), and obedience to the five constants (*merica*): benevolence, righteousness, proper rites, knowledge, and integrity (*ren, yi, li, zhi, xin*). His concern was primarily for these unchangeable principles, which, for him, originated from heaven (*tian*) and were fully exhibited in the *Zhou* dynasty.

Third, since the second century A.D., the most important modification of Confucianism happened in the Song dynasty in the 12$^{th}$ century, when Neo-Confucianism was born. Neo-Confucianism instilled the old system with many insights from Taoism and Buddhism, putting special emphasis on *li*. *Li* was the immutable principle that the whole universe was created by, which both natural and the human worlds had in common. The highest goal of an intellectual was to understand and practice this *li*, until reaching the final consummation, "union between heaven and person" (*tian ren he yi*) and becoming a saint (*shengren*). In sum, the major founders and reformers of Confucianism and their core teachings are without a doubt highly ideological.

One characteristic of being ideological is the conservative tendency of refusing to change in a changed environment. Confucianism's strong grip over Chinese intellectuals despite disastrous consequences was best illustrated in the painful transformation of China into a modern nation from 1842 to the middle twentieth century (Hsü, 2000). The first opium war from 1839 to 1842 humiliated the Qing, the heavenly dynasty (*tianchao*). With merely four thousand troops, later increased to ten thousand, the British army obliterated the pre-modernly equipped, corrupt, and poorly commanded Qing army. The foolishness and groundless audacity of the ruling elites of Qing was painfully exposed. But nobody exhibited a shred of doubt about Confucianism. For them, the problem was the lack of modern machinery, particularly weaponry.

Thus began the so-called Westernization Movement (*Yangwu Yundong*) from 1861 to 1895, led mostly by powerful and open-minded Confucian governors. One of the guiding principles in this process was "Chinese learning as essence, and western learning as application" (*zhongxue wei ti, xixue wei yong*), as advocated by one of its major leaders, Shanxi governor Zhang Zhidong. The pro-reform governors, who had deep concern for their country and were willing to do anything to strengthen it, were practical, capable, rational, intellectual, and entrepreneurial, and ranked among the most impressive leaders in Chinese history. The fact that it never crossed their minds that Confucianism itself might require a radical reform shows how strong Confucianism as an ideology was (金觀濤, 1988; 金觀濤&刘青峰, 1989; 金觀濤&刘青峰, 1993; 金觀濤&刘青峰, 2000).

These reformers' failure to critique Confucianism itself was inevitably exposed in another brief and disastrous war, the Sino-Japanese war, from 1894 to 1895. Among many shocking revelations of this catastrophe, an urgency to change the mode of governance reached a tilting point, resulting in the failed Wushu Reform in 1898. In 1911, a surprisingly successful revolution easily overthrew the vast Qing dynasty. However, even at this point, the intellectuals were not ready to abandon Confucianism, but focused only on a change of government. It would take another decade to tip the balance. In the 1919 New Culture Movement, some open-minded intellectuals engineered a nationwide assault directly on Confucianism, introducing democracy and science (*de xiansheng, sai xiansheng*) to the Chinese public. But their influence was limited to a small group of intellectuals and some urban citizens. For the vast rural side—more than 90% of the population—the rudimentary Confucian teachings and ethics would not be shaken until the cultural revolution in 1966.

Confucianism tenaciously gripped Chinese minds and extended long after the 1911 revolution. One revealing example was Mao Zedong's continual fight with his own CPC cadres against dogmatism. In 1930, Mao published a work translated as, "Anti-Bookishism" (*Fandui Benben Zhuyi*), arguing against the tendency to adhere to theories learned from books instead of letting field research and practical results dictate which theories to follow (Mao, 1966). In 1937, Mao published *On Practice* (*merica lun*) (毛泽东, 1975; Mao, 1973). Mao's main target in this work was dogmatism (*jiaotiao meric*), the tendency to hold on to dogmatic teachings regardless of the practical results. This was no doubt a struggle against two millennia of ideologically conditioned Chinese minds. Even though quickly enshrined in formal CPC orthodoxy, Mao's teaching on pragmatism never truly changed the CPC, and, ironically, Mao's own teachings were held as new dogmas.

Mao's true disciple on pragmatism was Deng Xiaoping, who popularized the so-called Cat Theory: "It doesn't matter whether the cat is black or white. It is a good cat if it can catch mice" (邓小平, 1989). Deng published this in 1962, and it was one reason for his downfall in the Cultural Revolution (靳志柏, 1976). Eventually, Deng fought back and successfully overrode ideological concerns of the party elders with his pragmatic approach.

Old trees have deep roots. Two thousand years of Confucianism gave Chinese intellectuals a strong ideological tendency to hold on to beliefs regardless of practicality. One of their beliefs is that an intellectual's public function is to "serve the state." The foundational documents for Confucianism are the "Four Books," the shortest of which is *Great Learning* (Legge, 1991). Its first sentence is known as the "three ultimate goals" or the vision for Confucian intellectuals: "The ultimate goals of great learning are to manifest true virtue, to transform the people, to reach perfect goodness" (Legge, 1991). Then it gives the "eight steps" to achieve these goals. These steps are: to observe and investigate this world, in order to increase one's knowledge, to purify one's motive, to correct one's will and mind, to establish one's character, to manage one's family and clan well, to govern one's country well, and finally to "manifest the true virtue" (Legge, 1991).

These eight steps are in sequence, covering the ways of gaining knowledge, personal integrity, family, country and the truth. It is a grand vision for life succinctly expressed. These eight steps are not just for intellectuals, but for everyone "from the emperor to the commoner." The Confucian intellectuals should educate and exemplify them. The first five steps are about the person himself. The sixth step is about his family and clan. In today's terminology, the first six steps are all about one's private life. The final step is about the transcendent truth. The only thing that this person needs to contribute to the public is to "govern the country." Therefore, according to the Confucian teachings, all personal study, discipline, and one's family are for the purpose serving the state well. Later, this dictum summarizes the two most important things a Confucian intellectual does, "to study and to govern" (*dúshū zuòguān*). In sum, Confucianism binds an intellectual's personal achievement and life goals with the welfare of the state.

The Confucian intellectual's relationship with the state, culminated in loyalty to the emperor. However, this relationship was not one of complete submission because Confucian intellectuals believed that the only way to serve the state well was through holding on to Confucianism. Therefore, sometimes, the most loyal thing to do was to speak against the emperor's will and hold to the true Confucian teachings. Many Confucian intellectuals were humiliated, demoted, and killed—sometimes with their entire families. These are the martyrs and heroes of Confucianism.

This intriguing submission yet independent relationship between the Chinese intellectuals and the emperor was one of most delicate and important political relationships in Chinese courts, because almost all officials were educated in Confucianism. For power, for conscience, or for both, the tensions and struggles in this relationship were often at the heart of the most crucial political events in Chinese history. On the one hand, the relationship between Chinese intellectuals and the ruling family was symbiotic, one providing political status, economic rewards, and state-enforced ideological monopoly, while the other providing ideological justification for the royal family and administrative technocrats. On the other hand, their relationship was one of mutual constraint, with the intelligentsia restricting the emperor's insatiable desire to gain unlimited power, and the emperor restraining any tendencies toward establishing a Confucianist "theocracy." Because both sides found it advantageous to be cooperative, whenever possible the Confucian officials would work with the emperor.

In sum, as an adherent of a highly politically aligned ideology, the ideal Confucian intellectual had only one occupation: as an official serving the state. As a group, Chinese intellectuals before 1911 were never independent from the state socially, economically, or ideologically; neither did they want to be. Indeed, they despised those who renounced the responsibility of serving the state. Whenever possible, Chinese intellectuals wished to contribute to the state, and many of them viewed themselves as the rightful guardians of proper state functioning. It was only when this became impossible from totally incompetent leadership or brutal oppression that Chinese intellectuals would retreat to personal pursuit of philosophy, arts, and live a semi-hermit life. During those times, Taoism and Buddhism (particularly Zen) were often their preferences.

As the People's Republic of China was established in 1949, Chinese intellectuals in general welcomed the new regime wholeheartedly, trying to accommodate whatever position they had to hold with the new orthodoxy, Communism. They genuinely participated in the CPC-led nation-building effort and attempted to craft a new symbiotic relationship with the CPC. Very few would have anticipated the tragic fate and profound disappointment ahead. This combination of hope and disappointment was one major factor that eventually set Chinese intellectuals free from their bond with the state.

### Two Attempts to Collaborate with the CPC and 1989

The communist regime initially enjoyed an amicable relationship with the intellectuals. Mao himself was an accomplished poet and writer. Compared to the rigidity and corruption of his opponents from the 1930s to the early 1950s, Mao stood out as a better choice for many educated Chinese intellectuals. With the traditional sense of political responsibility and facing the new reality of the CPC's rule, most Chinese intellectuals genuinely wished to be integrated into or work with the communist system. Many, even some of the best of them, tried very hard to understand, collaborate, and devote themselves to communism and the whims of Mao while maintaining some level of intellectual independence or integrity. However, this relationship gradually deteriorated after the mid-1950s, primarily due to the CPC's many attempts to gain total control of this group. Mao's personal leadership style and his Machiavellian political means, culminating in the Cultural Revolution, played a major role.

We mentioned that Confucianism taught Chinese intellectuals to serve the state whenever possible. But it also taught them that the only way to serve the state well was through holding on to the teachings of Confucianism. Therefore, it required Chinese intellectuals to maintain some level of independence, particularly intellectual and even ideological independence. While most intellectuals were eager to work with the CPC, this did not mean they would always say or do what the party instructed. Surprised, disappointed, and later angered on both sides, Mao was convinced that the intellectuals as a group were unhelpful, even subversive, to his nation-building project, and in need of "reeducation by the workers, farmers, and soldiers." This conclusion ensured the tragic fate of many intellectuals during the tumultuous Culture Revolution.

But the Cultural Revolution did not extinguish Chinese intellectuals' desire to contribute to the state. Like ancient intellectuals who were disappointed by foolish emperors (*hūnjūn*), this generation of Chinese intellectuals yearned for a "wise emperor (*míngjūn*)." They held fast and waited for a better time. In 1976, Mao died. In 1977, Deng was reinstalled and became the de-facto leader starting in December 1978. In 1980, Deng published an important speech, promoting political reform in the party and state (邓小平, 1980). In 1982 when reform-minded Hu Yaobang became the general secretary of the CPC, his reform-leaning policies further encouraged intellectuals and particularly students to participate and voice their opinions. But Hu's aggressive economic reform plans, anti-corruption effort towards princelings, and tolerance of student dissent gradually depleted Deng's confidence in Hu. After a wave of student movements from 1986 to 1987, he was demoted. Hu nevertheless retained his position in the Politburo,[41] and he was succeeded by Zhao Ziyang, also a reform-minded leader, who would retain this position until June 1989. The general open-mindedness of CPC policies during the 1980s and Deng's efforts to reform gave great hope to many intellectuals in meaningfully contributing to China's nation-building. After more than two decades of chaos and catastrophe in Mao's later rule, most Chinese intellectuals and the general public were greatly encouraged by the

---

[41] The highest authority within the Communist Party of China, typically has seven members.

reform and believed great progress on different fronts could be achieved. This optimism was one major reason why so many students dared to protest in the first place, which would be unthinkable in Mao's day. It was also precisely the reason Chinese intellectuals' disappointment towards the party-state was so profound after 1989.

Before our discussion of 1989 and its impact, it is important to know that the students who participated in this movement were *not* independent from the CPC; they were mostly responsible participants or stakeholders in the reform led by the CPC in the 1980s. During the 1980s, Chinese college students were one of the most prestigious groups in Chinese society. In 1977, the national college entrance exam was reinstituted in China. Among 5.7 million exam-takers, only 5% were accepted by colleges. From 1977 to 1988, there were a total 5.18 million of students admitted into college-level institutions from a total population of 1.1 billion in 1988. In that same year, the percentage of the college-level educated population in China was about 0.51%. Not only were college students numerically few, but they were treated as the future leaders for the nation and the CPC. College education was fully funded by the government until 1988. The CPC provided all tuition plus a stipend. Moreover, after graduation, all jobs were assigned through the government. Competition for a college graduate was fierce among different departments who recruited their new laborers through central planning committees. Therefore, college students typically had a number of choices, most of which provided much better compensation and benefits than available to the general public. In this period, almost no college graduates went into the private sector. Socioeconomically, they were the privileged group. Politically, college students in 1980s were the upcoming leaders for CPC's nation building effort. College students themselves also generally had a sense of ownership in the state. China was "their" China. This sense of responsibility helped propel students to protest against corruption, bureaucracy, and the leftist policy of some party leaders.

On April 15, 1989, the highly respected and reform-leaning former general secretary of the CPC, Hu Yaobang, passed away. In remembrance of him, students in Beijing began to protest for political reform for clean, open, and efficient governance. The number of protesters in Beijing grew to one million at one time and spread to hundreds of other cities. In these protests, undergraduate students were the main constituents, joined by other citizens. The leaders were mostly, if not all, students and professors.

The fate of the student movement in 1989 hinged on Deng. In a sense, the reform in the 1980s was what Deng had intended to do in the early 1950s. After wasting many years of his life in the Cultural Revolution, Deng used his position and influence to make as much progress as possible in 1980s. He supported Hu's and Zhao's efforts to reform and endured much pressure from the conservative senior leaders. However, for Deng, who spent most of his prime years fighting various battles, political stability—namely the CPC's solid control of China—was foundational. Therefore, in Deng's eyes, Zhao's failure in negotiating with students and his reluctance to use force showed Zhao as weak and unfit to lead China. Running out of patience, Deng decided to intervene directly. In early June 1989, the military effortlessly crushed poorly organized students and other protesters, and a nationwide purge of participants ensued. From that time until his death, Deng would firmly defend economic reform, but would never talk about political reform again in public. This use of force proved to all dissidents that the CPC would not hesitate to use force. However, in the long run, by choosing violence instead of a peaceful solution, the CPC lost significant support from intellectuals and pushed them to find an ideology outside of the current party-state system.

What happened in 1989 suggested to many intellectuals that their efforts would be fruitless and that their wishes were doesn't. Most students and observers were astonished by the brutal force employed by the CPC. This surprising turn crushed the young idealists' optimism and threw that generation into depression. After the shedding of blood, they knew through experience that any political reform not initiated from the very top was unwelcome, and attempts to achieve semi-independent participation were dangerous.

Such pessimism in turn forced Chinese intellectuals to renounce their responsibility to serve the state as partners (Weatherley, 2006). It was with this motivation that in early 1990s a sizable portion of Chinese intellectuals resigned from their state-given positions and went to engage in private economic endeavors. After all, if serving the state became impossible, why not spend the time and energy on self-interests? In that sense, this generation of Chinese intellectuals were forced into a "reluctant pragmatism." However, such "reluctant pragmatism" was not a happy place to be. To renounce the right of political involvement was especially frustrating for Chinese intellectuals, because traditional Confucian ideology held that "to serve the state" was the intellectuals' primary function. When Confucianism and communism lost their grasp on their minds and loyalty, Chinese intellectuals became ideologically and spiritually homeless.

### The Homeless Chinese Intellectuals: 1990 to the Present

Most Chinese intellectuals faithfully collaborated with dynasty after dynasty in the name of Confucianism for two thousand years, then paid a great price in attempting to establish a collaborative relationship with the CPC. What the CPC required was nothing less than total submission, which was difficult for many of them. Betrayed and shocked by the state that Chinese intellectuals attempted so hard to love, a generation of Chinese intellectuals therefore attempted to find an alternative (Salemink, 2012). Many of them began to engage in economic enterprises in the 1990s (*xiàhǎi*), pursuing material gains to alleviative their ideological loss. Feeling no responsibility to serve the state anymore and emboldened by sudden wealth, hedonism was a natural choice for many and a cause of the current rampant corruption.

Alienated and disenfranchised from the state, in the 1990s, Chinese intellectuals began to ask: where is my spiritual home? Some fell into cynicism and lost trust for any lofty talk of ideals and morality. Some became pessimistic and suicidal and gravitated toward the teachings of Buddhism or nihilistic philosophers such as Arthur Schopenhauer. Still others were intrigued by mystic experience and devoted their time and resources to esoteric Buddhism, Taoism, cults, and new forms of *Qigong*. *Qigong* was an ancient training method for gaining health, spirituality, and martial arts through the coordination of body movements, breathing, and meditation. This fad started in the 1980s and gained significant momentum in the 1990s. In the early 1990s, many new forms of *Qigong* were created by new masters. Their communal practice, promise of physical health, and desperately needed moral teaching attracted many followers, even among intellectuals and high government officials. The most famous of these new forms is Falun Gong. Though it only started in 1992, by 1999 Falun Gong claimed 90 million practitioners in mainland China, including many party members, scientists, and professors.

Still others began to explore Christianity, but in some unexpected ways. Since 1842, Chinese intellectuals have always been the most nationalistic segment in Chinese society. They resented foreign imperialism and the humiliation of China in the last two centuries. Because of their nationalistic sentiment, many of them have viewed Christianity as a tool of western imperialism. As early as the 1920s, a group of famous intellectuals led a nationwide Anti-Christian Movement (from 1922 to 1927). Ever since the PRC was established, the pejorative idea of religions as an "opiate of the masses" became orthodox. Even in the 1990s, to say there is anything good from Christianity was still a hard sell to intellectuals.

However, beginning in the early 1990s "cultural Christians," led by professor Liu Xiaofeng, successfully established themselves as a meaningful conversation partner in Chinese academia through translation of Christian thinkers' works. These young Chinese intellectuals began to promote Christian culture openly in China while simultaneously rejecting the fundamental Christian faith commitment. They never built a strong tie with established Christian churches: some of them were involved in churches while others were not, and the Chinese churches as a whole did not view them as speaking for Christianity. As a group, their relationship with Christian faith has been characterized by a flirtation rather than a serious commitment.

But some intellectuals were not satisfied with such superficial encounters with the Christian faith; they wanted to dive deeply into it. Many Chinese church leaders and observers recognized that since the early 1990s, large numbers of Chinese intellectuals had begun to accept the Christian faith. Many of them were educated in the very best institutions in China and had a bright future in society, yet decided to devote themselves to ministry at a young age. Before that, almost all Chinese churches were full of elderly, sick, female, and uneducated believers. But after the 1990s, young, well-educated—and later professional—people began to join the church in major cities and quickly rose to leadership roles due to their commitment to faith, better education, and a prime age fitting for ministry. Among the house church leaders I know in Beijing now, the vast majority of them became Christians in the early 1990s. Many of them have a nationwide reputation now. For Chinese churches, these new leaders have already brought profound changes many areas, such as preaching, church management, evangelistic methods, theological education, social participation, collaboration with Western churches, cross-cultural missions, and cultural participation. Under their leadership, Chinese intellectuals, professionals, and even government officials have been drawn into the churches at an accelerating speed.

It is not just external sociopolitical conditions that pushed these intellectuals to try the Christian faith. In and of itself, Christianity has several unique advantages in attracting Chinese intellectuals as compared to other alternatives. First, Christianity is a comprehensive faith that easily embraces all of life, ranging from mystical experience to active political engagement, from other-worldly supernatural phenomena to mundane daily life. In its comprehensiveness, Christianity resembles Confucianism, especially its Neo-Confucianism strand. By comparison, Buddhism and Taoism perform well in the mystic and otherworldly realms, yet have limited engagement with daily life. Second, the Christian faith has a proven record in inspiring highly acclaimed cultural, economic, and political achievements. New cults, theories, and *Qigong* have no historical bases to back their claim for truth. Third, Christianity is a cosmopolitan, global faith, starting from ancient civilization and leaving footprints on all continents. In this regard, only Islam and Buddhism can compete. However, Buddhism is confined to East Asia and lacks new scholars to produce new theories and practical guidelines for its followers in the modern world. Islam has made some progress in China but is limited mostly to the ten ethnic minority groups who are traditionally Muslim.[42] Fourth, even though Christians can fully engage in philosophical and theoretical discussions and produce outstanding academic work, Christianity is not just a philosophy or theory but a faith. Other philosophical traditions or social theories—such as Darwinism, communism, democracy, or libertarianism—if not elevated to a semi-religious level, cannot demand

---

[42] There are many reasons for the difficulty of the Han Chinese to embrace Islam. For example, Islam's dietary ban on pork alone poses serious difficulty for the mass conversion of Han Chinese, who generally view pork as indispensable to their diet.

the same level of commitment from its believer. These internal traits of Christianity, coupled with external forces, successfully attract a good number of Chinese intellectuals to commit to Christian faith. Of course, even though not explicitly mentioned, God is by no means excluded from this equation. I and many of my fellow Christians believe that God's will is ultimately at work behind all these forces.

## Into the Future

If we dare to peek into the future, we may surmise that three significant trajectories will continually push Chinese intellectuals to distance themselves from the party-state. Domestically, the growing size of the economically independent middle class will likely strengthen the intellectuals' independence from the party-state. Pundits are amazed by the rapid growth of the Chinese middle-class (Li, 2010; 2014), and some predict that China will have the largest middle-class population in the world by 2030 (Kharas & Gertz, 2010; Barton, et al., 2013). This economic independence and power will significantly boost the intellectual independence and power of the middle class. Economic freedom supports personal liberty and freedom.

Confucian social stratification recognizes four classes: intellectuals/officials, peasants, artisans, and merchants (*shi, mer, mer, shāng*), among whom the merchants are the lowest. Traditional Confucian intellectuals despised private economic endeavors and depended on the land, over which the state had total control. Their dependence on the state economically further tied them with the state politically. As more Chinese become economically independent, they will be less restrained by the state and therefore empowered to express their ideas. For example, many Chinese Christian parents are not happy with the state-run schools. Previously, they had no other choices. But now, many of them can afford to send their children abroad to attend graduate schools, colleges, high schools, or even elementary schools. Or, as is happening in many major cities, when a few families put their resources together, they can start their own private education. Mushrooming Christian private kindergartens and elementary schools in recent years have amazed many educators.

Another important domestic element to consider is the continual economic, social, and political reconfiguration in China, which ensures much unpredictability in the next few decades. This unpredictability will increase the demand for faith to sustain hope in this turbulent age. Economically, the state-owned enterprises, financial sectors, hukou system (the residency registration system that the state uses to control the distribution of social welfare), sustainable energy and environment, taxation and social security system, geographic inequality, and many other problems all demand further and deeper economic reforms. Socially, the force of urbanization will drive continual social adjustment. Chinese urban dwellers grew from 20% in 1990 to 56% in 2015 and are projected to reach over 70% as late as 2050, but that percent could come much earlier. Until then, the Chinese social structure will continue in a fluid state. The last and probably most difficult element is political reform. Externally, the CPC recognizes that a renewed popular support and legitimization for one-party rule is desperately needed for the long-term stability of China. Internally, the CPC needs a more stable power transfer mechanism that could be supported by most of its own members. Before the CPC figures out solutions and successfully implements them, the power structure in China would be unstable. In a time of so much unpredictability, faith in general—and Christian faith in particular—is much needed.

Internationally, the force of globalization will pull many Chinese intellectuals to think globally instead of nationally. By globalization, I mean the tendency of further integration and interdependence of culture, economy, and security on a global scale. This global integration will not be smooth or easy, but it is unavoidable. Like it or not, globalization will further limit the independence of nations, making nationalism much more costly. As a big country and major beneficiary of globalization, the general mood in China is pro-globalization. This will push more and more Chinese to think and act as cosmopolitan citizens, thereby further pulling them away from sole allegiance to the party-state (Brødsgaard, 2014).

Finally, the CPC as the ruling party in China undoubtedly will have a huge impact on Chinese intellectuals. As mentioned, the major challenge for the CPC is how to create a sustainable internal mechanism for power transfer and a sustainable justification of one-party rule with broad support from the Chinese public. Contrary to viewpoints of many western observers, I suspect that the CPC could figure this out (Plate, 2014; Irvine, 2016). The possible outcomes for the CPC fall along a spectrum. The worst would be some sort of Western-style democratic system in appearance but de-facto one-party rule, (e.g. Singapore.) And the best would be to create an ideologically and structurally unique system in China. In the past five years, the CPC led by Xi Jinping clearly aimed at the latter. The tightened political control, the emphasis on the CPC's absolute power, the "re-ideologizing" of the party, and further restraint on unofficial ideologies all point to serious effort to create a unique Chinese system. However, the lack of creativity in official ideology poses the most serious challenge to this effort, particularly when many intellectuals have already been alienated and are not ready to engage in such government-led efforts. The CPC has to produce an appealing new ideology to attract and convince Chinese intellectuals to realign with its political agenda. Right now, nationalism seems to be the only viable option. That is why the "Chinese dream" and the "revival of Chinese civilization" are the official talking points at this time.

Nevertheless, nationalism alone could not carry the CPC much further for two reasons. First, nationalism is at odds with globalization. Even if the CPC can successfully use nationalism as a banner to consolidate its support among Chinese, this nationalism will inevitably be a diluted version and must assume some cosmopolitan characteristics. China cannot be for China alone. Second, nationalism does not automatically justify the CPC. The nation of China and the CPC are two separate entities. Even though the CPC attempts to equate the CPC with the nation whenever possible with slogans such as "to love the nation is to love the CPC, and vice-versa," such logic will face increasing difficulty as the CPC's interests differ from public interests. Rampant corruption is a constant reminder to the public about this difference. Without significant political reform, this party/state narrative is not sustainable. The CPC cannot rely on nationalism alone but must create something unique that is persuasive enough to the public, particularly the Chinese intellectuals.

In sum, these forces will continue to pull the Chinese intellectuals away from the state. Of course, a lot of intellectuals are collaborating with the CPC and will continue to do so. And as the memory of the tragic events from the Cultural Revolution and 1989 gradually subsides, the CPC will be more likely to convince young intellectuals to work with the party-state. However, many intellectuals are suspicious of the regime. Empowered by their increasing economic power and many more available options provided by globalization, they prefer to find a new home independent of the party-state. Christianity now has the golden opportunity to win the hearts of many Chinese intellectuals, a rare chance since the first Nestorian missionary arrived in Chang'an in A.D. 638.

## A Few Suggestions for Ministry

I have shown that Chinese intellectuals are rooted in two thousand years of Confucian tradition. Confucianism shapes Chinese intellectuals in a highly ideological fashion, including the conviction that their public function is to serve the state. Based on such convictions, Chinese intellectuals as a community in general have successfully maintained a collaborative relationship with different dynasties over two millennia. As Communism replaced Confucianism as the official ideology and the PRC replaced the feudal imperialistic dynasties, Chinese intellectuals tried to establish a similar relationship with the CPC. The CPC also tried to woo the intellectuals. The results of such efforts, however, were disappointing and somehow surprising to both sides. The last tragic event was the forceful crackdown on the student movement in 1989. Such coercive methods, along with the diminishing effectiveness of the CPC's official ideology, pushed Chinese intellectuals away from the state.

Now, for perhaps the first time in two millennia, the majority of Chinese intellectuals have no desire, no responsibility, and no necessity to serve the state. By historical coincidence or the hand of God, they were thrown into a "reluctant pragmatism," a homeless state for many of them. As they are forced to look for a new home, the Christian faith stands out as a better choice for many as compared to other alternatives. Since the early 1990s, a sizable number of Chinese intellectuals have either flirted with or committed to Christian faith. Their influx has already profoundly changed the Chinese church. Looking into the future, I believe these factors will continually pull Chinese intellectuals away from the party-state, thus providing a golden historic opportunity to win many of them to the Christian faith.

For those who do ministry with the Chinese, I would like suggest a few thoughts. First, be patient and optimistic. Chinese intellectuals in our time are a proud, nationalistic, and cynical group, not the easiest people with whom to discuss faith. Frequently, as someone tries to share the Gospel with them, they ask blunt and difficult questions. However, in light of Chinese church history, for Chinese intellectuals to even consider Christianity is already a miracle in itself. It took the tragic experiences of the Cultural Revolution and 1989 for many of them to shift their eyes away from serving the state. We must be patient with them, be confident that our Christian faith indeed provides what they so desperately seek, and demonstrate it. It just takes some time for them to see it.

Second, a few talking points could be helpful. Christianity's comprehensiveness is capable of providing interpretation and guidance to all aspects of life, which would be intriguing to many. Our proven record of inspiring great cultural, social, and economic achievements debunks the idea that Christianity is just another superstition or an "opiate" to weaken believers' will. Emphasizing the cosmopolitan characteristics of Christianity would better serve the Chinese intellectuals in this global age. And, finally, it would be unwise to follow the liberal tendency to demystify or make our faith seem like just another ideology or theory. The faith commitment of more conservative believers is powerful in attracting many Chinese intellectuals.

My last suggestion is to encourage Chinese Christian intellectuals to use their minds and creativity to serve the church. Chinese churches since 1990 have made tremendous progress due to the influx of many talented people. I listed eight areas in which they have already contributed significantly. Take just one area, cultural participation, as an example. In our own church, we have begun to see Christian bands and music groups formed, producing high quality music, albums, videos, and concerts. We also have a group of painters, photographers, and calligraphers that produce faith-related art. These works are routinely displayed in our facilities and put on auction every few months to raise funds for ministry or charity. We have a media team producing daily Bible exposition videos and recording and distributing our sermons, seminars, events, and testimonies. There are also writers, journalists, and professors in our midst who engage in online or traditional publication. Recently, we began to see movie and TV producers, actors and actresses, and singers among us, some of whom are attempting faith-related works. Remember, I am only talking about their works in one area within one church. The great changes that are going on among Chinese churches are mostly unrecognized because they happen so quickly. As we continue to attract more Chinese intellectuals into our faith, it is crucial that we intentionally encourage them to use their God-given gifts, sanctified in God's truth, to express their faith and share the Gospel. To create truly contextualized ministry methods and Chinese theology may depend on how successfully these Chinese Christian intellectuals are able to use their gifts for Christ.

Apart from historical reasons, American churches have another huge advantage in serving Chinese intellectuals at this time. According to one recent study, in 2015, there were more than 304,040 Chinese students in American higher education institutions, and they are growing in number (Center on Religion and Chinese Society, 2016). They are here not just because of private motivations, but also because the sovereign God wants them to be. And I am convinced that God wants Christians to engage them too.

## References

Barton, D., Chen, Y., & Jin, A. (2013, June). Mapping China's middle class. *McKinsey Quarterly*, Retrieved from: http://www.mckinsey.com/industries/retail/our-insights/mapping-chinas-middle-class

Brockey, L. M.. (2007). *Journey to the east: The jesuit mission to China, 1579–1724*. Cambridge, MA: Belknap Press of Harvard University Press.

Brødsgaard, K. E.. (2014). Globalization and public sector reform in China. In K. E.Brødsgaard (Ed.), *Globalization and Public Sector Reform in China* (pp. 1–22). London: Routledge.

Center on Religion and Chinese Society. (Novermber, 2016). *Purdue survey of Chinese students in the United States*. Retrived from: https://www.purdue.edu/crcs/wp-content/uploads/2016/11/CRCS-Report-of-Chinese-Students-in-the-US_Final-Version.pdf

Charbonnier, J.. (2007). *Christians in China: A.D. 600 to 2000*. San Francisco, CA: Ignatius Press.

Gu, M. (2013). *Sinologism: An alternative to orientalism and postcolonialism*. New York: Routledge.

Hsü, I. C. Y. (2000). *The Rise of Modern China* (6th ed.). New York: Oxford University Press.

Irvine, R. (2016). *Forecasting China's future: Dominance or collapse?*. New York: Routledge.

Kharas, H. & Gertz, G. (2010). The new global middle class: A crossover from west to east. In C. Li (Ed.), *China's emerging middle class: Beyond economic transformation* (pp. 32-54). Washington, D.C.: Brookings Institution Press.

Legge, J. (1991). *The Chinese classics: With a translation, critical and exegetical notes, prolegomena, and copious indexes.* 台北市: 南天書局.

Li, C. (2010). Introduction: The Rise of the Middle Class in the Middle Kingdom. In Cheng Li (Ed.), *China's emerging middle class: Beyond economic transformation* (pp. 3-31). Washington, D.C.: Brookings Institution Press, 2010.

Li, C. (2014). A profile of the middle classes in today's China. In H. M. Hsiao (Ed.), *Chinese middle classes: Taiwan, Hong Kong, Macao and China* (pp. 78-94). New York: Routledge.

Mao, Z. (1966). *Oppose Book Worship* (May, 1930). Peking: Foreign Languages Press.

Mao, Z. (1973). *Über die Praxis.* Berlin: Red.-Kollektiv d. Roten Garde.

Mao, Z. (1981). *On contradiction: An annotated translation of the pre-liberation text* (Nick Knight, Trans.). Nathan, Australia: School of Modern Asian Studies, Griffith University.

Plate, T. (2014). *In the middle of China's future: What two decades of worldwide newspaper columns prefigure about the future of the China-U.S. relationship.* Singapore: Marshall Cavendish International (Asia).

Pomfret, J. (2016). *The beautiful country and the middle kingdom: America and China, 1776 to the present.* New York: Henry Holt and Company.

Salemink, O. (2012). Is protestant conversion a form of protest? Urban and upland protestants in southeast Asia. In J. Bautista & F. Khek Gee Lim (Eds.), *Christianity and the state in Asia: Complicity and conflict* (pp. 36-58). London: Routledge.

Standaert, N. (2001). Christianity in late Ming and early Qing China as a case of cultural transmission. In S. Uhalley & X. Wu (Eds.), *China and Christianity: Burdened past, hopeful future* (pp. 81-116). Armonk, NY: M.E. Sharpe.

Weatherley, R. (2006). *Politics in China since 1949: Legitimizing authoritarian rule.* New York, NY: Routledge.

吕实强. (2011). 近代中国知识分子反基督教问题论文集. 桂林: 广西师范大学出版社.

毛泽东. (1975). 实践论: 论认识和实践的关系–知和行的关系: 1937年7月. 北京: 人民出版社.

毛泽东. (1977). 矛盾论. 北京: 民族出版社.

邓小平. (August, 1980). 党和国家领导制度的改革. Paper presented at 中共中央政治局扩大会议, 北京.

邓小平. (1989). 怎样恢复农业生产（一九六二年七月七日）. in 邓小平文选:1938-1965年. 北京: 人民出版社.

金觀濤. (1988). 在歷史的表象背後: 對中國封建社會超穩定結構的探索. 台北縣新店市: 谷風.

金觀濤 and 刘青峰. (1989). 興盛與危機: 論中國封建社會的超穩定結構. 台北市: 風雲時代出版公司.

金觀濤 and 劉青峰. (1993). 開放中的變遷 : 再論中國社會超穩定結構. 香港: 中文大學出版社.

金觀濤 and 劉青峰. (2000). 中國現代思想的起源：超穩定結構與中國政治文化的演變 (第一卷). 香港: 中文大學出版社.

靳志柏. (1976). 不容抹杀社会主义和资本主义的区别——驳"白猫黑猫"论. 红旗, 4.

黃錫培. (2010). 回首百年殉道血：一九〇〇年義和團事件殉道宣教士的生命故事. Petaluma, CA: 美國中信出版社.

# 12. Key Steps on My Spiritual Path[43]

## By Wang Fei[44]

I was born in 1978, the very first year of China's one-child policy. I was destined to be the only child to my parents because my mother was a Communist Party member who was supposed to be a pioneer in the implementation of the policy. I was not as lonely in my childhood as readers might imagine. I had many playmates, including kids from my neighbors and my aunts and uncles, who were not much older than me. Looking back, now I can see this was the biggest scar in my life. It made our family fragile. My father died of throat cancer when I was completing the last year of university. Within a year of my father's death, my mother remarried a man twelve years her senior. After graduation, I worked in a city seven hours away by train from my mother's new home. I felt our family had been blown away by the wind. The old shabby house which had belonged to my father was empty. I have never visited that house since I left it. But it is still in my dreams, with the best father and mother in the world.

In recent years, for a time, I lived in the US while my mother still lived in China. Her loneliness and poor health were my all-time concerns when I was so far away from her. I imagined things could be a lot better if I had some siblings there to take care of her.

---

[43] *Editor's note: This middle-aged Chinese man offered to share a part of his life story so we could see how various people and circumstances have influenced his spiritual development. His comments are brief, but heartfelt. I trust that what he has written will still be insightful and inspirational to readers. He is an upstanding, outstanding individual, and I call myself blessed to have been entrusted with his story. - K.P.*

[44] *A pseudonym has been used to protect the identity of the contributor.*

## School Life and Atheist Education

I went to a neighborhood primary school when I was eight. I was good at language arts but horrible at math. I tried very hard to learn, but it was hopeless. Now, when I see that my son does not struggle with math, I feel so happy for him! Among all the subjects I learned at school, politics was the easiest one for me. Because my mother was a Party member, I had a lot of chances to read the Party's newspaper. The politics we studied in school centered around how glorious the Communist Party was. I knew the beautiful words to describe the Party by heart, so politics tests were easy. All we really had to do was remember answers to some questions like why the Communist Party was the only political party that could lead China to success and what the contributions of Chairman Mao were. We just had to memorize and keep repeating those answers until we finished our education. But now, I look back and see how those questions were like haunting ghosts following me through my whole school life.

Atheism is a major part of political education in China. All the students are taught to believe there are no gods in the universe and only the Party and its leaders can save China. Students are educated to be the future leaders and further constructors of a communist society. Even if they do not believe it, they simply accept the fact that what they learn in school and reality are different things. For example, in school, I was taught not to believe in God or any kind of spiritual things, which were said to be superstition. However, because my hometown was very poor when I was young, when people were ill, they could not afford to go or lacked the transportation to go to the hospital. They would have to go to a healer, like a witch doctor, for some cheap magical medicine, which usually was nothing more than paper ashes.

All Communist Party members are required to be atheists. All the important social positions like government workers, teachers, doctors and military jobs require people to be Party members. As a result, atheistic education remains very successful in the school system. I was recommended by my political teacher to become a Party member during my final year of high school because of my good grades in politics. But the whole process to become a real member stopped during my first year of university. I realized it was not what I wanted. I wanted freedom, and I wanted to explore more of the world before I could accept a certain belief. Looking back, I now believe that materialism and the pollution of our air and food is actually a result of atheistic education because Chinese atheists do not have respect for nature and pay no attention to spiritual life.

## Meeting Daughters and Sons of God

In 1998, I went to a university in a neighboring province and studied English language education. From that point on, I started to know Christian believers. All the early ones I knew were foreigners. I was amazed by their beliefs and their commitment to religion. They respected God and treated others equally, as their brothers and sisters. Sometimes, the English teachers explained their beliefs and their outlook on the world. From them, I first learned about God the Father and His Son, Jesus.

In 2002, I accepted a position to teach English back in my home province. I met more people from America who were teaching English at the same school, and I was excited to make new foreign friends. Those people had a lot in common. They were Christian believers and many of them were my age and recent graduates like me. We had a lot of time to be together. We shared our teaching experiences, and we watched each other's classes. I taught them Chinese, and they answered my English questions in return. Mutual trust between us was built on our daily life. Naturally, we started discussing our spiritual ideas as well. They listened to my thoughts, questions, and confusion about life. I listened to them talk about their love for Jesus Christ. I gained friendship, improved my English, and most importantly, I finally started to accept the existence of God and accept Jesus Christ as my life guide.

## Jesus Leads Me Out of Darkness

In 2012, after feeling restless and thinking for a long time about how to apply these new beliefs in my personal life, I decided to go out and explore the wider world. I moved to a far-off country and left my family behind in China, all in the name of trying to make a better life for them. The first few days away were so difficult for me. I stayed in a communal hotel. It was cold at night. Very soon, I went broke; I did not even have money for the simplest food! I suffered from sleeplessness. I started to talk to Jesus in my mind. I talked with him for the whole night. I talked about my life dreams, my father's death, and my worries for my family. He was such a wonderful listener, such a giver of wisdom for my life. The next day, a miracle happened. I saw a job advertisement, called the business, and got my first job there. I stayed in that area for half year before I went back to rejoin my family again. During that time, I was very happy and healthy with the blessings of Jesus. I will never forget what a sweet time of growth it was.

# 13. Americans Through a Chinese Looking Glass: How Portrayals of Western Culture and Interactions with Americans Influence Chinese Students' Perceptions of Christianity[45]

## By Lucas Tian[46]

After I gave a lecture about the influence of the Bible on Western culture at a Chinese university, a student asked a question that has been repeated many times in more than a decade of teaching in the country: "We all know that most Americans are Christians and that Christianity is about love and forgiveness," the student began. "So why are Americans fighting so many wars and why are American films and television shows so filled with sex and violence?"

I wished I had a simple answer. Given the number of times my Chinese students have over-generalized that "all Americans are Christians" and have observed that "most Americans" are overly sexual and violent and asked why "America loves war," I have often wondered if the generalizations were mere semantics—students not realizing that they were over-generalizing— or if they reflected actual Chinese bias

---

[45] *Editor's note: This author has lived and worked in mainland China for some time. In this article he draws from that experience as well as his graduate studies and strong background as an educator to present an extensive look at influences of American culture and politics upon the lives of Chinese young people and, potentially, upon their spiritual development. Many readers will find the ideas of this chapter at turns stimulating and challenging. One thing is certain: wrestling with such ideas is an essential part of understanding modern Chinese culture. - K.P.*

[46] *A pseudonym has been used to protect the identity of the contributor.*

against Americans. Either way, this was a stereotype which Americans—particularly American Christians—would need to address if they were to be taken seriously while working with Chinese people. Gu Chang-sheng, a retired professor of modern Chinese history at the East China Normal University in Shanghai, wrote that one of his conclusions after studying the history of the expansion of Christianity in China is that there is "too much confusion as to what is Christian versus what is merely Western civilization" (Chang-Sheng, 2009, p. 167).

My research at two Chinese universities, completed in 2008 and 2017,[47] suggests that Chinese people indeed see Americans through a complex set of lenses. Their stereotypes of Americans are more positive than negative, particularly after agreeable personal interactions with Americans; nevertheless, their views are mixed. On the one hand, Americans are most often viewed as kind, friendly, enthusiastic, confident, and outgoing. But on the other, we are associated with being very "open" about sexuality, overly violent, and supportive of war. Further coloring the matter is the complicated relationship China has with religion, particularly Christianity. Overwhelmingly, Chinese assume Americans are Christians. Yet Christianity is viewed with a mixture of curiosity, skepticism, animosity, and apathy because of the tarnished history of Christianity in China. Most important to the Chinese, missionary work gained its strongest foothold in China in the wake of the gunboats that plied the opium trade in the 1800s, which led to series of devastating treaties that humiliated China. This has made Chinese people view both Christianity and Westerners with skepticism ever since.

The source of these viewpoints is varied, but my argument is that the modern Chinese mindset about Americans remains closely connected with the historical actions of Westerners in China and around the world, popular media

---

[47] I e-mailed invitations to participate in the 2017 surveys to more than 500 current and former students at three Chinese universities between July 20, 2017 and December 31, 2017. I also asked students to share the survey with friends, so it is unclear exactly which current and former students were among the 59 who completed the survey; however, respondents ranged in age from 19 to 32 and said they had attended universities in nine different cities. They listed 33 different cities as hometowns. For the focus groups, I interviewed 28 students in October, 2008 at a university in Shaanxi province as part of an earlier research project while completing my Master's degree. This research had extraordinarily similar results to the results of the 2017 surveys, so I have included a mixture of comments from the 2008 focus group interviews and the 2017 surveys because the student's comments from this earlier research offers important insight into their thinking.

portrayals of American culture in TV and film, and depictions of America in Chinese news. The best way to counter these deep-rooted stereotypes is by presenting a compelling counter-narrative to the ideas that all Americans are practicing Christians and that modern missionary work is still intrinsically tied to the ideas of Christendom and cultural imperialism.

The central questions I sought to answer in my research were "How do Chinese college students perceive Americans in general?" and, more specifically, "What role do Chinese college students perceive Christianity to play in the lives and behavior of Americans?" We will later explore more of the historical answers for, certainly, historical contact between Chinese people and Americans—especially American missionaries—has had a profound impact on how Chinese people view American Christians today and, therefore, whether or not those Chinese people are open to considering Christianity as a viable option for their own personal spiritual beliefs. If we can take a step back and try to see American Christianity through Chinese eyes, we will not only discover much about American Christianity, but also see how we can better break down the walls that history has built between our cultures.

## Modern Background Research: Where are We Now?

Wike et al. offer insightful data from a poll conducted by the Pew Research Center in 2015. When asked their opinion of America in 2015, only 44% of Chinese people had a favorable view, while 49% had an unfavorable view. More than half of the Chinese surveyed (54%) believed the U.S. was trying to prevent China from becoming equally powerful. Younger people were not as suspicious towards the U.S. as the older generation: 59% of 18-to-29-year-olds in China had a positive opinion about the U.S., compared with just 29% of those ages 50 and older (Wike, et al, 2015). Unfortunately, the usefulness of this survey is limited, as it simply asked the binary question of whether Chinese people had a favorable or unfavorable view of America.

Wike and Devlin note that when Pew did a similar survey of Americans in 2018, only 38% of Americans had a favorable view of China, while 47% had an unfavorable view. More than 82% of those surveyed cited U.S. debt, Chinese cyberattacks, the Chinese impact on the global environment, the loss of U.S. jobs to China, and the trade deficit to China as somewhat serious or very serious issues affecting Sino-American relations (Wike & Devlin, 2018).

Allen cites older, but still relevant, data from Pew's 2005 and 2008 Global Attitudes Surveys, which asked questions that are a bit more helpful when discussing this topic. In its 2008 survey, 48% of the Chinese respondents had an unfavorable view of the U.S. China was one of the few countries in which American people were seen less favorably than the country as a whole. Only 38% of Chinese people had a favorable opinion of American people. When asked whether they see the U.S. as a partner, enemy, or neither, 34% called America an enemy, while only 13% called the country a partner. Pew's 2005 survey is even more applicable to my question because it adds insight into *why* Chinese people have largely negative opinions of American people. Only 35% described Americans as honest, while 44% described them as hard-working. Additionally, 57% of Chinese people described Americans as greedy, 61% saw them as violent, and 44% described them as both rude and immoral (Allen, 2005).

From this research and experience, we can conclude that American Christians hoping to share the Good News with Chinese people have their work cut out for them. Not only is Christianity unfamiliar to many Chinese, but if the messengers are seen as dishonest, greedy, violent, and lazy in the minds of a significant number of the Chinese people we interact with, these are huge obstacles to overcome. Trustworthiness and faithfulness are particularly important characteristics when it comes to being messengers of the Gospel, because Jesus emphatically claims to be the Way, the Truth, and the Life and expects his followers to be faithful stewards of his message (see Luke 16:10).

### Christianity in the U.S. and China

When Americans use the word "God," they are not always talking about the same being. According to a 2017 survey by the Pew Research Center, eight in ten Americans say they believe in God; however, only 56% say they believe in the God of the Bible (Cooperman & Smith, 2017). Only 56% of Americans and 74% of Christians believe that God is omnipotent, omniscient, and all-loving (Cooperman &

Smith, 2017). In spite of America's Christian roots, the nation is becoming more pluralistic.

These figures fall in line with the Barna Group's 2018 report about the waning influence of Christianity in America.[48] Whereas 75% of Elders and Boomers identified as Christians, among Generation X and Millennials, that percentage dipped to 65%, and for Generation Z teens, the number dipped further to 59% (Barna, 2018). Gen Z non-believers cited science, hypocrisy, and the problem of evil as the three biggest barriers to faith (Barna, 2018). These trends suggest that younger Americans identify themselves less with Christianity than older generations do.

Only 5% of the Chinese population identified as Christians as of 2011, according to estimates from the Pew Forum on Religion and Public Life (Liu, 2011). While the total number of Christians has increased in recent years, official government estimates put the number of Protestants at 23 million and Catholics at 5.7 million during the 2010 census. According to China's National Bureau of Statistics, its population increased to almost 1.4 billion in 2018 (Bodeen, 2019). If the Chinese Christian population remains at 5%, it is now approximately 70 million people. In a 2015 Gallup poll, 61% of Chinese people identified as "convinced atheists," 29% identified as "non-religious," and 7% identified as religious, with another 3% saying they did not know or choosing to give no response. This made China the country with the smallest percentage of religious people of all the countries included in Gallup's survey. It is not surprising to discover that many Chinese people do not knowingly have contact with Christians.

Another important survey investigated the prevalence of Christianity among college students at 12 universities in Xi'an. Of the 950 students surveyed, 1.4% were Christian; 4.1% were Muslim;[49] 8.7% professed belief in Buddhism, Taoism, or folk religion; and 85% had no religious belief (Wang, 2016). This data is similar to the 2012 Chinese Family Panel Studies from the Institute of Religion of Beijing

---

[48] The study delineated the generations according to the following birth years: Elders (before 1946); Boomers (1946-1964); Generation X (1965-1983); Millennials (1984-1998); Generation Z (1999-2004).

[49] While China's Muslim population officially accounted for 0.45% of the population in the 2011 Census, Xi'an is on the frontier of Western China, which has much higher concentrations of Muslim Hui and Uighur minorities. This may explain why there is a higher-than-normal percentage of Muslim students at universities in Xi'an.

University in 2012, which said that 89.6% of Chinese people had no religion, 6.75% were Buddhist, and 1.9% were Christians. Wang points out the difficulty of conducting this kind of research. He says, "It is possible that, under Communist rule in China, some religious people do not admit their faith, so that the true data is higher than the survey results suggest" (Wang, 2016).

A separate 2016 survey conducted by the Center on Religion and Chinese Society polled 960 Chinese undergraduate and graduate students who came to study in the U.S. The Center found that those who said they "completely believe" in a religion seemed to correspond most closely with "commitment to a religion" ("Purdue Survey," 2016). This survey is particularly helpful because it gives us a glimpse of how Chinese religious views changed as students lived in America and interacted with Americans. Before coming to the U.S., 1.3% of the students expressed "complete belief" in Protestant Christianity, but that figure quadrupled after spending time in the U.S., to 5.1% ("Purdue Survey," 2016). "Complete belief" in Catholicism also nearly doubled, from 0.3% to 0.5%. The percentage of students who said they "somewhat believe" in Protestant Christianity held fairly steady, moving from 12% to 12.9%, while it also increased from 4.4% to 5.1% for Catholicism ("Purdue Survey," 2016). For most other religions, students' beliefs held steady. After living in America, 2.3% said they "completely believed" in Buddhism, 1.4% in Taoism, 0.4% in Islam, and 0.4% in Chinese folk religion ("Purdue Survey," 2016). The rest professed no religious beliefs. Results from the same survey suggest that Chinese students living in America did not necessarily connect positive influences of Christianity with the morality of Americans. In fact, the majority thought that American democracy and freedom did not benefit from Christianity. This may be explained by their atheistic beliefs and communist education, but it indicates a strong bias against the role Christianity plays in American life.

In light of this, American Christians need to consider the personal views Chinese people likely carry about our faith. In the Xi'an survey, 51.7% of students said they oppose the work of Christian missionaries (who may be Chinese or foreign), yet 34% said they have respect for the Christian faith (Wang, 2016). Wang argues that this data indicates that although most are not Christians,

Students' attitudes toward Christianity are more respectful than antagonistic. While most of the students reported not liking missionary activities, they also indicated that young people are generally accepting of religious culture and have great regard for the social role of religion in the contemporary era (2016).

According to Wang's research, only 21% of the students surveyed had an interest in learning about Christianity. Wang also discovered that knowledge about Christianity led to more interest. Curiously, 12% of the students who said they wanted to learn about Christianity said they were opposed to missionaries, who could teach them about it, while 25% of those opposed to learning about Christianity were *not* opposed to missionaries (2016). These numbers are difficult to reconcile. Perhaps historical attitudes about missionaries have impacted the willingness of some Chinese people to even consider what missionaries have to offer.

The sources from which Chinese people are exposed to Christianity are also important. Most of the students Wang surveyed who were religious attributed their knowledge about Christianity to their family (48%), friends (19%), or from attending religious meetings (10%). Those who were not religious attributed their knowledge of Christianity to reading religious books (19%), browsing the Internet (19%), or being introduced through friends (18%). For students without family members who are believers, "their understanding of Christianity continues to come from the Internet, books, and other external sources, which makes it clear that college students' contact with Christianity is very limited" (2016).

About a quarter of the college students surveyed in Xi'an said they had had at least one encounter with a missionary before the time they were surveyed (Wang, 2016). Results from another survey about religion among college students in Guizhou province in 2011 revealed 23% of those who were religious developed their faith during college (Wang, 2016). However, almost 62% followed the same faith as their family members (Wang, 2016). These are important findings. They show that college is a time of great transition and change, but the influence of family is likely to be significantly stronger than that of anyone else for most students. The Chinese culture is deeply relational. God can certainly work in the hearts of anyone at any time, but if the Holy Spirit does not touch the lives of students with one of these two sources—a Christian family member or friend—before finishing college, it seems reasonable to extrapolate that their likelihood of becoming a Christian during or after college greatly diminishes.

But there is certainly an attraction to some of the cultural aspects of Christianity for some Chinese people as well. One Chinese friend, a professor who spent four years in London as a visiting scholar, said he brought his young daughter to the local cathedral even though they were not Christians so she could join the choir and learn about the culture. "We want to learn more about the Bible because we think the knowledge in the Bible is highly valuable and the text is beautiful," he said. Historian Philip Jenkins argues

> The Bible and the attendant Christian culture can exercise a real attraction for non-Christians, who are fascinated by its ideas and its literary qualities, even if they might ultimately be repelled by the claims of the religion as a whole (Jenkins, 2006).

He points to another example, essayist and journalist Xiao Qian, who was a vigorous critic of the faith, yet "a devout lover of church music," Christmas carols, *The Messiah*, and hymnals and who said, "I'm fond of religious architecture too. I love to sit in an empty cathedral, smell the incense and gaze at the painted glass. I love many passages from the Bible, especially 1 Corinthians, chapter 13" (Jenkins, 2006). One student told me that she also enjoys sitting in the pews in a Catholic church built by foreigners more than 200 years ago in her hometown of Chongqing and appreciating the quiet environment on weekdays. "It is so peaceful and beautiful," she said. "I really like the atmosphere."

The average Chinese person has little personal contact with Americans. Most of the students I have taught in China had never personally met any foreigners, let alone an American, before they enrolled in the university. Some had never even *seen* a foreigner in person. So their stereotypes about foreigners are shaped not by personal interaction with Americans, but by other sources: news, movies, and what they are taught by their Chinese teachers. As a result, Chinese people often see foreigners as strange, exotic creatures. Unsurprisingly, their stereotypes about

Americans have a deep impact on the willingness of Chinese people to accept the claims of the Gospel.

For some, the strangeness of Christianity actually acts as a magnet to attract them. "It's exciting and interesting," said one seeker. "It is a different way of thinking that is very appealing to me." But for most, the poles of the magnet are reversed, and it repels them. "I see Christianity as something strange and foreign that I cannot accept," said a recent university graduate who now works in Shenzhen.

### History

A vital factor to keep in mind when considering why Chinese people often hold similar points of view about foreigners is that the Chinese tend to have a much longer collective memory than Americans. For example, many Chinese people today, including Chinese Christians, still openly express strong dislike, even hatred, for Japan because of atrocities committed during World War II. "I can forgive almost anybody, but how can I forgive the Japanese?" said one Chinese believer. According to a 2016 Pew Research survey, only 14% of Chinese people had a favorable view of Japan (Stokes, 2016). Those surveyed overwhelmingly saw Japanese people as arrogant, violent, and dishonest. Japanese leaders have repeatedly offered apologies for the nation's actions during WWII, yet, only 10% of Chinese people believe that Japan has expressed sufficient remorse, according to the Pew study. Only 2% said they did not think Japan needed to apologize (Stokes, 2016).

Contrast this with Americans, who generally have little animosity for Japan or Japanese people in spite of Japan's WWII attacks on Pearl Harbor and inhumane treatment of American POWs. According to a 2015 Pew Research Survey, 61% of Americans believe that Japan has either sufficiently apologized for its actions during World War II or does not need to apologize (Stokes, 2015). In contrast with the Chinese view, Americans typically see Japanese people as honest, hardworking, unselfish, and non-aggressive (Stokes, 2015). While Americans and Chinese people both suffered brutal Japanese attacks during WWII, the Chinese endured a much longer period of suffering, causing scars on the national conscience that have taken much longer to heal than those inflicted upon Americans.

## Foreign Stereotypes

Americans need to remember that China's relationship with the Western world, like its relationship with Japan, has been complicated and has left scars that have taken a long time to heal. One reason for this is that, historically, Chinese people have long had a "Sino-centric" worldview: the civilized center of China (literally the "middle kingdom") was seen as surrounded by the people of various countries or regions who were different and "often thought to be barbarians, or at least as lacking Chinese superiority. In general, those that were further away were seen as less civilized" (Agøy, 2016).

Using Confucian ideas of hierarchy, Q. Edward Wang (1999) noted that the Chinese judged people by their willingness to adopt the majority Han lifestyle. Wang argued that in section 4, chapter 16 of The *Analects,* Confucius saw Chinese values as superior to those of outsiders, going so far as to say that, "if remote people are not submissive, all the influences of civil culture and virtue are to be cultivated to attract them to be so" (Wang, 1999). He also pointed out that the Chinese referred to foreigners *and* any non-Han Chinese as either "raw" 生 ( meri) or "cooked" 熟 (shú), according to how closely assimilated they were into Chinese culture (Wang, 1999). "Civilization in this case usually meant geographical closeness to and cultural similarity to China," wrote Agøy (2016) in his discussion of Wang's ideas. "China sought to dominate foreign countries by spreading aspects of its culture to them; something that at times was given particular emphasis." Of course, America did not even exist and China's contact with the Western world was limited at that time, but aspects of China's Sino-centric worldview from this period continue into modern times.

China is a nation that tried to surround itself with walls. The commonly used word for foreigner, *wài guó rén* (外国人) literally means "outside country person." Another word historically used for Westerners, yì, 异 often had negative connotations. The first translation given in four modern Chinese-English dictionaries for 异 is "different," followed by "strange" or "unusual." Historians note that China's acceptance of foreigners has ebbed and flowed over the centuries. According to Erling Agøy (2016), the Early Táng dynasty welcomed foreigners and foreign influence in the period before the An-Shi Rebellion of 755-63, when General An Lushan declared himself emperor of a rival northern dynasty. Then, during the Middle Táng dynasty, a Confucian resurgence movement was launched, which caused the majority Hàn Chinese to develop hostility toward foreigners (Agøy, 2016). After this period, China's openness to foreigners ebbed and flowed, according to the attitudes of various emperors and later post-imperial leaders.

      Historians note that as far back as the Ming Dynasty in the late 15$^{th}$ century, China has adopted a much more inward-focused foreign policy, even as other countries tried to expand trade relationships with China. It was during this period that the most famous parts of the Great Wall of China were built to keep out the foreign invaders. Perhaps a big reason for the turn inward is that, while the Táng and Míng dynasties were distinctively Hàn Chinese, the Yuán dynasty was established when Mongolian ruler Kublai Khan became the first foreigner to conquer China in 1271. This led future Han emperors to display greater apprehensiveness and fear of other surrounding nations. Historians Stephen Neill and Owen Chadwick offered an excellent description of how China selectively closed its doors to foreigners in the 1500s:

> China proved for a long time far less accessible to the Gospel than Japan. The well-known Chinese xenophobia kept the doors of China entirely closed, except as the Chinese themselves expressed it, to members of subject races who come to pay tribute, to Muhammadan merchants who come to trade under the guise of paying tribute, and to foreigners who wished to settle in the empire, being lured by the good fame of Chinese virtues. (Neill & Chadwick, 1990)

The final dynasty, the Qīng, was also not Hàn Chinese, but rather, founded by Manchurians in northeastern China. When Sun Yat Sen, founder of the Republic of China, led an uprising against the Qīng Dynasty in 1911, he wanted China to get out from under what he considered the "foreign yoke" of the Manchus (Teon, 2016).

      One of the frequently cited reasons Chinese people see Christianity as a "foreign religion" more than Buddhism is due to the complicated history China has with Christianity. Buddhism, originating in India, made its entry into China at an earlier date—around the first century AD—and was more willing to blend its forms to fit with Chinese culture, even allowing syncretism with Taoism and Confucianism. Thus, from the Chinese point of view, Buddhism, is more "cooked," whereas Christianity is "raw." Most Chinese are unaware that Christianity's roots are in the Middle East, not Europe. They also do not realize that its first documented entry into China actually dates back to the arrival of a Syriac monk named Alopen from the Church of the East (also known as the Nestorians) in A.D. 635. The relatively few Chinese people who are aware of Italian Jesuit missionary Matteo Ricci, who became the first known foreigner to enter the Forbidden City in 1601 at the invitation of Emperor Zhu Yijun, are often more impressed by his language learning skills and contributions in the fields of astronomy and mathematics and translations of Confucian classics than they are in his calling to share the Gospel in China. Perhaps these or other historical touchpoints might make Christianity feel slightly less "raw" to the Chinese.

Chinese people often have a much more antagonistic view of Protestant missionaries who came to China starting in the early 1800s. These missionaries who arrived in the wake of the powerful East India Trading Company brought the Gospel, but many were also complicit with British imperialism because they saw it as their only way to enter the country. Initially, the East India Trading Company refused British missionaries, including Robert Morrison, passage because it was opposed to the work of missionaries in China. So, Morrison caught a ride aboard an American ship in 1807 and pretended to be an American for months before admitting he was British (Pomfret, 2016). He studied Chinese, then got a job as a translator with the East India Company, which by this time had changed its anti-missionary policy, and now found missionaries "indispensable because of their linguistic skills" (Brown, 1986). Most of the missionaries were conflicted about entering the nation on gunboats or using the opium trade to enter China, but they did it anyway. Writing from Shantou, Guangdong in 1856, British missionary J. Hudson Taylor, founder of China Inland Mission, acknowledged the toll the opium trade was having on the Chinese:

Not less than 32,000 pounds of opium enter China every month at this port alone, the cost of which is about a quarter of a million sterling. After this you will not be surprised to learn that the people are wretchedly poor, ignorant and vicious . . . The people have no love for foreigners (Wallis, 1985). Although some governments and many missionaries denounced the opium trade, and most missionaries later took advantage of other ways to enter the country, the Western-backed drug trade continued until 1917.

The Chinese government still reminds its citizens about this period of "foreign aggression" in classrooms, museums, news broadcasts, and patriotic displays on a regular basis. As a result, the Chinese particularly remember the series of "unequal treaties" imposed upon China by foreign powers seeking to gain trade advantages in the 1800s, which humiliated the Chinese. While Americans were not directly involved, German missionary K.E.A Gutzlaff helped draft the British treaty after the First Opium War, which led to the British annexation of Hong Kong and forced the opening of treaty ports in Shanghai, Guangzhou, Fuzhou, Xiamen, and Ningbo, "thus signaling to the Chinese that Western power and Christianity were one and the same" (Yeo, 2002).

Though Americans stayed out of the Opium War, they still quickly took advantage of the opportunities offered by the British in the aftermath. The first American missionary, Elijah Bridgman, and the first medical missionary Peter Parker, also an American, helped draft the Wangxia Treaty in 1844, which gave Americans the same rights to live, trade, build churches and proselytize in the treaty ports as the British, further demonstrating the convoluted role of missions and foreign diplomacy. The later Treaty of Tianjin of 1858, required China to tolerate Christianity, giving Americans, British, Russians, and French the right to travel and conduct missionary activities throughout China, in addition to opening eleven more trade ports and granting foreign ships the right to navigate the Yangtze River. "Patriotic Chinese of every persuasion, Christians and non-Christians alike, deeply resented the humiliation which was imposed by the unequal treaties," wrote Brown (1986). The treaty also contained provisions which "granted Christian converts the protection of foreign laws" (Brown, 1986). Historian Kenneth Scott Latourette wrote that, "This provision, in part, removed Chinese Christians from the jurisdiction of Chinese officials . . . it led to abuse, because not infrequently Chinese professed conversion to obtain the assistance of the missionary and the Consul in lawsuits" (Brown, 1986). As a result, the Chinese often blamed the "foreign devils" for interfering in Chinese affairs. Anti-foreigner sentiment and anti-Christian sentiment continued to rise.

Brown argues that Christians were still seen as too foreign. The vast majority of missionaries lived in treaty ports, separated from Chinese populations:

> In spite of all their good works, the missionaries had not been able to rid themselves of the taint of foreignness. Christianity was still a foreign religion, and its foreignness, rather than any distinctive Christian dogma or practice, made it offensive. As the human body reacts to a foreign object in its blood stream and seeks to reject it, so the Chinese body politic was reacting to the foreign presence in its midst. (Brown, 1986)

Neill and Chadwick suggest that had the missionaries done a better job of *assimilating* to Chinese culture, the Chinese may have been more accepting. "The missionaries were not altogether free from blame. Some had been less than discreet in making use of the privileges assured to them under the treaties" (Neill & Chadwick, 1990). As early as the 1830s, some were better known for hobnobbing among the elite in Beijing or Shanghai than winning souls (Pomfret, 2016). Most 19th century Chinese "were comfortable with their culture of Confucius, Buddha and the Tao, and showed little interest in the holy goods the missionaries were hawking. In the first twenty-seven years of their missionary work in China, Protestant missionaries claimed only ten converts" (Pomfret, 2016).

Some, like Issachar Jacox Roberts of Tennessee, took some positive steps towards accommodation, donning a floor-length Chinese gown and preaching to a leper colony on the outskirts of Guangzhou where his first convert was a beggar (Pomfret, 2016). But he also sometimes displayed an "exasperation with, even a hatred of, Chinese culture," wrote Pomfret because he and his Baptist colleagues wanted to "cast aside the old China and create a new one, modeled on America." Roberts later hoped for a "blitzconversion" of China as he accepted an invitation to join his former student Hong Xiuquan, leader of the Taiping Rebellion, which would go on to kill millions. Before the massacres began, he declared, "Never were the prospects for usefulness with God's blessing brighter . . . China will be revolutionized, Christianized, and a great multitude saved through these means" (Pomfret, 2016). After the failure of the rebellion, the Qing court demonized the West and turned Chinese sentiment against Christianity. "From 1860 on, the fires of a xenophobic, anti-Christian hatred would burn in many Chinese hearts, stoked by those in the upper class and others with bad memories of the Taipings," wrote Pomfret (2016).

That is not to say that all missionaries were unsuccessful. Perhaps the most well-known missionary from the 1800s was J. Hudson Taylor, who first arrived in China in 1853, famously bucking the trend of huddling in missionary compounds and treaty ports, heading inland and trading proper British attire for Chinese clothing, convinced that the Gospel would take root in China only if missionaries affirmed Chinese culture. He followed Paul's example, arguing, "Let us in everything not sinful become like the Chinese, that by all means we may save some" (Bunn, 2015). At the time of Taylor's death in 1905, the agency he founded—China Inland Mission—had 825 missionaries, 500 Chinese helpers and claimed more than 25,000 Christian converts (Piper, 2014).In 2013, the Chinese government in Zhejiang province had a positive enough memory of Taylor and his first wife Maria to hire an archaeologist to exhume and move their graves, where a warehouse had been built, to a nearby church, where they were buried in a memorial garden (Berry, 2013).

Like Taylor, American Dr. Peter Parker, who was the first medical missionary to be sent abroad, arriving in 1834, also believed that "healthy respect for the culture" was among the "keys to China's kingdom," but unlike Taylor he wanted to "heal" China to help it become stronger and embrace Western values in the process, (Pomfret, 2016). In contrast, Americans John L. Nevius, Rufus Anderson, and Lottie Moon, emphasized building the indigenous church and took great pains to separate the Gospel from "civilization." For example, Anderson, who led the American Board of Commissioners for Foreign Missions, was so upset when Parker eventually went to work as a diplomat, translating for the American Legation to China, that he resigned from the Board (Beaver, 1979). He said he "found in the apostolic record no evidence of an aim to change and transform a society and, therefore, he opposed the efforts and apparatus for furthering 'civilization' which had prevailed until then. They were complicated and costly and, in his view, deflected concentration from the rightful objective" (Beaver, 1979). Moon, a Southern Baptist, lived alone in a rural Shandong village, preaching to Chinese men and demanding that women be allowed to become ministers starting in the 1870s (Pomfret, 2016).

A Chinese civil servant named Wèi Yuán (魏源) saw these abuses and wrote a Chinese response to the Opium War called *The Illustrated Treatise on the Maritime Kingdoms* (海国图 or Hǎiguó Túzhì), published in three editions, in 1843, 1847, and 1852, which offers a helpful portrayal of how Chinese people saw foreigners at the time, in their own words (Leonard, 1984). "Wèi portrays foreigners as dangerous and vicious. Though China might have something to learn from them, the portrayal of them are clearly negative," writes Agøy (2016), adding that he saw "Westerners as not primitive, though still aggressive."

Although Western missionaries may have gained access to Chinese through these treaties, Bishop K.H. Ting, former president of the China Christian Council argues that these compromises damaged their witness to the people of China. "The recognition of the historical relatedness of the missionary movement to Western economic, political and military penetration into China is all-important to any understanding of what Chinese Christians have strived to do and be, and to any consideration as regards relations with Chinese Christians" (Brown, 1986).

Some American missionaries saw themselves as culturally superior to the Chinese. Jason Chang argued that they saw American values and Christianity as intrinsically intertwined:

> They crossed the Pacific with a sense of the innate superiority of Western Christian values and saw themselves as part of a benevolent crusade to bring the heathen Chinese out of the darkness of their ossified traditionalism and into the light of a new modern Christian era. Theirs was imperialism without any apparent territorial designs; they sought hearts and minds, not land. (Chang, 2018, p. 122)

In 1886, William Ashmore, a Baptist missionary who had recently returned from China, told participants at a week-long Bible conference to "look upon missions as a war of conquest, and not as a mere wrecking expedition," leaving a strong impression on a young John Mott, who later led evangelistic crusades in China (Mott, 1889, p. 7). In 1910, Methodist missionary D.L. Anderson, in a support letter home, similarly wrote that, "the conquest of China will not simply be taking advantage of an opportunity, but a bitter war with an adversary of greater power and more strongly entrenched, than the Church found in her conflict with the Roman Empire" (Varg, 1960, p. 15). No wonder Chinese people saw missionaries as conquerors—it seems some of the missionaries saw themselves as conquerors as well.

The "unequal treaties" amplified Chinese anger and distrust of the West, eventually leading to the Boxer Rebellion in 1900, in which at least 30,000 Chinese Catholics, 47 foreign Catholic priests and nuns, 1,900 Chinese Protestants, 134 foreign Protestant missionaries, and 52 missionary children were killed (Gu, 2009). In retrospect, Chairman Mao Zedong later declared the Boxer Rebellion an "anti-imperialist and patriotic movement of the Chinese people" (Gu, 2009, p. 139). Christianity's fraught political relationship with China continued well into the 20th century. Part of the trouble in the eyes of today's Chinese is that many Americans living in China during China's revolutionary period, particularly missionaries, stood on the side of the Nationalists and their leader Chiang Kai-shek, largely because he professed faith in Jesus and endorsed Christianity, which gave them a sliver of hope that he might usher in an era of pro-Christian government. Soon after the death of Sun Yat Sen in 1925, Chinese Communists sermonized against "imperialistic foreign devils" and Communist Party founder Chen Duxiu, declared that he who "advocates that America is China's friend is a traitor to the Chinese nationalist movement" (Pomfret, 2016, p. 190). In 1929, the Communist party began charging that "American missionary, health, and education activities were 'only a disguise of liberalism.' Anyone who doubted that, said Chen Duxiu, 'is a traitor'" (Pomfret, 2016, p. 206).

Chinese Bishop K.H. Ting claims that the politics of missionaries undermined their faith in God, not to mention their love for the Chinese:

Why do Chinese revolutionaries reject the God of the Christians? Because many Christians all over the world stood on the side of Chiang Kai-shek, the enemy of the Chinese people; and because in 1949, when the People's Liberation Army was about to cross the Changjiang (Yangzi) River in pursuit of Chaing Kai-shek forces, some missionaries and their Chinese colleagues led Christians in praying that the soldiers of the People's Liberation Army would drown in the river. That was certainly a very political, reactionary and brutal prayer. (Yeo, 2002, p. 175)

Interestingly, Chiang, who earlier courted the support of the U.S. later developed disdain for America. In 1926, he told American reporter Lewis Gannett that "Thinking men hate America more than they hate Japan . . . Americans come to us come to us with smiling faces and friendly talk," but in the end, the U.S. emulates China's enemy Japan rather than living up to its promises to help China (Isaacs, 1958, p. 202). Chiang continued his scathing criticism:

> That is what is behind the anti-Christian movement in China. Your missionaries write 'charity' over their doors, and I do not deny that many of them are good men who do good work. But in the end they make it easier for American policy to follow that of the other imperialist Powers. So because we have been deceived by your sympathetic talk, we end by hating you most. (Isaacs, 1958, p. 202)

American evangelist and Nobel Peace Prize winner John Mott, longtime leader of the World Student Christian Federation and the YMCA, visited China nine times from 1922 to 1949 to conduct mass evangelistic meetings, but later drew the ire of Chairman Mao. "He openly exhorted Christians not to cooperate with the Chinese Communist Party and its new regime . . . promising that (American) churches would continue to give them financial aid and pray for them," wrote Gu (2009, p. 60). "No wonder Mott became the 'number one enemy' of the Chinese Communist Party. It is easy to see why he was the first missionary to be singled out in the accusation campaign by the high-ranking Party officials" (p. 60).

In an editorial in the "People's Daily" on August 30, 1949, Chairman Mao declared that "Christianity is a spiritual aggression from the West" (Gu, 2009, p. 204).

Earlier that month, in a report to Congress, U.S. Secretary of State Dean Acheson declared the vital role American missionaries had played in developing cultural ties between the U.S. and China, declaring the U.S. was China's "close friend and benefactor" (Acheson, 1949, p. 10). Acheson's White Paper may have raised Mao's displeasure with the declaration that "American missionaries, through their religious, educational, and medical work, had played a very large part in spreading Western concepts of thought ever since the opening of China to intercourse with the West, and in developing a close cultural tie between the United States and China" (Acheson, 1949, p. 20). Perhaps it would have been better for the American government *not* to have voiced its support for the role of American missionaries in China. Then again, the Chinese were likely already well aware that a large percentage of the missionaries working in China were Americans and of America's pride in the work they had done.

In 1950, Chinese Premier Zhou Enlai accused "American imperialists" of using Christianity as a "tool against China" and emphasized that Chinese church leaders needed to break ties with them so that "imperialism will never again be able to manipulate the Chinese church" (Gu, 2009, p. 57). The "Manifesto of the Chinese Christians," which was published September 23, 1950, and signed by more than 400,000 Chinese believers, declared that the basic task for Chinese Christians was "to give full support to new China and the leadership of the Chinese Communist Party, to oppose imperialism, and to take part in the effort to build an independent, prosperous, and powerful new China" by severing ties with foreign missionaries and building a self-sustaining church (Gu, 2009).

By 1952, the Chinese government had expelled more than 11,000 Christian missionaries. Any who remained were denounced and imprisoned. American mission boards were accused of sending missionaries as spies for the U.S. government and "stirring up 'cultural aggression' in China and poisoning the minds of the Chinese people" (Gu, 2009, p. 57). Neill and Chadwick (1990) argued that,

> The Chinese Christian found himself in a situation of grave perplexity. If interest in the West was to be regarded as a crime, then every Chinese Christian was automatically a criminal. The Gospel had come to him from

>the West . . . Now he was assured that Christian missions had been simply a part of the cultural aggression of the West against the East. (p. 430)

This is exactly what Western Christians did *not* want to see. Millions of Chinese Christians were forced into hiding or put into labor camps by the time the Cultural Revolution began in 1966.

This is not just a "back then" historical issue. Recent "anti-foreign" propaganda campaigns have also turned public sentiment against foreigners. In 2015, China's Education Minister Yuan Guiren, a former president of Beijing Normal University, told a conference of college academics that they should "by no means allow teaching materials that disseminate Western values in our classrooms" (Gu, 2009, p. 57). In 2017 and 2018, officials at the university where I teach in China explicitly told American teachers not to talk with students about "anything other than English, especially religion." Several American Christians working in the city were questioned regularly by police; others were sent home and told never to return. Eric Fish (2016) of *Foreign Policy* writes that,

> The Communist Party's fears of foreign ideological infiltration were laid bare with the leak of Document 9, an internal communiqué instructing cadres to stop universities and media from discussing seven taboo topics: Western constitutional democracy, universal values, civil society, neoliberalism, the Western concept of press freedom, historical nihilism, and questioning whether China's system is truly socialist.

Fish (2016) goes on to say that the circulation of Document 9 in 2013 led to a crackdown on public protests and brought down lawyers, journalists, and anyone else who has been outspoken against government policy. Pomfret (2016) wrote that the party was ordering "heightened vigilance" against "false ideological trends" and that China "had declared war on American ideas" (p. 612). He noted that in 2015, Minister of Education Yuan Guiren published an essay "demanding that China's textbooks be cleansed of 'wrong Western values' and warning teachers and college students that they could become victims of brainwashing by 'hostile forces'" (p. 613). Carl Minzner, a specialist in Chinese law and politics at Fordham Law School, told *Foreign Policy* that the campaign is now poised to reach deeper into academia (Fish,

2016). "This is big and dark," Minzner said. "This is several years in the making and it will likely roll out in colleges over the next several years. We don't know how far it will go" (Fish, 2016). In 2014, President Xi praised ultranationalist blogger Zhou Xiaoping, who berated "the tendency of young Chinese to worship the West and declared that America was treating China and the Chinese in the same way that Hitler had treated the Jews" (Pomfret, 2016, p. 612-613).

Another sign of the recent state of paranoia about foreigners is a 2016 anti-espionage campaign featuring cartoon posters warning Chinese women not to give away state secrets to handsome Western men, lest they turn out to be foreign spies (Coonan, 2016). When China implemented a new law, putting NGOs under the oversight of the ministry of Public Security, it cited suspicion of foreigners as one of the motivating factors. "A minority of foreign NGOs, through the means of funds and some methods, are able to harm China's national security interests and [undertake] some other illegal criminal activity," said Hao Yunhong, head of the Ministry of Public Security's foreign NGO management office (Beech, 2016).

Yeo (2002) argues that the political commitments of missionaries serving in places like China, where anti-imperialist tendencies are strong, can sometimes be a hindrance. In the early 1900s, "They held democracy against communism" and aligned with the Nationalists, Yeo writes, seeking to "use Christian values to reform and save China, but they were walking a tightrope of being understood as fulfilling the political agenda of the imperialists—the Westernization and Christianization of China" (Yeo, 2002, p. 175). While Woodberry and Shah (2004) argue that there is "compelling cross-national evidence of a causal association between Protestantism and democracy" (p. 48) they say that the association is contingent upon a wide variety of factors including religious pluralism, the "mutual independence" of church and state from one another, robust volunteerism, and mass education. Their research suggests that democracy has historically been more likely to develop in countries that were colonized by predominantly Protestant empires than Catholic or non-religious countries. But, other than Hong Kong and Macau and several treaty ports, China was not colonized.

For Christianity to thrive in China, Western Christians must be willing to loosen their grip on the need to push the idea of democracy and specific Western values. Democracy is not the Gospel. Neither are a vague set of "Western values." If spreading democracy becomes as much of a goal as spreading the Gospel, Christians are missing the point. Democracy may not even be what the Chinese seek. "Many Westerners seek this lack of democracy in China as a deficiency to remedy," writes Mike Falkenstine in *The Chinese Puzzle* (2012, p. 154). "Contrary to popular belief in the West, most Chinese do not see the development of democracy as one of their nation's top needs of the future . . . A plunge into potential political chaos would hinder the development of the country" (Falkenstine, 2012, p. 154). Besides, contrary to many Americans' beliefs, God does not favor one political system over another. Yeo (2002) argues that:

> Pauline theology does not prohibit Christian involvement in politics; otherwise, to be a Christian would be to assume a politically passive role. Paul's theology cautions Christians not to use the name of God to justify one's political stance, such as thinking that democracy is the divine economy and that communism is satanic. (p. 17)

Despite many missionaries having positive motives, Chinese perceptions of missionaries as imperialists are deeply ingrained and unlikely to change soon. Some Chinese acknowledge that Christianity's mark on China is not entirely negative, but they are a distinct minority. Retired modern Chinese history professor Gu Changsheng took considerable risk to counter prevailing thought and argue that "most missionaries in China were not agents of imperialism" (Gu, 2009, p. 148). His 1981 book *Missionaries and Modern China* was the first book published in Communist China to include not only the negative contributions of missionaries, but also their positive legacy, including the introduction of Western sciences; establishing schools, hospitals, publishing houses, and other philanthropic enterprises; and "acting as bridges to form a link between the cultures of East and West" (Brown, 1986). Gu wrote, "The charge that Christianity is a 'foreign religion' in China can no longer be substantiated by the facts. It is no more 'foreign' than Buddhism or Islam, for these too were originally imported" (Brown, 1986, pp. 220-221

## My Research

In an attempt to discern both positive and negative opinions about Americans, how those opinions changed after Chinese students entered college, and which sources of information Chinese people find the most influential in forming their opinions about Americans, I surveyed students using a Web-based questionnaire and conducted focus groups. In order to find out how strongly these opinions are linked in the Chinese mind with Christianity, parts of my research focused strongly on the persuasiveness of various religious beliefs in America and about students' perceptions of American religious beliefs. The questions were designed to discover any correlations between each student's perceptions of America and religion in America.

Since I had observed that most Chinese college students, particularly those studying English, had their first personal contact with an American at the beginning of their college experience, I began by asking for some demographic information, including how many Americans they had contact with both before and after coming to college. Of the 59 valid responders from the 2017 survey, 54% said they had never met or had a conversation with any foreigners, let alone any American, before starting college. Two-thirds of respondents said they had never met an American before college. Surprisingly, 10% of the students surveyed said they had met nine or more foreigners before college, but only one student had met nine or more Americans. Almost 19% of the students had met two or more Americans before college.

However, college was an eye-opening experience for the students. Almost 93% of respondents said they had met an American by the time they took the survey. More than seven in ten students said they had met at least three Americans by the time they took the survey, a natural outcome of most surveyed students being English majors.

My research revealed several things about how Chinese college students perceive Americans. These can be grouped into four main areas: perceptions of Americans as a whole, perceptions of religion in America, and changes in Chinese perceptions and the influence of American politics in China.

## Modern Chinese Perceptions of Americans as a Whole

The words students used to describe Americans give a glimpse of their attitudes toward them. When asked to write any five words they would use to describe Americans, only 10% of words students chose had negative connotations, while about 77% of the words had positive associations. Another 13% of the words were more "neutral" in their meanings, mostly regarding appearance and observable traits such as: tall, strong, fat, and white. But most described personality traits or character descriptions. Some of the most commonly chosen words were "friendly" (25%), "kind/warm" (24%), "outgoing" (22%). 19% chose one of the following descriptors: "confident," "free," "enthusiastic," "humorous." Other descriptors they chose included "open" (17%), "serious" (12%), or "wealthy" (12%). A minority of students referred to Americans as "arrogant" (7%), or used a smattering of other negative words like "infantile," "selfish," "egotistical," or "unpredictable." When asked to identify how closely they currently associate several words with Americans, students also tended towards positive descriptions of Americans. For example, about three-quarters of students said that they closely associate the word "freedom" with Americans. Six out of ten closely associate the words "polite" and "happy" with Americans.

The most difficult word to categorize from my survey results was "open." While most Americans might interpret this word positively, as in "willing to consider new ideas," about 75% of the students I interviewed in focus groups used the words "open" or "open-minded" as a negative descriptor of American behavior. When asked why, they described the sexuality they see in American movies. "American people are really open," explained one student. "They don't care about saying something about sex in public, and they easily have sex with others." Another student said, "They just live the life to enjoy themselves." Another added, "They do what they want to do when they want to do it, and they love who they want to love." Students agreed that this sort of behavior is unacceptable in Chinese society.

Several students further noted the prominence of sexual promiscuity and violence when asked about what they learn about Americans through films and television. In focus group interviews, students watched an episode of *Friends*.[50] During a follow-up discussion, students overwhelmingly agreed with the idea that Americans are "brave," "outgoing," "friendly" and "humorous." However, they also described the characters as "lazy," "rough," and "too open" with sex. About two-thirds of those who participated in focus groups and those interviewed who were familiar with the television show agreed that the behaviors of the characters were representative of "most Americans." Students focused much attention particularly on the sexual element of the show, visibly squirming and covering their eyes. "I think these things are common among Americans," said one, "not in China." Yet, in a personal interview, a student voiced surprise that one of their American teachers (a Christian) had given a lecture on sexual purity. The teacher "said, 'Don't have co-habitation before you are married,' so I think that maybe the films and television are not real American life."

When asked to identify how much influence various sources of information have had on their opinions of American people and culture, 34% of respondents said classroom education with Americans had a "very large" impact on their opinion. When added to the students citing classroom education as a medium or large influence, 74% of those surveyed listed their American teachers as one of the biggest influencers on their opinions of Americans. Personal contact with any Americans was right behind, named as a "very large" influence by one-quarter of respondents and at least a medium influence by seven out of ten surveyed. "Personal contact with Americans makes me really understand Americans, I can talk to them face to face, and share thoughts," wrote one student, who acknowledged that the second biggest influence was likely the Chinese media. "I see them every day," said another student, who has a class with an American teacher each day of the week. "They can subtly influence me." Another student wrote, "After contact, I think Americans are very

---

[50] Curtis, Michael, and Greg Malins, writers. "The One Where Ross and Rachel . . . You Know." Friends, directed by Michael Lembeck, produced by Betsy Borns. National Broadcasting Company. (February 8, 1996). In this episode, two characters, Ross and Rachel, have sex on their first date, one character falls in love with a man her father's age, and two other characters slothfully spend the entire episode sitting in their new recliners, refusing to even answer the door.

good, do things very seriously, and take responsibility. They have had a great influence on my studies."

The third biggest influence was foreign movies or books, which 66% of respondents cited as a medium or large influence. "The American entertainment industry is very effective," said one student. "It can reflect Americans' true daily life," explained another. Focus groups and interviewees rambled off a long list of films they have drawn their opinion of America from, ranging from *Top Gun, Avengers,* and *James Bond* to *Gone with the Wind, Titanic,* and *Frozen.* They also mentioned television shows like *Friends, The Big Bang Theory, Game of Thrones,* and *Breaking Bad* as favorites. "I've seen a lot of American films and TV shows," one student said with a smile. "Too many."

Pomfret notes, however, that the American entertainment industry is now catering to Chinese audiences, even employing Chinese censors to vet films during the film-making process, so the glimpses American entertainment gives Chinese people of Americans must get past Chinese censors. "After 1997, it stopped making films that were critical of the PRC," wrote Pomfret (2016, p. 620). "As China grew into the world's second-largest movie market, Hollywood labored to shed its image as the polluter of Chinese minds" (p. 620). Perhaps Chinese censors do not mind American entertainment that makes Americans look bad, just entertainment critical of China.

Relatively few students expressed the belief that the behavior of television characters may not be representative of Americans as a whole. Chinese students said they see significant overlap between American entertainment and real life. "I think American films can often reflect [real] life in America," one student declared. "I just think the high-tech films are somewhat beyond real life." However, a few students expressed that their interaction with American teachers had shattered some of their stereotypes about Americans. One said, "I know from you that not all Americans are [like this]." However, others said their exposure to films was more significant than limited interaction with one or two Americans. "I've seen lots of films and books," said one student, noting that many of them contain similar levels of sexual promiscuity as in *Friends*. "So I think that most Americans act this way."

Interestingly, 27% of respondents, said that their family members' opinions of America had no influence on how they see Americans. Another 24% said their family had very little influence, so the majority said their family had very little or no influence. Only 19% said family members have either a medium or large influence in how they see Americans. Their friends had a slightly larger impact on their worldview, with 63% saying they had little to some influence.

Additionally, when asked to identify what they saw as the top two motivating factors for Americans to teach English in China, students overwhelmingly pointed to a desire to learn about Chinese culture (58%) as the top motivator. The next largest factor (31%) was "because they want to spread Western culture," which may be related to subtle connections Chinese people have about Western imperialism. This was followed by the desire to travel (29%). Surprisingly, nobody surveyed pointed to a desire to find a Chinese girlfriend or boyfriend as a motivating factor. Notably, few students (8%) selected "because of their religious beliefs," and none said that American English teachers in China were motivated most by a desire to help the Chinese people, even though most of these students had heard from at least one American teacher that faith and helping were among the reasons Americans came to China. Perhaps this should not be surprising, given the Pew Foundation's findings that 61% of Chinese people perceive Americans are greedy (Allen, 2005). It is likely that these answers were influenced by their knowledge of the reasons their American English teachers have shared, but it is useful to see which aspects students understood and retained.

| *What do you think are the top two motivating factors for most Americans who come to teach English in China? (Please select two.)* | |
|---|---|
| To learn about Chinese culture. | 59% |
| To spread Western culture. | 31% |
| Because they like to travel. | 29% |
| To make more money than they would in America. | 15% |
| They want the adventure of living in China. | 14% |
| They think it will improve their ability to get a good | 12% |

| | |
|---|---|
| To improve cultural relations between China and | 10% |
| To learn Chinese. | 10% |
| Because of their religious beliefs. | 8% |
| To find another job in China. | 5% |
| They want everyone to speak English. | 3% |
| They do not like life in America. | 2% |
| For some other reason. | 2% |
| To find a Chinese girlfriend or boyfriend. | 0% |
| To help Chinese people. | 0% |

## Chinese Perceptions about American Religion

I wanted to know what students' stereotypes about religious believers in America were because of the frequently held Chinese belief that all or most Americans are Christians. The results of my survey were surprising. When asked to estimate the percentage of Americans adhering to various religious beliefs, Chinese students overwhelmingly showed awareness of a diversity of beliefs in America, even if they could not quite pinpoint how prevalent different religious beliefs are. According to a 2015 Pew Survey, 70.6% of Americans identified themselves as Christians, 22.8% as religiously unaffiliated, and 5.9% as other non-Christian faiths (1.9% as Jewish, 0.9% Muslim, 0.7% Buddhist and 0.7% Hindu, and 1.8% other religions) (Wormald, 2015).

In comparison, the Chinese students underestimated the percentage of American Christians and overestimated the percentage of American Muslims, Buddhists, Hindus, Jews, and atheists. Most students rightly saw Christianity as the most prevalent religious belief in America. They estimated, cumulatively, that 46% of Americans are Christians, a number which corresponds closely with the percentage of self-identified Protestants in the U.S. The range of estimates individual students gave for how many Americans are Christians was quite large, from 10% on the low end to 90% on the high end. Interestingly, almost one-third of the students estimated that 30% or less of Americans are Christians. Significantly, students also estimated the prevalence of Islam in America to be much higher than expected, at 10%. Three in ten students chose this answer specifically. While 56% of the students estimated the population of America to be 10% or less Muslim, some students estimated the Islamic population as high as 30%. These are surprisingly high estimates. It is unclear why Chinese students would perceive that the U.S. has such a large Muslim population.

Additionally, students also vastly overestimated the prevalence of Jews (9%), Hindus (6%) and Buddhists (6%) and other religions (7%) in the U.S. These religions cumulatively account for almost 6% of Americans, according to Pew's research, rather than the 28% estimated by Chinese students. The students came a bit closer to estimating the cumulative percentage of agnostics, atheists, and "religious nones" (17% combined), which Pew put at almost 23%. This suggests that Chinese people have a distorted view of just how religiously diverse the U.S. is. It is diverse, but not *that* diverse. Focus group studies and personal interviews revealed that students indeed perceive most *Caucasian* Americans to be Christians. But they assumed that the adherents of other faiths were primarily among minority populations. So, perhaps, they are overestimating the size and influence of these minority populations in the U.S. or which types of ethnic and racial groups adhere to which religions.

After watching an episode of *Friends* in a focus group, about 70% of the students said that they thought all the characters were Christians, even though the episode contained no explicit references to religion. About 11% said they thought the characters were Muslim and another 11% said the characters were probably not religious. The remaining 8% were split evenly between Judaism and other religions. When asked why most thought the characters were Christian, students pointed to the prevailing culture. "Maybe the TV show doesn't tell us what they believe in, but in my mind, most Americans believe in God, so I think they are Christians," said one student. Another noted that a character exclaimed "Oh, my God," so she assumed they were Christians. Some saw the characters' sexual behavior as particularly contradictory to what they knew about Christianity, but others did not. A few of the minority who said they thought the characters were not religious pointed to the Bible for support. "God doesn't [want] people . . . to live like this. He doesn't like sex before marriage," said one student. "If they are Christians, they should obey God, so I think they have no religion."

Additionally, the students interviewed pointed to the violence in American movies as incongruous with what they knew about Christian beliefs, yet they saw it as common among Americans. "In the films I've seen, probably some are Christians, but some are [sic] no religion," said one student. "Some of their actions [are bad] . . . they do some things that God forbids like murder and adultery."

While many students had difficulty articulating specifically why Chinese people perceive America as overwhelmingly Christian, several students pointed to history, expressing the belief that most Americans have simply continued the religious beliefs of their ancestors who migrated to America from Europe. "In America, I think they . . . learn about [Christianity] from their parents," one student said. "So they don't think about it much, they only follow their parents."

## Changes in Perceptions

Tellingly, many of those surveyed had a change in attitudes between the time they enrolled in college and when they took the survey. The biggest changes took place in their attitudes about morality, respectfulness, politeness, war, and wealth. Before college, only 27% of respondents said they would have closely or very closely associated the word "moral" with Americans. That number had risen to 51% at the time of the survey. Before college, 80% would have at least partially associated the word "war" with Americans. That number had dropped to 61% at the time of the survey. They still saw Americans as imperialistic, but a bit less so, with 71% associating the word with Americans before university and 58% at the time of the survey. At the same time, the number of students who did not associate "imperialism" with Americans or only "a little bit" increased from 27% to 37%. There was also an increase in the percentage of students who used the word "loving" to describe Americans, from 37% to 54%.

When asked to explain which words "very closely" describe Americans, students often said they were motivated by personal relationships with foreign teachers and watching TV and movies. "I was in contact with a lot of Americans," said one. "They *all* emphasized their belief in Christianity, and I think they are humorous and friendly." Another said, "I think some stereotype images do not change any more such as war. But I think these words more closely describe the U.S. government [and] less closely describe people." One said their point of view was adversely affected by America's friendly relationship with Japan. Some students said they had not changed their viewpoint through interaction with Americans, but most admitted that their point of view had changed a bit over time. One noted, "As time goes by, I know more information and reconstruct [sic] my [view] about the world."

Americans may be surprised that Chinese people still associate words like "war" and "imperialism" with us when we have not been involved in a war with China since the Korean War, but perhaps it should not be surprising. According to the Centre for Research on Globalization, as of 2019, America had been at war for at least part of 222 out of 239 years—93% of its existence as an independent nation.

It is clear from this research that the perceptions of Chinese college students regarding Americans shifted somewhat after they arrived at college. Students more strongly associated words like "war" and "rude" with Americans before they came to college. In most cases, the students characterized Americans with positive words such as "loving," "kindness," and "generous" much more strongly after coming to college than before, suggesting that something in their college experience affected their view of foreigners. Many students attributed the changes to having met and interacted with an American for the first time. "After meeting Americans, I see that we are all human beings," said one student. "Maybe we're different in some ways, but mostly we're the same." Others attributed the attitude changes to other sources, including their friends and the media. While there is certainly a correlation between first-time interaction with Americans in college and use of favorable terms to describe Americans, it is not clear whether this impact came specifically from American teachers.

### American Politics in China

Finally, I was curious about the effect political news might have had on Chinese students' view of Americans. Particularly, I wanted to know whether the divisive American political climate following the 2012 and 2016 U.S. Presidential elections might have impacted Chinese views of Americans. When I asked students how four U.S. presidents had affected their opinions about Americans, about 71% of respondents said that Barack Obama gave them a positive view of Americans, whereas only 5% said he gave them a negative view. "He improved the relationship between China and America," said one student. "He is a great person, I admire him very much," said another. "I think he is very inspiring." Many praised his speaking abilities. "He is friendly to China, and his speech is very positive, he loves his country very much." One of the few voices of dissent did not like how Obama involved America in international affairs. "We don't like the fact that he used a few neighbor countries and our Taiwan to provoke us Chinese," he said. "Mind your own business."

Students had a much more negative view of Donald Trump. Eight times as many respondents (41%) said President Trump gave them a negative impression of Americans. Only 14% said Trump gave them a positive impression of Americans. One student called him "an American, in the traditional sense." The survey was conducted less than a year into Trump's first year in office, before Trump imposed new tariffs on many Chinese goods and American warships passed through the Taiwan Strait, but also before Trump had well-received personal meetings with Chinese President Xi Jinping, so it is possible that Chinese attitudes toward Trump have changed since the survey was taken.

The students were much less certain about the impact of Presidents George W. Bush or Bill Clinton on their opinions of Americans because most of what they knew about them came from textbooks rather than current affairs in the news. "I don't know too much about him," was a frequent response, as was, "I was very young at the time."

| How has each of the following U.S. Presidents affected your opinion of Americans? | | | | |
|---|---|---|---|---|
| | Negatively | No change | Positively | Not sure |
| Donald Trump | 41% | 19% | 14% | 27% |
| Barak Obama | 5% | 10% | 71% | 14% |
| George W. Bush | 14% | 39% | 12% | 36% |
| Bill Clinton | 7% | 31% | 31% | 32% |

## Conclusions

The guiding questions for my research were: "How do Chinese college students perceive Americans in general?" and, more specifically, "What role do Chinese college students perceive Christianity to play in the lives and behavior of Americans?" My research shows that the answer to these questions are varied. It is clear that they see Americans overwhelmingly as Christians, but they also see us as through a variety of different lenses. As described above, they chose three times as many positive words as negative or neutral words to describe Americans.

Survey responses regarding religion defied many of my expectations. For example, while I was spurred to research this topic partially because of the frequency of comments that "all Americans are Christians" and that "Christianity is a Western religion," my hypothesis that Chinese students see *almost all* Americans as Christians, based on frequent similar comments in the past, proved to be faulty. My research indicates that, while Chinese college students strongly associate Christianity with America, it is a weaker correlation than previous anecdotal evidence suggested. They clearly saw America as a predominantly Christian country; however, students estimated that slightly less than half of Americans are Christians, which is a far cry from "all Americans."

In order to gain an understanding of how Chinese college students perceptions changed through their interactions with Americans, it was helpful to see how they perceived Americans before and after most had their first interactions with Americans. It was clear, from the way they replaced more neutral descriptions like, "tall" with positive descriptions like "kind," and swapped negative descriptions like "imperialism" and "war" for "moral" and "respectful" that their opinions of Americans improved through these interactions.

It was encouraging that my respondents generally held Americans in higher regard than did the general the Chinese population. According to the Pew Global Attitudes Survey, only 38% of Chinese people had a favorable opinion of American people (Allen, 2005), but most Chinese students I surveyed shared favorable opinions of Americans. Whereas 44% of Pew respondents called Americans immoral, only 5% of the students I surveyed said the same word "closely" described" Americans and

24% said it even "partially" described Americans. This disparity may suggest the students chose generous terms because they did not want to offend their teacher, even in an anonymous setting. However, is also possible that Chinese college students majoring in English have a more favorable opinion of Americans than the average Chinese population because they have more interaction with Americans. If this is the case, those who interact with the Chinese should draw encouragement from the fact that their opinions of Americans seemed to improve after interacting with Americans. Obviously, Americans are not the only ones who can bring them the message of Christianity, but if we do, the Chinese are open to hearing the Gospel from us if it is not presented in a culturally arrogant way. This requires not only proper contextualization to recognize the ways Chinese people think, but also humility in how we approach the task.

In focus groups, students overwhelmingly said they thought that the sexual promiscuity in *Friends* was unacceptable, but probably similar to the behavior of most Americans. Moreover, most indicated a strong belief that the characters were Christians because "most Americans follow this religion." It is plausible to conclude that the students see Christian behavior as matching the behavior of the television characters. This is disconcerting because the TV characters' behavior contradicts Biblical teaching that sex should only take part in the context of marriage. However, this moral norm is eroding in American society. According to a 2016 Barna study, only half of Americans and three-quarters of Christians strongly agree that "choosing not to have sex outside of marriage is healthy." This is a point where there is a disconnect between Biblical teaching and the practice of Americans, even many American Christians. Among the Chinese, this is hurting our witness.

Many Chinese students also see a disconnect between Christianity and the violence and sexuality that fills American films. Though some students suggested that there was not a need to connect a person's religious beliefs with their actions, clearly we *do* need to connect the two. As James put it, "Faith by itself, if it is not accompanied by action, is dead" (James 2:17, NIV). American Christians who work with and love the Chinese need to be aware of these stereotypes. It would be wise to do our best to be careful not to deliberately or inadvertently promote potentially offensive stereotypes through our own ignorance.

Purdue's study, which found that Chinese students studying in America overwhelmingly did not believe that the moral standards of Americans benefited from Christianity, and overwhelmingly disagreed with the idea that American democracy and freedom benefited from Christianity, should also be an eye-opener for American Christians ("Purdue Survey," 2016). Is it possible that strong bias against the role Christianity plays in American life may have a connection to the ways that Americans, even Christians, are seen as complicit in America's moral failures?

## Where Do We Go From Here?

The primary focus of this chapter is not politics, but politics and religion are so intertwined in America that sometimes we forget how politics impacts international ministry. I suggest that one important way that American Christians working with Chinese people can react to this information is by making it clear, both in the U.S. and abroad, that Americanism and Christianity are not the same. Many American values certainly overlap with those of Christianity, but it is the *church*—the body of believers—that is the "city on a hill," *not America*. As China—and the world—sees America repeatedly applying Biblical language to itself, claiming to be a "chosen people of God" the Chinese are understandably confused.

Stanley Hauerwas wrote an op-ed in *The Washington Post* arguing that this was "clearly a theological claim that offers a kind of salvation." He points out, correctly, that "Christians believe that only God demands 'total allegiance' and that 'Christians are devoted to God, not to any nation'" (Hauerwas, 2017). However, in his 2011 essay "The Death of America's God" Hauerwas argued that part of the reason for the title of his essay is, that, "For Americans, faith in God is indistinguishable from loyalty to their country" It is when these lines have been crossed in China, and American and other Western missionaries have had mixed allegiances to the kingdom of God and the kingdom of their birth that imperialistic tendencies have crept in and damaged Christian witness.

One reason Chinese people still see a strong connection between Christianity and American democracy is because many Americans refuse to acknowledge that America is becoming more pluralistic. Hauerwas (2011) argues that the god of many Americans is not the God of the Bible:

> Americans continue to maintain a stubborn belief in a god, but the god they believe in turns out to be the American god. To know or worship that god does not require that a church exist because that god is known through the providential establishment of a free people. This is a presumption shared by the religious right as well as the religious left in America. Both assume that *America* is the church.

Similarly, America's blend of Christianity and civic religion would likely look foreign to the early church, wrote author and theologian Preston Sprinkle (2019):

> No Christian in the first 300 years after Jesus would have pledged allegiance to Rome during a church gathering. Roman flags didn't stand next to Christian flags in first-century churches, and followers of Jesus viewed themselves as citizens of One: One Lord, One baptism, One kingdom of sojourners scattered across the earth as colonies of heaven. Christians in America [and in China, I might add] are more like Israelite exiles living in Babylon than Jewish kings reigning in Israel.

Sprinkle (2019) points to Jeremiah, who encouraged the exiles to "seek the welfare of Babylon" while living in Babylon in Jeremiah 29:7, as a model for modern Christians. "While Christians should submit to the state, pray for its leaders and render qualified obedience to its laws, to pledge allegiance is a profoundly religious act. It's a religious statement infused with divided loyalties and borders on syncretism." Musician Derek Webb (2005) put it well when he sang, "My first allegiance isn't to a flag, a country or a man, my first allegiance is not to democracy or blood. It's to a King and a Kingdom."[51] As Christians, we should love our country and be proud of it, but we should are resident aliens whose true citizenship is not on earth. Our primary purpose on this earth is not to serve our country or its values, it is to serve the kingdom of God. And that means that sometimes we must be

---

[51] Sadly Webb, in recent years, gave up his allegiance to Christ's kingdom, and instead now espouses atheism, but his words still ring true about to whom an American Christian's first loyalties should lie.

countercultural. The writer of Hebrews calls heroes of the faith like Abel, Enoch, Noah and Abraham "foreigners and strangers:"

> All these people were still living by faith when they died. They did not receive the things promised; they only saw them and welcomed them from a distance, admitting that they were foreigners and strangers on earth. People who say such things show that they are looking for a country of their own. If they had been thinking of the country they had left, they would have had opportunity to return. Instead, they were longing for a better country—a heavenly one. (Hebrews 13:13-16)

Politics can be a minefield for Christians to navigate in the U.S., but even more so in China. Hwa Yung, longtime bishop of the Methodist Church in Malaysia, a country which has a sizeable Chinese community, argues that the 2016 Presidential election harmed America's image abroad:

> One of the things that America has stood for in the past was moral leadership and character. Over the past few decades, it has slowly dissipated. In this election you have produced two candidates, both of whom are deeply flawed in character. The question people around the world are asking is, "Is this what America is today?" The election has done great damage to your moral standing in the eyes of the world." (Shellnut, 2016)

If bitter election campaigns are damaging Christian witness globally—and in China in particular—it is imperative to figure out what must be done to restore the essence of true Christian witness extended from the lives of Americans to the lives of their Chinese friends, apart from the political arena. I contend that it begins with *dignified dialogue* with those whose religious, political, and cultural views are different from our own. Alexander Lindsay argues in *The Modern Democratic State* that the origins of American democracy came from Puritan and Quaker congregations in which "the dignity of the adversary made dialogue not only necessary but possible" (Hauerwas, 2014). I do not think baiting opponents into arguments about pet issues with endless streams of unverified memes on social media accomplishes this goal. Without *dignified* dialogue, democracy too easily becomes a shouting match. I fear that is what Chinese people see: American Christians turning our violence inward upon each other in the mud we sling back and forth. For a culture that values harmony and relationships above all else, why would the Chinese want to embrace such chaos, either as a political system or as a Christian philosophy that they believe is inextricably associated with it?

The close alignment of Evangelical Christians with a president whose goal is to "Make America Great Again," in part by engaging in a trade war with China, has been particularly confusing to some Chinese observers. According to the Pew Research Center, 58% of Protestants as a whole, and 81% of white evangelical Christians voted for Trump (Smith & Martinez, 2016). Yet, my Chinese friends have expressed confusion about Trump's religious beliefs. "Is he a Christian?" one Chinese believer asked me, before listing several of the scandals he was aware of, including divorce and accusations of various crimes. The fact that many American Christians voted for a man whose life departs from traditional Christian values in significant ways has only served to muddy these perceptive waters for many Chinese people.

Hauerwas (2010) argues that the downturn in Christian practice among younger generations in America is because of this syncretism the American church has made between the civic religion of America and the church. The goal of the church, he argues, is not to establish any particular nation as the next edifice of Christendom; it is bringing forth the kingdom of God by proclaiming the Good News of Jesus.

> I love America and I love being an American. The energy of Americans, the ability to hew out lives often in unforgiving land, the natural generosity of Americans, I cherish. But I am a Christian. I cannot avoid the reality that American Christianity has been less than it should have been just to the extent that the church has failed to make clear that America's god is not the God we worship as Christians. [Hopefully] that will leave the church in America in a position with nothing to lose. When you have nothing to lose all you have left is the truth. So I am hopeful that God may yet make the Church faithful even in America. (Hauerwas, 2010

If American Christians want to see the Father's kingdom firmly planted in the hearts of the Chinese, as well as the hearts of their fellow Americans, we need to make sure they see our faith as distinct from our nationality and our culture. Chinese people do not need to abandon the Middle Kingdom to enter the Kingdom of God. In fact, they'll be more effective emissaries of God's kingdom if they remain faithful citizens of both. While it is clear that our faith does play a significant role in the history and values of America, we need to be careful not to equate America with God's Kingdom. Clearly, there is much to be done to better understand *how* we are perceived, both as Americans and as Christians. Sometimes in assimilating and contextualizing to Chinese culture, it might even be helpful to be willing to apologize for the negative actions of our own country. This will take humility, patience, care, and much more listening. But this work is worth doing.

With this goal in mind, I echo Hauerwas' prayer for the church. I think Christians who are working with the Chinese should make it a point of emphasis to distinguish more clearly between typical American values and Biblical values whenever possible, even if that means having to divest and de-emphasize some of the importance we place on American socio-political values and strive to adapt to their culture as much as possible. Is not this the root of contextualization? As the Apostle Paul put it, "Now, even though I am free from obligations to others, I *joyfully* make myself a servant to all in order to win as many converts as possible . . . I have adapted to the culture of every place I've gone so that I could more easily win people to Christ" (1 Cor. 9:19, 22, The Passion Translation, 2017).

## References

Acheson, J. (1949, August) The China White Paper, vol. 1, Department of State Publication 3573. Far Eastern Series 30. Retrieved from https://archive.org/details/VanSlykeLymanTheChinaWhitePaper1949/page/n9

Agøy, E. T. (2016, Autumn). Portrayal of Foreigners in Traditional Chinese History and Literature. Retrieved January 15, 2019, from https://www.duo.uio.no/bitstream/handle/10852/54557/EAST4591-Master-s-Thesis-in-East-Asian-Culture-and-History—Erling-Hagen-Ag-v.pdf

Allen, J., (2005, June 23). American Character Gets Mixed Reviews: U.S. Image Up Slightly, But Still Negative. Retrieved January 22, 2019, from http://assets.pewresearch.org/wp-content/uploads/sites/2/2005/06/Pew-Global-Report1-6-23-05-final-with-Morocco-note-and-topline.pdf

"America Has Been at War 93% of the Time – 222 out of 239 Years – Since 1776." (2019, January 20). Retrieved January 23, 2019, from https://www.globalresearch.ca/ merica-has-been-at-war-93-of-the-time-222-out-of-239-years-since-1776/5565946

Barna, G. (2018, January 24) Atheism Doubles Among Generation Z. Retrieved February 13, 2019, from https://www.barna.com/research/atheism-doubles-among-generation-z/

Beech, H. (2016, April 29). China Campaigns Against 'Western Values, but Does Beijing Really Think They're That Bad? *Time*. Retrieved January 23, 2019, from http://time.com/4312082/china-textbooks-western-values-foreign-ngo/

Berry, C. (2013, June 1). Hudson and Maria Taylor's Graves Found in China. *OMF International News*. Retrieved February 13, 2019, from https://omf.org/nz/2013/06/01/ meric-and-maria-taylors-graves-found-in-china/

The Bible, The Passion Translation (2017), Broadstreet Publishing Group

Bodeen, C. (2019, January 21). Report: China population growth continued to slow in 2018. Retrieved February 13, 2019, from https://www.yahoo.com/news/china-population-rises-15-23-million-2018-rate-044134157.html

Brown, G. T. (1986). *Christianity in the People's Republic of China*. Atlanta: John Knox Press.

Bunn, A. (2015, Summer). "Heroes and Heretics," *Urban Medical Mission,* issue 43:3. Retrieved February 14, 2019 from http://admin.cmf.org.uk/pdf/nucleus/sum15/sum2015.pdf

Burana, L. (2016, November 18). Jesus wept: How can you call yourself a Christian if you voted for Donald Trump? Retrieved January 23, 2019, from https://www.salon.com/2016/11/19/jesus-wept-how-can-you-call-yourself-a-christian-if-you-voted-for-donald-trump/

Carlson, B. (n.d.). China Loves Trump: The people love a winner, leadership loves a dupe. Retrieved January 22, 2019, from https://www.theatlantic.com/magazine/archive/2018/03/trump-china/550886/

Carriere-Kretschmer, E. (2018, June 18). Some Positive Signs for U.S. Image: Global Economic Gloom – China and India Notable Exceptions. Retrieved January 21, 2019, from http://www.pewresearch.org/wp-content/uploads/sites/2/2008/06/2008-Pew-Global-Attitudes-Report-1-June-12-2pm.pdf

Chang, J. C. (2010). *Liberal Imperailism, The Rise and Fall of Liberal Imperialism in U.S.-China Relations and the Origins of the Cold War, 1898-1945* (Unpublished doctoral dissertation, 2010). University of Michigan. Retrieved January 21, 2019, from https://deepblue.lib.umich.edu/bitstream/handle/2027.42/78943/jasoncc_1.pdf

Gu, C. (2009). *Awaken: Memoirs of a Chinese Historian*. Bloomington, Indiana: AuthorHouse.

Coonan, C. (2016, April 20). China warns against 'Dangerous Love' with foreign spies. *Irish Times*. Retrieved January 19, 2019, from https://www.irishtimes.com/news/world/asia-pacific/china-warns-against-dangerous-love-with-foreign-spies-1.2617278

Cooperman, A., & Smith, G. A. (2018, April 25). "When Americans Say They Believe in God, What Do They Mean?". Retrieved January 11, 2019, from http://www.pewforum.org/wp-content/uploads/sites/7/2018/04/Beliefs-about-God-FOR-WEB-FULL-REPORT.pdf

Curtis, M., & Malins, G. (Writers), Lembeck, M. (Director), & Borns, B. (Producer). (1996, February 8). The one where Ross and Rachel . . . You Know

[Television series episode]. In *Friends*. New York: National Broadcasting Company.

Engelhardt, T. (2017, December 6), *Overwrought Empire: The Discrediting of U.S. Military Power*, The Huffington Post. Retrieved on February 22, 2019 from https://www.huffingtonpost.com/tom-engelhardt/us-military-power_b_1951026.html

Falkenstine, M. (2012) *The Chinese Puzzle* (2nd edition), China Resource Center Press.

Fish, E. (2016, February 9). China's Youth Admire America Far More than we Knew. *Foreign Policy*. Retrieved January 21, 2019, from https://foreignpolicy.com/2017/02/09/chinas-youth-admire-america-far-more-than-we-knew-surprising-survey-results-ideological-university-crackdown/

Gallup (2018). Religion. Retrieved Feb. 13, 2019, from https://news.gallup.com/poll/1690/religion.aspx.

Grybroski, M. (2016, September 27). Philip Yancey Dumbfounded Evangelicals Support Trump, 'Who Stands Against Everything That Christianity Believes'. Retrieved January 23, 2019, from https://www.christianpost.com/news/ meric-yancey-dumbfounded-evangelicals-support-trump-who-stands-against-everything-that-christianity-believes.html

Hauerwas, S. (2010). *Stanley Hauerwas on America's God: Lecture at Church of the Incarnation*. Lecture presented in The Living Church, Dallas, Texas. Retrieved July 6, 2011, from http://www.livingchurch.org/news/news-updates/2010/3/9/ mericas-god

Hauerwas, S. (2011, August 9). *The Death of America's God*. Retrieved July 6, 2016, from https://www.theaquilareport.com/the-death-of-americas-god/

Hauerwas, S. (2014, Tuesday 24 June 2014).Can Democracy be Christian? Reflections on How (Not) to be a Political Theologian. Retrieved January 9,

2019, from https://www.abc.net.au/religion/can-democracy-be-christian-reflections-on-how-not-to-be-a-politi/10099212

Hauerwas, S., & Willimon, W. H. (1989). *Resident Aliens: Life in the Christian Colony*. Nashville: Abingdon Press.

Hauerwas, S. (2017, January 27). Christians, don't be fooled, Trump has deep religious convictions. *The Washington Post*. Retrieved January 23, 2019, from https://www.washingtonpost.com/news/acts-of-faith/wp/2017/01/27/ mericas s-doesn't-be-fooled-trump-has-deep-religious-convictions/

International Institute for Strategic Studies (15 February 2019). *The Military Balance 2019*. London: Routledge. Retrieved on February 22, 2019 from https://www.iiss.org/-/media/files/publications/military-balance-2019/mb2019-defence-budgets-branded.ashx?la=en&hash=C560EFFEC61FA0816B61B8A005215F0510F449EC

Isaacs, H. (1958). Scratches on Our Minds: American Images of China and India. New York: The John Day Company.

Japan's Apologies for World War II. (2015, August 14). *New York Times*. Retrieved January 15, 2019, from https://www.nytimes.com/interactive/2015/08/13/world/asia/japan-ww2-shinzo-abe.html

Jenkins, P. (2006). *The New Faces of Christianity: Believing the Bible in the Global South*. New York: Oxford University Press.

Kumar, A. (2016, March 27). Max Lucado: Some of My Church Members Are Upset by My Anti-Trump Blog. Retrieved January 23, 2019, from https://www.christianpost.com/news/max-lucado-some-of-my-church-members-are-upset-by-my-anti-trump-blog.html

Leonard, J. (1984). *Wei Yüan and China's Rediscovery of the Maritime World*. Cambridge (Massachusetts); London: Harvard University Asia Center. Retrieved January 12, 2019, from http://www.jstor.org/stable/j.ctt1tfjd0q

Liu, J. (2011, December 11). The Size and Distribution of the World's Christian Population. Retrieved January 19, 2019, from http://www.pewforum.org/2011/12/19/global-christianity-exec/

Lu, Y. (2011, November 11-December 22). "Research on the religious faith of college students and young teachers in universities—A case of Guizhou province." (高校青年教师和大学生宗教信仰问题研究—以贵州省高校为例). Paper presented at The Conference Proceedings of Social Science Academic Annual Meeting of Guizhou, Guiyang, China, November 11, 2011 to December 22, 2011.

Lucado, M. (2016, February 26). Max Lucado: Trump doesn't pass the decency test. Retrieved January 23, 2019, from https://www.washingtonpost.com/posteverything/wp/2016/02/26/max-lucado-trump-doesn't-pass-the-decency-test/

Mott, J. R. (1889). *The American Student Missionary Uprising, or, History of the Student Volunteer movement for Foreign Missions* (Student Volunteer Series, No. 1). Chicago: SVM Papers.

Neill, S., & Chadwick, O. (1990). *A History of Christian Mission* (Second ed.). London: Penguin Books.

Piper, J. (2014). *The Ministry of Hudson Taylor as Life in Christ*. (2014, February 14). Retrieved June 12, 2019, from https://www.desiringgod.org/messages/the-ministry-of-hudson-taylor-as-life-in-christ

Pomfret, J. (2016). *The Beautiful Country and the Middle Kingdom: America and China, 1776 to the Present*. New York: Henry Holt and Company, Kindle Edition

Purdue Survey of Chinese Students in the United States. (2016, November 16). Retrieved December 17, 2017, from https://www.purdue.edu/crcs/wp-content/uploads/2016/11/CRCS-Report-of-Chinese-Students-in-the-US_Final-Version.pdf

Shellnutt, K. (2016, November 16). Global Evangelical Leaders: Trump's Win Will Harm the Church's Witness. Retrieved January 23, 2019, from https://www.christianitytoday.com/news/2016/ mericas/global-evangelical-leaders-trump-win-will-harm-churchs-witn.html

Smith, G. A., Martínez, J. (2016, November 09). How the faithful voted: A preliminary 2016 analysis. Retrieved January 23, 2019, from http://www.pewresearch.org/fact-tank/2016/11/09/how-the-faithful-voted-a-preliminary-2016-analysis/

Sprinkle, P. (2019, February 15). What Christians Can Learn from Colin Kapernick: Exploring the big questions about allegiance, faith and the Bible. Relevant Magazine

Stokes, B. (2015, April 7). Americans, Japanese: Mutual Respect 70 Years After the End of WWII. Retrieved January 15, 2019, from http://www.pewresearch.org/wp-content/uploads/sites/2/2015/04/Pew-Research-Center-US-Japan-Report-FINAL-April-7-2015.pdf

Stokes, B. (2016, September 13). Hostile Neighbors: China vs. Japan. Retrieved January 15, 2019, from http://www.pewglobal.org/wp-content/uploads/sites/2/2016/09/Pew-Research-Center-China-Japan-Report-FINAL-September-13-2016.pdf

Teon, A. (2016, March 18). The Chinese Revolution of 1911—The Founding of the Republic of China. Retrieved February 14, 2019, from https://china-journal.org/2016/03/18/ merica-revolution-1911-founding-republic-of-china/.

Ting, K. (1979, November). *Facing the Future or Restoring the Past?* Address, Toronto, cited in Brown, 27

Ting, K. H. (1984). A Chinese Christian's View of the Atheist. In *Chinese Christians speak Out- Addresses and Sermons* (97). Beijing: New World Press.

Trump, D. (2016, January 16). Presidential Candidate Donald Trump at Liberty University. Retrieved January 29, 2019, from https://www.c-span.org/video/?403331-1/ meric-trump-remarks- liberty-university Trump's comment begins at 6:38 and ends at 7:00 in the video.

Trump, D. (2017, January 20). The Inaugural Address. Retrieved February 13, 2018, from https://www.whitehouse.gov/briefings-statements/the-inaugural-address/

Varg, P. A. (1960). *Missionaries, Chinese, and Diplomats. The American Protestant Missionary Movement in China, 1890-1952*. Princeton, New Jersey: Princeton University Press.

Wallis, A. (1985). *China Miracle: A Voice to the Church in the West*. East Sussex, Great Britain: Kingsway Publications.

Wang, C. (2016, May). Research Note: Chinese Students' Attitudes Toward Christianity in Xi'an, China. *Religions*, 7 (58), 3-4. Retrieved January 11, 2019, from http://www.mdpi.com/2077-1444/7/5/58/pdf

Wang, Q. E. (1999). History, Space, and Ethnicity: The Chinese Worldview. *Journal of World History,10*(2), 287. Doi:10.1353/jwh.1999.0029. Retrieved February 14, 2019, from http://muse.jhu.edu/article/18312.

Webb, D. (2005). A King & A Kingdom [Recorded by D. Webb]. (2005). On *Mockingbird* [CD]: Derek Webb, Cason Cooley.

**What Americans Believe About Sex (2016, January 14). The Barna Group, Retrieved February 16, 2019, from** https://www.barna.com/research/what-americans-believe-about-sex/.

Wike, B., Stokes, J., & Fetterolf, J. (2017, June 13). U.S. Image Suffers as Publics Around World Question Trump's Leadership. Retrieved January 12, 2019, from http://assets.pewresearch.org/wp-content/uploads/sites/2/2017/06/25100416/PG_2017.06.26_US-Image-Report_Full-Report.pdf

Wike, R., Stokes, B., & Poushter, J. (2015, June 23). Global Publics Back U.S. on Fighting ISIS, but Are **Critical of Post-9/11 Torture.** Retrieved January 19, 2019, from http://assets.pewresearch.org/wp-content/uploads/sites/2/2015/06/Balance-of-Power-Report-FINAL-June-23-2015.pdf

Wike, R., & Devlin, K. (2018, August 28). As Trade Tensions Rise, Fewer Americans See China Favorably. Retrieved January 19, 2019, from http://www.pewglobal.org/wp-content/uploads/sites/2/2018/08/Pew-Research-Center_U.S.-Views-of-China_Report_2018-08-28.pdf

WIN/Gallup International Survey, VOP (EOY) 2014. (2014). Raw data. Retrieved January 12, 2019, from https://www.washingtonpost.com/blogs/worldviews/files/2015/04/WIN.GALLUP-INTERNATIONAL-RELIGIOUSITY-INDEX.pdf.

Woodberry, R. & Shah, T. (2004). Christianity and Democracy: The Pioneering Protestants. *Journal of Democracy* 15 (2), 47-61. Johns Hopkins University Press. Retrieved February 21, 2019, from https://muse.jhu.edu/article/54681.

Woodberry, R. (2006). Reclaiming the M-Word: The Legacy of Missions in Non-western Societies. Review of Faith & International Affairs. 4. 3-12. 10.1080/15570274.2006.9523232. Retrieved February 21, 2019 from https://www.researchgate.net/publication/254285240_RECLAIMING_THE_MWORD_THE_LEGACY_OF_MISSIONS_IN_NONWESTERN_SOCIETIES.

Wormald, B. (2015, May 12). America's Changing Religious Landscape. Retrieved January 5, 2019, from http://www.pewforum.org/2015/05/12/ mericas-changing-religious-landscape/

Yeo, K. (2002). *Chairman Mao meets the Apostle Paul: Christianity, Communism, and the Hope of China.* Grand Rapids, MI: Brazos Press.

# 14. Chasing Knowledge: A Young Chinese Woman Reflects on the Empty Intellectual Spirituality of Her Generation[52]

## By Yang Xiaoxiao[53]

"Do you want to be a Christian?" The very first question I heard as a non-believer was from a young female preacher. It was 1999, and, as a six-year-old, I had just traveled from north to south, from an ancient political center to a modern transportation hub. The south was new and cool and different, much more developed than an old heritage town left behind. They even spoke a different dialect, a dialect that sounded like a high-class language. I was too young to grasp the idea of the cost of discipleship. I thought if Jesus knocked on my door, why not open my door and welcome Him? What harm could He do? I certainly did not have a clue about what it would be like to become a Christian in a closed communist country.

China, the country I was born in, the country I have deeply loved and been passionately devoted to serving, does not lead me or my generation to God's Kingdom, for we do not know God. The truth we stand by is not God's truth. Instead, Marxism-Leninism, Mao Zedong's thought, Deng Xiaoping Theory, the Three Represents, and the scientific outlook on development, and, nowadays,

---

[52] *Editor's note: This chapter reflects the point of view and observations of a young Chinese woman. Some of her statements are certainly critical, a point that will not always make them well-received. I applaud her bravery to name things unequivocally as she sees them. - K.P.*

[53] *A pseudonym has been used to protect the identity of the contributor.*

President Xi's "Chinese Dream" are our theoretical guidance, to which we must adhere. One of our textbooks says, "We must unswervingly follow the path of socialism with Chinese characteristics." CCTV news reports, "Our general task is to achieve socialist modernization and the great renewal of the Chinese nation." The Communist Party teaches us, "Always be prepared to strive for the great cause of communism." The ideology of atheism has occupied our body, our mind, and our soul. We cannot believe what we do not have. That is why our hearts are hardened, just like Pharaoh's heart in the Bible.

### "Do Not Believe in Christianity; Believe in knowledge."

Growing up in elite parts of the public school system, I was used to being one of only a few Christians among thousands of other students. The eyes of my generation were so fixed on worldly security. In my schooling years, knowledge became most Chinese students' idol, sharing the largest group of followers. But what is knowledge? In Chinese, we called it 知识 (zhī shi). The word 知 (zhī) means understanding and the word 识 (shi) means recognition. However, when we look it up in our traditional Chinese dictionary, it explains knowledge as when "people get the understanding of objective things through the practical activities of class struggle, production struggle and scientific experiment." (Baidu dictionaries, n.d.) Tracing back, the word "knowledge" is from the verb to "know," and the second element means to "obscure." *The Oxford Dictionary* defines knowledge as the theoretical or practical understanding of a subject. In common terms, it means facts, information, and skills that are acquired through experience or education.

So, what is the Biblical interpretation of knowledge? *Baker's Evangelical Dictionary of Biblical Theology* (1996) notes, "Knowledge is not the possession of information, but rather its exercise or actualization." Proverbs 1:7 (NIV) states, "The fear of the Lord is the beginning of knowledge." Later, Proverbs 2:6 (NIV) says, "For the Lord gives wisdom; from his mouth come knowledge and understanding." We know God gives knowledge as a gift. True knowledge from God is found in our deep appreciation and relationship with the Lord.

Therefore, we need to make a clarification here: the knowledge that the majority of young Chinese people worship is not knowledge from God, but knowledge from the world. What does this kind of knowledge do for our generation, the millennial Chinese generation? Why does this particular type of knowledge have such a huge influence in schools and eventually make us follow it in a way that we do not even know we are worshipping the wrong kind of god? Bacon said, "*Scientia potentia est*" meaning knowledge is power (Bacon, 1597). God told Adam and Eve to choose the tree of life and *not* to choose to tree of knowledge [of good and evil]. Unfortunately, we failed God's command since day one. To understand the effects of this on recent Chinese generations, it is important to study the historical and cultural background.

## Historical Background

The People's Republic of China was founded on October 1, 1949 and a few years after that, the Great Leap Forward occurred—a radical political reform policy that was not a success. This was Chairman Mao's attempt to modernize our nation's economy. He hoped that by 1988, China would build an economy that could compare with America's. There were two major areas of reforms: agriculture and industry. Unfortunately, Mao's program led to the closing of many factories and resulted in many social conflicts. Everyone was so anxious because they were scared to be scolded for no reason.

Several years later, the country experienced the Cultural Revolution. This movement lasted from 1966 to 1976. Our country suffered greatly from this ten-year period of chaos. Initially, the Communist Party of China (CPC) wanted to develop the economy. Nevertheless, Chairman Mao was concerned that both the economy and the government would slide into capitalism, and therefore would not be able to carry on true Communist ideology and heritage. One of the popular posters at the time said, "The Chinese People's Liberation Army is the great school of Maoism." During that time, law and order were completely redefined and torn apart. Economically speaking, the Chinese government had very limited resources. Additionally, our foreign relations at the time was going through a lot of setbacks with developed countries. The situation was indeed troubling. Looking back, we see this social movement has greatly hindered our country's economy, education system, and social structure in the long run.

Educationally, the Cultural Revolution laid the foundation for a society in which many young Chinese today worship "knowledge" as their God. In most schools, students were forced to hand in their textbooks and teachers were dismissed. No one attended regular, formal school anymore. To make matters worse, college graduates were forcibly sent to disadvantaged areas of the countryside to be reeducated by the poor and lower-middle peasants and do huge amounts of heavy labor work. This is what we called the "down to the countryside movement." The purpose of this movement was to eliminate the "three major differences," which are the difference between workers and peasants, the difference between the city and country, and the difference between physical and mental labor. According to Patricia Buckely, approximately 17 million youth were sent to rural areas as a result of the down to the countryside movement (Ebrey, 2005). For many college graduates at the time, this movement permanently changed their lives. Some of them remained in the countryside and continued their labor work even after the movement ended. Some of them left their families and loved ones behind. While some of them were fortunate enough to escape those conditions, many hard changes were still taking place around them.

In 1977, our country restored the nation's testing system after having put it on hold for 12 years. The College Entrance Exam (Gao Kao) was originally designed to solve the issue of ensuring fairness in college student acceptance and enrollment. My parents came from that era, and so did our nation's current top leaders.

Chairman Deng Xiaoping was concerned that the country was far behind the United States and the Soviet Union in technical development. He knew this generation needed that exam to channel the nation's pool of academic talent toward meeting national needs. But before they took it, that young generation had suffered from the Cultural Revolution and the down to the countryside movement. Because they took the chance to study for the first college entrance exam, they were able to change their lives and social class. Without knowledge, these current top leaders could not climb up the ladder to become the top one percent. Without the college entrance exam, their children and their grandchildren would still be in the countryside, probably thinking they would never have a different future. To that generation, knowledge became a strong weapon. It gave them power, favor, and privilege.

Nonetheless, this idea of college entrance exams was not groundless and baseless. It was inspired and adopted from the imperial examination system that dated back to the Sui Dynasty. This imperial examination system had 1300 years of history, and the main test material was about classics, literary style, and Confucianism. The purpose for creating this test was to select elites to govern, and the emphasis was about learning how to acquire "people skills" for the state bureaucracy. Here is what they were taught in their ethics classes: to govern the country (and bring peace to all), one should first be able to govern one's family; to govern one's family successfully, one should first learn to govern oneself. Likewise, in *The Analects,* Confucius described an ideal state of politicians in ancient China with the following:

> At fifteen I set my heart upon learning.
> At thirty, I planted my feet firm upon the ground.
> At forty, I no longer suffered from perplexities. N
> At fifty, I knew what were the biddings of Heaven.
> At sixty, I heard them with a docile ear.
> At seventy, I could follow the dictates of my own heart;
> for what I desired no longer overstepped the boundaries of right.

Hence, there were a large number of students who tried to take this test so that they could increase their social class and serve the emperors. Sometimes, a scholar did not step outside his gate, yet he knew the happenings under the sun. As an old Chinese saying goes, "When a man attains enlightenment, even his pets ascend to heaven."

In contemporary China, if you pass the college entrance exam and get into a prestigious university such as Tsinghua University or Peking University, you'll be guaranteed a promising career. In today's world, you'll be perceived as "a winner in life." There are only three subjects that the education bureau tests in this exam: Chinese, English, and math. Along with that, we have a division of subjects in high schools: liberal arts and science. If you are a liberal arts student, you will study politics, history, and geography and only be tested on that portion. If you are a science student, you will study chemistry, physics, and biology and only be tested that portion. In 2019, there was a major education reform of the college entrance exam. Take Guangdong province as an example; the change will cover the students who entered high schools in the fall of 2018 and later, allowing them to have up to 12 combinations of subjects instead of the current two choices between arts and science for their exams, in accordance with their hobbies, interests and specialties, according to the education authority in Guangdong. To be more specific, students are required to take Chinese, math, and English. For electives, students have to choose between physics and history. Among politics, geography, chemistry, and biology, students can mix and match two subjects together. If you are not in China, it is easy to underestimate the influence of being a liberal arts student versus being a science student. If you choose to former, it means limited majors to choose from in college. The stereotype is your work will be automatically associated with a lower income and less important jobs. Though we are only 15 or 16 years old at the time, we need to make this life-or-death decision about our future. Some of my classmates even made that decision when they were in middle school. The Chinese people are determined to get on the road of success from an early age.

Compared with the American "No Child Left Behind" policy, the Chinese philosophy of education is: "Do not let the children fail at the starting point." If you get into a high-quality kindergarten, you can get into a prestigious elementary school; if you get into a prestigious elementary school and middle school, you can get into a prestigious high school; if you get into a prestigious high school, you can get into a prestigious university. Since the day we were born, our families have been preparing and training us to get a good score on the college entrance exam. For our parents, the competition starts when we are three years old. If we compare the ancient and modern Chinese systems, we learn that the students back then wanted to be influential politicians, and the students today want to be accepted into good universities. Essentially, they are reshaping the social system and becoming the backbone for the country.

## Cultural Background

In China, students need to apply to become a "young pioneer" when they are in elementary school. Usually, the participants range from ages six to fourteen. This young pioneer movement is the preliminary step of joining the Communist Party. As we grow up, we can apply to be a member of the Communist Youth League at the age of 14. We can even prepare ourselves to join the Communist Party as a senior in high school. According to People.cn (2010), the nation's top news agency, there were 130 million young pioneers in China as of 2010. Of these, 90 million were from the countryside. The Young Pioneers constitution also summarized that there are three leadership levels. The top is the Pioneer Battalion (Da dui), the middle level is the Pioneer Companies (Zhong dui) and lastly, the Pioneer Squads (Xiao dui). Each team has two people for management: one leader and a vice team leader.

When I became a young pioneer in third grade, I was proud that I got my red scarf, because young pioneers are often called "Red Scarves." This was what separated me from the rest of the crowd because this is the only uniform for young pioneers. When people saw me wearing my red scarf, they would know I was a diamond in the rough. If I were not a young pioneer, our teacher would not choose me for the merit student (three-good student) award. In Chinese, "three-good" means good in study, attitude, and health. Without this award, I will be one step behind others in my cohort.

When I was in fifth grade, I was proud that I got to be elected as a leader for the Pioneer Company. My role was to take over a class every Thursday afternoon, use this class to lead students to learn about the Communist Party, and organize group activities. The benefit that accompanied this was that I got to stand in front of the entire class during the national flag raising ceremony every Monday, and I could also be a lead singer when we sang our national anthem. To me, these honors were imbued with a deep sense of national pride. For example, I taught my peers stories about Lei Feng—who Chinese people call a "communist legend of China." Chairman Mao complimented Lei Feng as a selfless and modest soldier. The nation soon started a "Follow the examples of Comrade Lei Feng" campaign. When I was first asked to read his biography in front of the class, I was so touched by his story that my eyes were filled with tears. I could not get enough of his story. I thought I needed to be a good young pioneer like Lei Feng, sacrificing for the future of our country. Little did I know this was a slippery slope that leads people to embrace atheism. Lei Feng was my role model, not God. My patriotism became my idol. My loyalty—if so called—was shown in my dedication to my role as a young pioneer, not my identity in Christ.

As an emerging young adult, after I received the Gospel message, I have never stopped asking myself this question, "What's going on with our generation?" I realized I had forgotten to ask, "What's going on with me? Why do I believe what I believe? What is my cause?"

This is 21st century. Even though we Chinese might appear to those in the West that we only have limited resources to understand the Gospel, we know Christmas is the celebration of Jesus Christ's birth. We know there is some kind of God who controls the universe. We know churches exist in China. What is more, we may not reject the idea of Jesus Christ. Why is it so hard for us, the younger generation, actually to become Christians? Is it because we do not have access to churches? Not really—according to Chinaconnection.org, there are over 15,000 legal protestant churches in China and 35,000 groups of Christians are now meeting legally in homes ("China's church," n.d.). An interesting phenomenon that I noticed while I was attending middle school and high school was this: the majority of my classmates heard about the local church's location, even though they had never been there, and they were non-Christians. Nonetheless, whenever I came across a new Christian friend in my school, the first thing they would say was "I never knew that such and such town/city/province had a church." Another response I heard more often in recent years was, "So are Christians the same as Catholics? They are the same, right? All that Western religion stuff."

Truly, I was indeed a minority, but I never felt excluded by society. I went to school, I made friends, and if I got a decent job in China and I were climbing the ladder, my boss might ask me to join the Communist Party. Nothing seemed wrong. Everything was right.

The young generation today are portrayed as the most vulnerable group in China by the media, especially for people who were born during the 1980s and 1990s. They had too much confusion about work, life, and love. For this particular group, they are the foundation for their families, because most of them are in their mid-20s to mid-30s. They have to raise kids as well as support their parents. They are anxious and depressed. They are eager to find "God," yet still want to be the masters of their own lives. For some reason, they think they have already found an answer to "God," and this could be Confucius, Buddha, the Communist Party, or other options. Although my former classmates constantly say, "You must believe in knowledge and nothing else; don't be superstitious," a large group of them are devoted Buddhists. They even write down "Buddhavacana"—the Buddhist scriptures—as their daily practice. How ironic!

From my perspective, Buddhism, along with atheism, has been deeply rooted in our hearts because of the influence of our classic literature. "Cessation of all the Defilements," the "Four Noble Truths," and other works that we usually write about in our Chinese essays. I recall in middle school that my Chinese teacher taught us this poem written by a famous Dharma Master. It says,

> There is no wisdom tree; (菩提本无树)
> 
> nor a stand of a mirror bright, (明镜亦非台)
> 
> Since all is void, (本来无一物)
> 
> where can the dust alight? (何处惹尘埃)

To a group of young students, it does sound like "wisdom" and "knowledge." What else did we learn about Buddhism in our Chinese classes? We studied eight virtues, which include filial piety, fraternity, loyalty, trustworthiness, propriety, righteousness, incorruptibility, and a sense of shame. We pondered eight sufferings, including suffering of birth, of aging, of sickness, of death, of separation from loved ones, of association with the unbeloved ones, of not getting what is wanted, and of five clinging-aggregates. The 6th Dalai Lama, Tsangyang Gyatso, who lived a few centuries ago, has poems which have received much media attention in recent years because they have captured the young generation's hearts. One of his popular poems says,

> I went to a holy Lama,
>
> And asked for spiritual advice.
>
> But I was unable to change my mind,
>
> So again I drifted to (my) lover's side.

He also wrote in his poem *Ten Admonishments*,

> Albeit, ever to meet is to know!
>
> If ever is as such, better not to meet.
>
> Alas! How could I part with you eternally,
>
> thus not in the gyre of endless lovesickness?

The young generation was fascinated by the emotions that came from this poem that they even adopted the poem and continued to finish the poem as follows,

> Had better not to meet, and thus you would not fall in love;
>
> Had better not be in acquaintance, and thus you would not be drowned in lovesickness;
>
> Had better not be in company, and thus you would not mutually owe;
>
> Had better not cherish, and thus you would not recall;
>
> Had better not fall in love, and thus you would not mutually abandon;
>
> Had better not see face to face, and thus you would not meet;
>
> Had better not hurt, we would not fail to be loyal;
>
> Had better not promise, and thus your love would not continue;
>
> Had better not depend, and thus you would not snuggle;
>
> Had better not encounter, and thus you would not be in reunion.
>
> Albeit, ever to meet is to know! If ever is as such, better not to meet.
>
> Alas! How could I part with you eternally, thus not in the gyre of endless lovesickness?

This poem, which has a strong Buddhist background, has touched our generation deeply. We were influenced by his way of writing, both consciously and unconsciously. Chao Fan Comics, a start-up animation company founded by young college graduates in China, recently created a comic book series in regard to Tsangyang Gyatso. Their Weibo account, as of June 2017, has over 10,000 followers who participate and comment regularly. They are planning on publishing this series not only in Chinese, but also in French. Tsangyang Gyatso, even 311 years after his death, is now "Instafamous," the new face of Tibet, and goes viral on all sorts of internet fiction sites. We should be aware that Tsangyang Gyatso was the Sixth Dalai Lama, and all of his work shared his religion, so through social media nowadays, we just help him publicize his religion. The social media feels it is right. The authority thinks it is right. And we are fine with it.

What everyone needs to know is this: these platforms are magnets for Chinese youngsters. *Sina Weibo* is the Chinese twitter. According to the 2015 Chinese Campus Weibo Development Report, Weibo had more than 52 million young users. 70 percent are college students, and 30 percent are high schoolers. In Beijing, Hubei and Jiangsu, student users had multiplied greatly, resulting in the overall growth in the national increased by 23.37 percent. More recently, Beijing has replaced Guangdong Province, becoming the area with the largest number of college students that are active on Weibo. At the same time, 110 top colleges and universities have opened their official microblog accounts. Among Weibo users, college students are significantly more active than high school students. According to Weibo's Senior Vice President Cao Zenghui, there are 439 million active users on Weibo. 61 percent of the active users are between ages 16 to 25 (Sina, 2019).

Furthermore, Internet fiction is now the major resource for the making of TV shows and films. Qidian.com did an online survey (2016) to research different age groups about internet fiction. Among 548 surveyed, 66.7 percent of the readers fall into the age group between 13 to 20. Another 26.4 percent of the readers are between 20 to 30. If Tsangyang Gyatso's story was headed back to the big screen with a mega-production company like the one producing the movie *Confucius*, the influence would be immeasurable. That *Confucius* movie grossed 18.6 million dollars and was a box-office hit in 2011. What about sharing Tsangyang Gyatso on Wechat, an app that is taking over the country and has 549 million monthly active users (as of 2015) (Kosoff, 2015)? The nation will definitely hear his ideology and testimony.

Here is the struggle: How can our generation convert to Christianity when our Chinese classics have a Buddhist way of thinking and when our political textbook is all for communism? Will this not more likely to lead us to cultural and moral relativism?

Our generation has access to all kinds of information, but we seldom put a filter on that information. Another tough situation we cannot ignore is this: Why would our generation choose Christianity when we might have to face being misunderstood by our parents and older colleagues, when other religions are the majority in this country and when we may face setbacks in the workplace because of what we believe? What is best for us now? That is the thing with our generation—"What's good for me *now*?" We want that instant gratification, not heaven after death. But Dietrich Bonhoeffer explained in his book *The Cost of Discipleship* (1937),

> Costly grace is the Gospel which must be sought again and again and again . . . Such grace is costly because it calls us to follow, and it is grace because it calls us to follow Jesus Christ. It is costly because it costs a man his life, and it is grace because it gives a man the only true life.

What the young generation does not realize is that everything has a cost; even not being willing to pay the cost is also a type of cost. When we purposely choose the Internet over religion, when we purposely choose money over religion, when we purposely choose communism over religion, there is still a cost we have to pay.

As young adults, we, the future of China, are not being persecuted like the older generation. At the same time, we also share the freedom of religion if we do choose to have one. Article thirty-six of the Chinese constitution states, "Chinese citizens enjoy freedom of religious belief, including these five state-recognized religions: Buddhism, Catholicism, Daoism, Islam, and Protestantism." Additionally, it bans discrimination based on religion and it forbids state organs, public organizations, or individuals from compelling citizens to believe in—or not to believe in—any particular faith.

As the young generation, we do have a choice. Yet, in terms of religion, we just sit here and choose nothing. We give our attentions to the K-pop stars such as Exo and BTS; we spend our time and money endlessly on Taobao.com (Chinese Amazon); we are addicted to entertainment and materialism. Apparently, there is no time and no room for God. As a matter of fact, we worship ourselves in a way so that we are almost like our own god. Christianity, on the other hand, is on our back burner: not needed, unnecessary. Hudson Taylor, a British missionary who spent more than 50 years in China and the founder of the China Inland Mission said, "Unless there is an element of risk in our exploits for God, there is no need for faith." Even though this was what I experienced five to ten years ago, this situation still reminds me of the IKEA effect, which was researched and named by Michael I. Norton, Daniel Mochon and Dan Ariely. What they believe is this: labor alone can be sufficient to induce greater liking for the fruits of one's labor (North, Mochon & Ariely, 2011)

    Undoubtedly, this "IKEA" way of thinking is reflected in the way youngsters in China perceive Christianity. They have not been invited to a church, found a home church, or been involved in a church ministry. No effort, therefore, no interest. It is all too easy, not to mention the fact that they have been taught communist theories throughout their entire school life. "Rome wasn't built in a day." The important matter is we need to set a fire down in their souls. That means we must keep inviting them to church, letting them hear the truth in black and white, trying to build intentional relationships like what God does with us, etc. If they do not already have an example of what a Christian is like, we need to be that example, that salt and light.

### Inside a Three-Self Church Experience in Southern China

    When the pastor asked me that question, I decided to follow Christ. I did not know as a six-year-old how it would affect my life and the type of balancing act I would have to perform in connection with my education and the attitudes of my friends. I went to a Three-Self church down in the south during my entire childhood. Church was my sanctuary, my home, and my safe place. I did not even realize I was in a "three-self," government regulated church. In China, "three self" refers to self-governance, self-support, self-propagation and respectively reject foreign influence on church leadership, financing, and church multiplication. This is known as a patriotic movement.

    After I got into middle school, I realized something different about my church. As I walked in every Sunday, somehow I knew I did not belong there. The seats were filled with senior citizens, people with special needs, or young children. Our buildings were old and outdated. We kept donating money, but it was still a slow process to get a brand-new building in use for our ministry.

"Should I even be here?" I would ask myself. The sermon was too difficult for me to understand, the worship style was not contemporary, and I could barely find any friends. I did get a seat at the table; I was not a stranger—but why did I not feel welcomed? Why did I feel disconnected? Every minute seemed like torture. It was heart-wrenching every time I listened to God's preaching looking for a way I could relate. Who were *my* people? Who were *my* Christian friends? According to the *Telegraph*, the number of Christians in Communist China is growing so steadily that it by 2030 China could have more churchgoers than America, and Protestant congregations in particular have skyrocketed since churches began reopening after Chairman Mao's death in 1976 (Phillips, 2014). But at that time, I did not have them, and I did not see them around me at all.

Where are the young people? Jesus said in Matt 18:14 (NIV), "Let the little children come to me, and do not hinder them, for the kingdom of heaven belongs to such as these." But here is the situation. As I looked around me, the young people were gone, the middle-aged came and went, and only the old stayed. In order to reach young people, we need to know what is occupying them through a social and cultural context. On the other hand, we need to pay attention to the economics of religion, which was first brought up by Adam Smith, then later developed by Rodney Starks and William Sims Bainbridge. What Adam Smith analyzed was the effect of competition and government regulation for religious denominations on the quantity and quality of religious services (Smith, 1776). The Stark-Bainbridge theory of religion, however, explored religious involvement, particularly with rewards and compensators. In both their books, *The Future of Religion* (1985) and *A Theory of Religion* (1987), they discussed religious involvement as a precursor of the more explicit recourse to economic principles in the study of religion.

Some of you may wonder, what does this have to do with China? These theories are so foreign and seem so irrelevant to the young adult Chinese market. China, a country that has a strong supervision of religious practice, would be compatible with Adam Smith or Rodney Stark. Surprisingly, back in 2006, a Chinese professor named Fenggang Yang, published a study called *The Red, Black, And Gray Markets of Religion in China* in *The Sociological Quarterly*. Yang (2006) adopted the theories above and proposed a triple-market model: a red market (officially permitted religions), a black market (officially banned religions), and a gray market (religions with an ambiguous legal/illegal status.)

According to Yang (2006), a red market can be labeled as "the open market," though it was not equally open to all religious group and needed to be colored with the official Communist ideology. Black markets, on the other hand, are conducted underground or in secrecy. Lastly, the gray market, which was being categorized as both legal and illegal, or neither legal or illegal, is the most difficult to demarcate because of its "ambiguous" and "amorphous" nature. The key to this model is to understand the gray market. There are two main practices worth summarizing: 1) illegal religious activities of legally existing religious groups, and 2) religious or spiritual practices that manifest in culture or science instead of religion.

He also concluded three main propositions. First, to the extent that religious organizations are restricted in number and in operation, a black market will emerge in spite of high costs to individuals. Second, to the extent that a red market is restricted and a black market is suppressed, a gray market will emerge. And third, the more restrictive and suppressive the regulation, the larger the gray market is. The trend is this: with the expansion of Christianity, more and more Christian organizations that belong to the "gray market" are now being listed under the "red market" (Yang, 2006).

Though Yang's study results have been around for a number of years, we need to realize that the management level still does not want to be a player in this. And the reason is simple: this is determined by the current Chinese politics and reform status. For Chinese authorities with their understanding, any religious organization is not necessarily just a religious organization. It can become a political organization, a social organization, or even raise up as a military power. In Chinese history, we have learned that an organization's political power and military power can trump its religious power. So far, our country is trying its best to build a solid system like the ones in Western countries. However, it might be too soon presently to adopt Yang's proposal as completely applicable to the Chinese environment.

### So . . . What is Next for This Generation?

Five years ago, if a young evangelist knocked on my door, and I were not a believer, I would have asked this: "Is it worth it? Is it worth it to experience a God like that? Is it worth it to live a life for Christ and His Kingdom?"

Charles Van Engen et al, commented in their book *Footprints of God: A Narrative Theology of Mission* (1999) that mission is "relational." They also noted, "The Gospel story is mission in the street, an incarnational identification with the poor, sick, powerless and oppressed." While doing ministry, it is crucial to comprehend the despair aspect of hope, and how to embrace suffering. Our vision should help us "critique the past, to reinterpret it and build upon it" (1999). Our preaching should call young people to repentance and faith, not cultural and moral relativism. I firmly believe the beauty of the Gospel will be shown in the full context of humanity. For this purpose, we need to aim at creating a church environment that includes authenticity, solves commonly asked questions related to Christianity, and shares a sense of urgency and belonging. Why do people go to church? The answer is simple—they want to be heard and find answers. Why do they stop going to church? The answer is also quite simple—nobody hears their struggles and nobody answers their questions.

Another question I would like to ask directly to the young, non-believers is this: "What if I want to live out my Christian life in China? Would that be difficult? What is *my* cost of discipleship?"   Personally, it might mean I have to sacrifice my time to explain to my family why I believe what I believe and hope that they will not think I am crazy. I will miss out on the promotion that my boss originally planned to give because I chose not to join the Communist Party. More important, I might never be able to get promoted again. It might mean when I publicly announce my faith, the administration would like to have a conversation with me. It might mean I have to go through a lot of heartache in personal friendships and relationships because the majority of my acquaintances are not Christians. Warning against idolatry, the apostle Paul wrote specifically in Corinthians 6:14 (NIV): "Do not be yoked together with unbelievers. For what do righteousness and wickedness have in common? Or what fellowship can light have with darkness?" To the majority of us Chinese, if we truly are convicted and repent, this "Jesus deal" is all or nothing.

If I go back to 1999, when a close family member of mine decided to follow Jesus, I think of how, in a million years, she might never have thought of herself as a "preacher." She was in her 50s when she converted. A decade passed, and she dedicated herself to serve many family churches. Now, whenever she has time, she reads the Bible from beginning to the end, though her education level is only elementary. She always hosts Bible fellowship meetings and invites people to come. She is one simple example, and a microcosm of today's Chinese Christians. Although times have changed, there is still a large number of Chinese Christians who might not have any educational background and have a low literacy level. From my perspective, she has gone through the biggest change in the nation's short history. Even now, she is enduring enormous stress from suffering when she tries to preach in an atheist country. However, whenever they see her, people can feel her joy, energy, and passion for the church and Christ's mission.

In Acts 1:8 (NIV), the Great Commission itself calls the church to be a witness "to the ends of the earth." Therefore, when we preach, it is vital for us to practice what we preach and understand comprehensive contextualization. For instance, according to Scott Moreau (2012), contextualization has to speak to seven aspects: the doctrinal or philosophical dimension, ethical/legal dimension, mythic or narrative dimension, social or organizational dimension, the ritual dimension, the experiential dimension and the material dimension. Moreau (2012) also points out that contextualization is the art of translating ideas into a particular situation, place, or culture. It is fundamental to successful intercultural communication, which makes contextualization essential in sharing one's faith. We must think how to do share our faith in a smart and more impactful way. We need to understand what contextualization is, and how to apply it to our particular mission field.

In the East, there is still a stereotype that being a missionary is just an old-fashioned idea, and they do not seem relevant in a normal person's life. It feels like missionaries are staying in their own bubble and never really bonding with others.

However, if we start to implement the idea of "smart mission," it will be easier for us to understand other people's culture, upbringing, and spiritual needs.

My point is this: just because we Chinese are in a communist-ruled country and that might lead to more challenges, it does not mean there should not be any missionaries and there should not be any Chinese Christians. The book *Encountering Theology of Mission: Biblical Foundations, Historical Developments, and Contemporary Issues* written by Craig Ott et al., states, "The heart of mission: God's deep compassion, seeking and saving the lost, freeing from sin and Satan." To me, the joy of suffering as a young Chinese Christian comes when I realize God's presence. It is the togetherness with God that gives a special bond with church and friends. And because of that, this new generation might be capable of doing what Mother Teresa said: "Do small things with great love."

## References

Aldridge, A. E. (2000). *Religion in the contemporary world: A sociological introduction.* Wiley-Blackwell.

Bonhoeffer, D. (November 01, 1991). The Cost of Discipleship. *Christian History, 10,* 4.

Chinese Campus Weibo Development Report (2015). *China Daily.* Retrieved from http://www.chinadaily.com.cn/dfpd/dfcmhlw/2015-08-20/content_14123592.html

Lehmann, D. "Rational Choice and the Sociology of Religion", in Bryan S. Turner (ed.), *The New Blackwell Companion to the Sociology of Religion,* Wiley-Blackwell, 2010, 181-200.

Engen, C. E., Thomas, N. J., & Gallagher, R. L. (1999). *Footprints of God: A narrative theology of mission.* Monrovia, Calif: MARC.

Ebrey, P. B., & Walthall, A. (2014). *East Asia: A cultural, social, and political history.* Guangdong reforms college entrance exam. (2019). *China Daily.* Retrieved from http://www.newsgd.com/news/2019-04/25/content_186920841.htm

Kosoff, M. (Aug 10, 2015). *This Chinese messaging app is taking the country by storm—and Facebook should pay attention.* Business Insider. Retrieved from http://www.businessinsider.com/wechat-why-it-dominates-china-2015-8

Moreau, A. (2012). *Contextualization in world missions: Mapping and assessing evangelical models.* Grand Rapids, MI: Kregel Publications.

Norton, M. I., Mochon, D., & Ariely, D. (July 01, 2012). The IKEA effect: When labor leads to love. *Journal of Consumer Psychology 22,* 3.

Ott, C., Strauss, S. J., & Tennent, T. C. (2010). *Encountering theology of mission: Biblical foundations, historical developments, and contemporary issues.* Grand Rapids, MI: Baker Academic.

Phillips, T. (2019). *China on course to become 'world's most Christian nation' within 15 years.* Retrieved from https://www.telegraph.co.uk/news/worldnews/asia/china/10776023/China-on-course-to-become-worlds-most-Christian-nation-within-15-years.html

Qidian.com online survey (2015). Retrieved from https://wenku.baidu.com/view/dbc2a717d5bbfd0a795673dd.html

Smith, A., & Cannan, E. (1994). *An inquiry into the nature and causes of the wealth of nations.* New York: Modern Library.

Stark, R., & Bainbridge, W. S. (1985). *The future of religion: Secularization, revival, and cult formation.* Berkeley: University of California Press.

The Digital Tail. (2019). *The Active Weibo User has reached 430 million.* Retrieved from https://www.sohu.com/a/292443492_465976

Yang, F. (February 01, 2006). The red, black and gray markets of religion in China. *Sociological Quarterly, 47,* 1.

## 15. Outside Influences and Personal Challenges: A Belief Journey[54]

### By Mia Pan

I am from Shenzhen, a newly-prosperous city near Hong Kong, where my grandparents and parents have lived since the 1990s. I would like to share some things with you about my family background and my perceptions about life, values, and spirituality.

Even though they have a few similar characteristics, my parents and maternal grandparents are quite different. Not only are they from different generations, but I also think my parents are more open-minded. My grandparents are a little bit traditional but not overly so. Because they live in such a big city, they can accept more things than older people living in small villages. And they are very willing to travel, so they have been to several foreign countries and traveled to nearly every part of China.

My grandparents were a part of the generation that built up Shenzhen into the city it is today. My grandfather had a job that was beneficial for our family,

---

[54] *Editor's note: The following contribution is a narrative of an interview I conducted with a female Chinese student in 2017. Over the next couple of years, Ms. Pan's thinking developed further as she processed some major life events, including getting married. After reading over this chapter in 2019, she said, "My perception about family and life has changed!" With her permission, I am including both the original essay and some additional life summary paragraphs she added to reflect her current views. Doing so shows a fuller evolution in her thought process and sense of personal maturity over time. This collection of thoughts is invaluable as a reflection of the complex thought processes common for today's Chinese young people, expressed in a far more forthright way than many Chinese people ordinarily would be willing to articulate. - K.P.*

developing urban infrastructure, so that was good for both us and our community. When I was a child, I traveled with them a lot. In fact, my first flight on an airplane was when I was one year old. I think I was the youngest passenger on that flight.

My grandpa and grandma are a little bit different. My grandpa received somewhat higher education, though both got college degrees. My grandma is more of a people person and she was kind of a drama queen before. She really liked to gossip about our relatives, and she was extremely sensitive. But it provided a lot of fun and entertainment for our family because no one else was talking about those kinds of things. We would often tease her about it. She had a serious illness years ago. I do not know the name in English, but I can describe it. It is something like when people lose their body's "balance." For some people, day and night is messed up, so they are in a bad emotional state. It was more of a mental problem. While she was sick, she was always yelling at people and not being nice, fighting with anybody. Some of the triggers made sense, but most of them did not make sense. She would readily show her anger, even though our family was taking good care of her. We went to the hospital to get her some medication. And even now she must take medication every day to control those issues. But it is not just mental, I guess. It is also partly physical too. She is really taking the medicine to deal more with then physical symptoms. The mental side of her sickness might become aggravated with more medicine. When we are on medicine for such a long time, I think it can make the problem worse. But in her case, it is not that bad, and it is being controlled right now.

This all happened almost fifteen years ago, when I was very young. I only remember a lot of fighting. My grandfather and parents were getting along with each other for the first several years of the situation—they really discussed this a lot with each other. Over time, they started to fight about it. Both my grandpa and my mom had strong opinions. They each felt we should do this or we should not do that. They really believed in themselves and their own opinions. Looking back, however, I see we had each other to depend on all the time, to get through that hardest initial part of her illness. Therefore, in the end, I think that was a good growing experience for the family.

I would say that my mother and her mother are more strong-willed than many average Chinese women. As a result, most of our family dynamics were a little bit different, especially while I was growing up. My mom is a teacher and has a long commute, taking about one hour each day to get to her workplace. It is pretty far away. So, my dad is the one who cooks every day. He even prepares boxed lunches for my mom. And sometimes breakfast. He does a lot of housework. My dad also works, but he has a lot of time to work from home. Though I do not know all the details, I know he had more work flexibility after he opened his own business. As a result of this, combined with my mom's personality, our family was different from the traditional house where the mom may work outside the home and still do most of the cooking—or the grandparents may live with the family and do all the cooking and housework.

There were various types of spiritual ideas influencing my life growing up. My paternal grandparents are very different from my other grandparents. My father's family came from and lived in Hubei Province, which is north of Shenzhen, in the middle of China. My father's mother died about seven years ago. I do not have many distinct memories of her. But she was not a very strong-minded person. She was always quiet and did the housework. She was a Christian. I do not know how old she was when she began to practice that religion. But now I know she was the one person who was always praying for me—the one person in the world. However, we did not talk that much when I was young because I did not see her much. I did not visit her for years at a time because she was in the north. Even during my visits, I saw she did not talk much at all with my grandpa. They had their own kind of communication. Yet, without words, I still remember she could still communicate a lot. This was so opposite of the way my other grandparents expressed themselves! My dad's father is still alive, and he is kind of a strange person. It is like he is in another world, his own little world. We do not talk much, and we do not have serious communication. I guess that is because we have not really had enough time together. I know my grandmother was a Christian, but I have no idea if my grandfather ever joined her in that belief or how he felt about her choosing that belief.

In terms of spirituality, my parents and maternal grandparents do not have a very exact or strongly defined belief. But from my childhood until now, they always go to the Buddhist temple. They do not really follow any Buddhist practices or ceremonies but just go to the temple perhaps twice a year. They are busy with life and work, so they do not have time to go more often. I do not think they intend to earn any merit or luck by going to the temple; it just gives them something to believe in, I guess. To help them feel well and have a peaceful mind. In my family we do not really believe we have to pray for something. If we want good things to come to ourselves, we must try hard to get it or gain it on our own. It is not like we can pray and receive it as an answer to prayer. We believe that we earn things by our effort and hard work—not just by praying and waiting. First and foremost, we must have a belief in ourselves. That is the biggest reason we go to the temple. To have a peaceful mind and to see the religious beliefs and practices. It will inspire our life to make us stronger through our own willpower. Going to the temple brings my relatives some personal inspiration. But it also helps them to focus mentally so they will not feel too tired or stressed out while they are working so hard. However, my dad has enjoyed listening to passages from the audio Bible. After my grandmother passed away, he found comfort in that and thought it was very peaceful.

Since I was an only child and grew up with these types of relatives, I felt a little lonely and had some misunderstandings with people at school. I did not like my school life in China. In fact, I really hated it. I did not have many close friends I could talk to. I was still always trying to be nice to others, but I felt lonely because I could not really understand the ideas of others and they could not completely understand me. And sometimes I was bullied by others. Nevertheless, I was a good student and my teachers liked me. However, there was a period where I was only an average student. This was influenced by my health because I had to have two surgeries on my ears. During that time, I developed a changing impression about religious beliefs.

When I was young, we went to the temple more often than my family does now. As a result, I had a deeper impression of Buddhist rituals. I was sick almost constantly through much of my childhood, having a persistent cough or cold, so my parents treated me well. When I was sick, they would just take me with them to their workplace and watch over me very closely. During primary school, I was often with my mom because my mom is a teacher. Later, when I had the surgeries and I was in the hospital, I always prayed to Buddha. But in the end, I found that it was not working! At that time, I was about 12 years old, in middle school. I thought to myself, "Gosh, what's going on? You pray for something, but it is not really helping that much and not helping you get through this." After that, even though my mom still went to the temple sometimes, I did not pray in that way, like, "Oh, please help my ears to get better." I got so upset that I guess I lost my belief in Buddhism. I have never really talked to my family about that because my parents are not so devout in their belief. They just have some spiritual mindset but are not heavily involved in those things because they are so busy with their work.

From that time until now, I have experienced an ongoing change in my beliefs and my outlook on things. I would say I had a belief, but it was not that strong. I did not belong to any organized religion or group of believers. Sometimes my teachers in elementary or middle school would tell me and my classmates directly, "You need to believe this," or "You should not believe that." But as I got older and for the first two years of my college life, I felt things were becoming crazy in China. The economy started to grow. All the beliefs, mindset, and culture-based stuff was not growing fast enough to keep up with the economy, so they were not on the same level of development. It seemed like people were kind of messed up all the time, kind of like in the 1960s in America. At that time a lot of people were focused on freedom and basic rights, but they did not have strong beliefs or opinions about personal religious life. It is kind of like my situation now. But for most of the people I talked to, their life is going along okay and is fairly peaceful.

As the economy has spiraled up, the culture has kind of veered off to become all about materialism. When my Chinese friends want to get married, first they must get really good jobs and then they work hard to save up money so that they and their future spouse can have a new house, a new car, new everything. But for what? They keep working and working but their life feels empty because they work hard to have all those things on the outside. But what is going on with their heart?

I used to believe, "OK, the only reason I will get married is because I love that person very much. Otherwise, I do not want to get married. There's no point for me to marry." I do not want to marry just for the sake of having a child. Even when you create a child, you have a responsibility to give it a loving home. You must be a good parent and provide them with a good education. You should be responsible. But at the same time, I do not want to do everything only out of duty. I want to do it out of love.

Yet, I feel horrible because of the people around me. Some people think the same way as me. They are becoming more open-minded. I would say about 60% of the young people around me do not want to be like that, just doing things out of duty instead of out of love. But they do not have a brave and strong opinion to control themselves. They always think, "Oh, my mom and my dad supported me for my whole life to this point using all their money. I have to listen to them!" As an example, a friend of mine is thinking now that she is done with her internship, she might simply go home to China, *or* she might join a website like *Match.com* to try to hurry up and find someone to marry, just because her parents say it is time for her to marry. She would rush forward to marry someone she does not really know or love just so she can have a child and go through all the steps she is supposed to follow in her life without having any sense of deeper purpose about it. But that is the wrong way to think. Because their parents do not have that much education. And they just become socially "numb" in a way. In some ways, it is like their life is pointless. That includes their ideas about marriage and everything related to that. Our parents do have some life experience, often more than us, but just because they have more experience than us, that does not mean that we always have to listen to them. We must make our own way in life.

I have discussed this with my parents, and they agree that there is no point in me marrying a person I do not like. But they encourage me to not give up and to not be so picky, to find something I can like about another person. Love is a great thing for people, and you should not give up on it, but you do not have to be carried away by crazy romantic thoughts. In that way, you can end up in a situation where someone could take advantage of you.

I honestly feel I would put myself at a disadvantage if I just went the way I *had to* go. Some people say, "Oh, if you follow the same path as everyone else, you will have success, but if you take your own path, it may feel like it is a big risk because you are not doing what everyone expects you to do." Yet, I think we will still be happier because we are doing something different and unique. If you follow your heart and you make the right choices, then you actually will be in the best place no matter what other people say.

However, it is still a little confusing and scary because my parents support me in my independent thinking, yet at the same time, they say, "You have to take a risk and just try." But I do not know what or who should I try? It is like I am saying, "I want to follow my heart and do the thing that's right for me." And my parents are saying, "Ok, that's fine. Do it!" But I still do not know what that is. So, then they are saying, "Well then, just do *something*! Because until you try *something*, you will not be able to find what that best thing is." But even that cycle of communicating and thinking can seem empty and pointless.

I feel the gap between the generations, those 20 years, shows that their thinking is very different. Our parents' generation have gone through a difficult time. They had to struggle for their life and for their money. The newer generation has that worry, but it is not as deep. We do not really understand that feeling of helplessness. So, when I talk with my mom and dad, they always have something about this in mind, like they feel more pressure to move forward. This has been even more strongly influenced by the one-child policy. In those families, the parents are so focused on their child doing everything in the very "correct" way. We are their only child; they want to make sure everything is okay for us.

In their mind, there is a starting point and a good ending point, and there is a "successful" way to move from beginning to end to really be successful and achieve the ultimate goal for a good life. And that is the way they want their children to be. Since our generation is still young, they always direct us in this way. Because before, they always had to do everything on their own, and they were very brave to create the way for us. They do not want us to face that pressure. They encourage us to make some choices, but they do not want us to go off and do something crazy, to stray too far from that path.

And that way of thinking really drives me crazy. If I stay to close to their straight line, there is no room for me to take a risk, to go off and try something of my own. But I do think that if more young people, especially young Chinese women, would stand up and say, "I can do something different. I *want* to do something different!" that would cause even more of a problem in China where, right now, there are so many more men than women. Because of the gender gap, there are more men than women who are looking for someone to marry. I have even heard of some Chinese men who must go to other countries to find a wife because there are not enough Chinese women for them to marry who are within the same age group. If more Chinese women declared that they did not want to get married or follow that traditional path, it would probably cause more trouble for the men. But that is okay! We already have such a high population. Why shouldn't a woman be allowed to do what is best for her, even if it is not what tradition demands?

Another aspect of my current spiritual confusion is tied to different cultural influences. Belief in fate is a very traditional Chinese thing. And that belief might normally have a big effect on how I see my situation and if I try to branch out and do something different or if I just follow a traditional path and wait for things to happen to me. Since I came to America, I have attended church a few times. And the people there are like a family. They have a strong belief with all the other members around to support everyone. They go to church often and meet with people and have spiritual support at that time. Many of them even read the Bible often.

But for me in my family, we have never done anything quite like that in the span of my whole life. We do not have those strong belief-centered activities to take part in. But we do have some traditional teachings such as those sayings of Confucius that are already in our minds and shaping our thinking. Like when I talk, I already have those ideas there which are influencing me. But I think there is another difference between my viewpoint and the traditional ideas. One reason why my family does not pray much is tied to my dad's work. He is a financial analyst and analyzes everything for a living, so he must think about all things carefully. I think I get that habit from him. When we think about things so much and try to come up with a logical explanation for the details, that also keeps us from relying a lot on spiritual thinking or religion.

Young Chinese people today also watch a lot of movies from America, Korea, Japan, India, and other countries. I cannot speak for everyone, but for me, I have been in a period where I am being exposed to all those different cultures and ideas. And I am at a point where I still do not have a stable opinion of my own, with my thinking being influenced by so many ideas. That is the reason I feel confused right now. There are too many choices to consider. And people tell me to follow my heart—but I still do not know what is in my heart!

I also realize we do not have a strong sense of pride to guide us. I mean, we are proud of our country, but too many cultures from other countries have gotten through to us and influenced our own culture. We have tried a little bit of this and a little bit of that. Yet, I will note that in a lot of other Chinese families, they have a stronger sense of belief than my family does. They would do more things like praying. There are people who have a stronger belief or religion because they are not influenced or encouraged by other outside cultures so much. They focus more on traditional ways and do not want to think outside the box and explore other ideas more readily.

Yet, even though many Chinese people are proud of their culture, there are so many more influences from the outside, that if they do open up they will start to question what they believe and why they should hold on to their own culture. Because the cultures all start to blend together and they kind of lose their own identity. The world is more global, and every country is developing. We want to say, "America has the best economy now . . . " But ten years in the future it might be Russia or some other country. There is no point in trying to guess and make predictions. We just have to go around and learn about and explore all those other cultures.

In a way, it is connected to what I said earlier. If the economy is shooting up like this, but the culture is developing and increasing at a much slower rate, then there is a higher chance that members of that community will be influenced more by outside cultures and the people may feel very confused from a cultural standpoint. I have even seen a lot of these influences since I have lived in America, like how Disney will teach us to "just follow your heart." But I have always said to myself, "What if my heart is not right?" Sometimes I follow my heart's desire only to find out later that it was bad, and I made the wrong choice.

At the same time, I do not think you can ever say something is "wrong" or "right" because it might be that your choice for this time and place is right. But it is not until ten years later that you find out that was not a good idea. So, in those types of decisions, there is not a definitive "right" or "wrong." There are certain basic things like murder that are always wrong. But there are other things we cannot say are right or wrong because right now they may be okay but later we will find they were really not okay. At some points, our judgment is clueless. Besides those fundamentally wrong things, the judgment or the decision about wrong and right always depend on the person and where he/she is at. In America this freedom of personal and individual choice is a really good thing, but in China, there is an opposite view about this.

From my observations, I would say it is still a blend of the culture's standards and individual judgments, but I think I think most Chinese people would say we should still follow the standards of the group and collective culture. That is kind of a traditional thought, but it is also connected to the brainwashing we undergo today. I think there is a kind of brainwashing that happens in American culture, but it is not the same as what we have in China. Americans cannot always notice it, but they still have it.

I now view Christianity as a Western religion most of the time. I have several Indian friends who are also Christians, and I know there are Christians from African countries. And they are certainly going to worship in different ways because they come from different cultures. But I would say that originally Christianity was an American religion but then it was taken to those other countries. Because America was already a big melting pot. That is the point. You are very diverse here.

But I recognize that if I had not come to America to study and I had stayed in China, then my view of Christianity would probably be very different. Because in China I did not really trust anything, at least not as much as compared to here. I thought so many [American] people are Christian and trusting that kind of idea is good. We could tell you have churches everywhere. It is still a very important part of American culture.

And I feel it is even stronger here. When you learn the Bible in a good or correct way, it is very good for you and important. But in China, a lot of people do not really know what the Bible is. They just start a church and are teaching other people, but they are often misleading others or have a wrong side of their teaching so that they are really dangerous. It is a little bit like Falun Gong and other groups that teach crazy or harmful things. I did not really believe in those things because I do not want to be brainwashed or led along by bad ideas.

Yet, when I came to America, I even found there were some people who have very strange and even harmful ideas. We must be discerning and carefully everywhere, in China and even here, because we do not know what other people will teach us. Recently, I met a man on my university campus, and he was even working in our computer lab for a while. He was going around talking to people and telling them some strange, non-traditional things. I think the English words used would describe him as being a member of a cult.

Ironically, some Chinese friends have accused me of being in a cult! That is simply because I had ideas that were different from the normal ones and I was not afraid to discuss them with other people. I was telling people, especially girls, "You do not just have to listen to your parents, you can just do what you need to do and stand up for yourself." And they looked at me strangely and thought I was trying to brainwash them. I guess that is not a sign of a *religious* cult, but simply having personal ideas that are so different from traditional values in a collectivist culture can be a very hard thing to deal with.

It is hard for me to offer a full opinion of the Bible because I have not read the whole thing. But from the small parts I read, I think most of the stories are from ancient times. Some of them inspire me a little bit. But I have to take a lot of time to try and understand them deeply. Since I cannot understand deeply, I feel clueless at some points when I try to understand this system of belief. At the same time, I feel my attitude is changing. Before, I had a much more carefree attitude, saying, "Okay!

Maybe today I'll read just a little bit . . ." It was just about reading some information. Then, I got a copy of my own and reading became more personal. I would say that now I have read the Bible sincerely, with the attitude that if I could understand it, maybe I could believe it.

The main reason why I have gone to church here is because most of the people around the church are devout and very nice people. I can see that they are trying to be better. Maybe they had a really hard time in their life before. But since they came to church and believed in that, they have something good to make themselves brave and provide them with emotional support. When I enter a church building, even though I do not believe all those things, I feel the love and goodness of the people around me. And then I feel inspired too.

All in all, though, living in America has been difficult because I have had a lot of life experiences and some of them have been quite hard. At the same time, I have been feeling like an outsider, like someone who cannot go deep in the relationships with most of my American friends. When I first arrived here, I was very eager, excited to learn everything, and very open. In hindsight, I know I was too naïve. I think I was too innocent because I grew up being kind of sheltered by my family. During my time here and while going through those painful experiences, I have matured. Even though my heart has been hurt, I have still tried to remain open-minded. Yet, if I am honest, I know I have kind of closed myself off from others and I am more withdrawn now than I was before.

When I think of Chinese people in general and those I know specifically, I automatically think of Buddhism. I know that most of them are not what we would call devout and they do not go to the temple often, but in their heart, they think in Buddhist ways. If people want to become members of the Communist Party, they should not really believe in God. But there is a part of our cultural roots that leads us to think in Buddhist ways anyway.

However, I think we can kind of divide people into several levels. In some families, they just hold onto some ideas to inspire their lives, and for other families they just use it when they are going through a very hard time, praying to get through all that. Those people simply use the prayers as a way to get a better life for themselves. That is their definition of "belief." I have observed different stages for how devout people are and how closely they follow all the beliefs and rituals.

At the other end of the spectrum, I have one friend whose family are really strong Buddhist believers. They all live in China now. Both of her parents work for the government. So they are not allowed to go out and worship that freely. They can apply for permission to do that, but it is very hard for them. She has been my longtime friend, from childhood until now. We have known each other for over ten years. Every summer, or during any school break, her mom will take her to some mountain or other Buddhist holy site. They visit a lot of temples and stay out in natural places. They are cut off from phones and TV, and they eat a simple vegetarian diet. They just sit with the monks and nuns and pray for about twenty days at a time. I guess it is what you would call a spiritual retreat. My friend thinks it is great. She always wants me to join them, but I have never gone. They completely cut themselves off from any city life and related things that can distract them. To be honest, sometimes I cannot understand that. I guess we simply come from family backgrounds that are too different.

Even as far back as middle school, this same friend has always had issues with guys. I am the one who has been like her counselor, listening to her life stories and drama. That drove me crazy because I had to listen to a lot! So sometimes we would temporarily end our friendship on WeChat for a few days. I would say, "If you're just going to keep talking to me forever about your guy stuff, I'm not listening anymore! You've been talking about it forever, but you never show any improvement. It is still the same old way of thinking!" It is annoying because I think, "Why are you letting those guys treat you like that? Try to move on and live your own life and take a better path." Why do women stay with men who are not good when they do not really like those men deep down? I do not get it.

Still, I am wondering if it has something to do with her parents and her relationship with them, with her dad. I see the way my parents interact and how they look for love and acceptance, whether from each other or from other people they know. Sometimes I do not like their way of thinking, but I can see how the beliefs and actions of the parents will strongly influence the child. And no matter what culture a person comes from, I think that makes such a big difference. If the parents teach something to their kids that is rooted in a faith that is very strong, the child can learn how to make sound and level-minded decisions and do things based on those guiding principles, not just based on what other people think or how they feel in the moment of the situation. They have some sort of standard to measure things with.

To be honest, since my family does not really have that, my relatives change their minds all the time. And they have times when they are messed up too. That is the hard part. I guess everyone must be messed up for a while and then change their mind and then are messed up a while longer until they figure out how to grow in this life. However, when I return to that idea of having something objective to hold on to as a firm foundational belief, I think that is the biggest difference I see between my family and Christian families I have met in America.

Sometimes, describing things and understanding concepts between languages—Chinese and English—can be tricky. Take, for example, the words faith, religion, and superstition. But if you ask me how I understand these words as a Chinese person, I think I'll break it down like this. first, religion is more like an official belief. And it involves a group of people doing the same thing. They have strong support through joint belief and outward action. Faith for Chinese people is very different, and it is kind of hard to define. I have one friend who is so positive and impressive all the time. Those kinds of people put a lot of passion into everything because they have a strong "faith." It is like a natural passion shining out of their mindset. So in the Chinese mind, I would say faith is tied to hope or optimism. By being so positive all the time, we think good luck should naturally come to such faithful people all the time. There are not too many Chinese people like her, who are so naturally positive all the time. They face their struggles and never give up, and it is because they hold so much hope in their heart that keeps them going.

Finally, superstition is perhaps the hardest for me to nail down. I know that a long time ago Chairman Mao would tell our people, "You shouldn't believe in religion because religion is just superstition." I guess that was also a sign of people not being enlightened or being uneducated. And I have heard that most Americans think of superstition as old-fashioned or backward traditions which invite good or bad luck.

But I think for most of us, no matter which country we are from, if someone from outside our culture asks us why something is considered lucky or unlucky in our traditions, most of us can only say, "I'm not really sure, it is just a belief that people have or use to have." As we all become more well-educated, we may find some scientific or better explanation for these things. And yet, that is another mysterious and hard-to-define thing in the minds of Chinese people. I guess there are some things that science and logic can never explain. And there are some things about the hearts and minds of my people that cannot be fully explained either.

### *Ms. Pan's Additional Life Summary (2019):*

I lived in Zhuhai and Shenzhen, which are in the southeast part of China, with my parents and grandparents. I am glad that I am loved by all my family members and grew up in a nice environment that my family provided for me. Growing up in a typical Chinese family, I built myself personally through family and school. And I am so proud of my family, since they give me the important lessons in life which are to be kind and demonstrate responsibility.

In my family, different generations had a hard time understanding and communicating with each other. As the only child, I often felt pressure and emotions because of the unhappiness of our family. However, books and education have been a great help to me. Reading psychological books and learning from others helped me to rebuild my personality and repair the relationships between family members. I think belief is another guide for me to understand the relationship with family and myself. I am a Buddhist. In Buddhism, it is important to love your family and yourself, and this system teaches me to respect people, animals, and myself.

# Epilogue: A Clearing on the Way

## by Kaylene Powell

Years have passed since a colleague first approached me with the offer of this writing opportunity. And, oh, the mountains and valleys I have seen along my own journey in the meantime!

Grace, sharp as ever, is now successfully settled into her freshman year of college a couple of states away, continuing on her own path, discovering now for herself more clearly and firmly what she believes. And, as before, as her aunt I could not love her more nor be prouder of her exactly as she is.

My contributors, God bless each one, have been patient (sometimes painfully so, I know) as I juggled communicating and editing with other work and life demands. Looking back, however, I can see with crystal clarity that this culminating work is what it was meant to be, and that it could never have resulted in what it is now if I had tried, somehow, to rush the work. Each contribution was, in its own way, necessary, and the formational process that some of the contributed pieces had to go through in order to fit within the whole was well worth the time, the waiting, and the intense effort made on the parts of the writers and editors polishing the final material for publishing.

A little further down the road readers will be holding a finished copy of this book in their hands. If those readers have reached this point, they have joined us, Chinese and non-Chinese contributors alike, for a little while on the same leg of the misty path. A path of exploration and contemplation, a path of learning and insight, a path of questioning and—perhaps—concluding anew.

Readers have read about more traditional Chinese beliefs, values, and ways of thinking. They have considered when and how spiritual ideas with non-Chinese origins have influenced—and continue to influence—the Chinese. They have seen how history and politics have intersected with and greatly impacted those strains of development on both macro and micro scales, in thoughtful and intensely personal examples. And they have been exposed to some projections for how the spiritual lives and viewpoints of many Chinese may continue to develop or expand in the future. Many stories have yet to be told, and other aspects of these related topics can certainly be further explored, experimentally applied, or written about in the years ahead.

This is, by no means, the end of the journey, but perhaps, merely a clearing in the path, an opportunity to take our bearings before choosing a path forward. All of us—the contributors to this book, the editors, and you, the reader, are moving on in life, encountering various ideas and being shaped by all types of influences. We may now part ways, so to speak, stepping off between different clusters of bamboo in the dense forest. But as we walk on, may we do so with a mixture of greater knowledge, greater discernment, and greater humility. For a soul should keep its feet on the path, but that same soul should support an open mind, an open heart, and an open hand to be offered to another journeyer when paths intersect in new clearings and new groves, further along the way.

www.ingramcontent.com/pod-product-compliance
Lightning Source LLC
Chambersburg PA
CBHW050204240426
43671CB00013B/2239